ISBN 978-1-330-57217-7
PIBN 10080344

1 MONTH OF
FREE
READING

at

www.ForgottenBooks.com

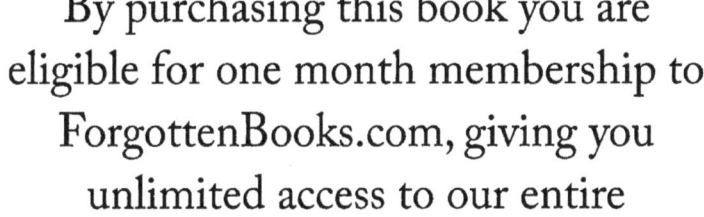

By purchasing this book you are eligible for one month membership to ForgottenBooks.com, giving you unlimited access to our entire collection of over 1,000,000 titles via our web site and mobile apps.

To claim your free month visit: www.forgottenbooks.com/free80344

English
Français
Deutsche
Italiano
Español
Português

www.forgottenbooks.com

Mythology Photography **Fiction**
Fishing Christianity **Art** Cooking
Essays Buddhism Freemasonry
Medicine **Biology** Music **Ancient
Egypt** Evolution Carpentry Physics
Dance Geology **Mathematics** Fitness
Shakespeare **Folklore** Yoga Marketing
Confidence Immortality Biographies
Poetry **Psychology** Witchcraft
Electronics Chemistry History **Law**
Accounting **Philosophy** Anthropology
Alchemy Drama Quantum Mechanics
Atheism Sexual Health **Ancient History**
Entrepreneurship Languages Sport
Paleontology Needlework Islam
Metaphysics Investment Archaeology
Parenting Statistics Criminology
Motivational

MAN AND HIS DIVINE FATHER

BY

JOHN C. C. CLARKE, D.D.

CHICAGO

A. C. McCLURG & CO.

1900

PREFACE

This book aims to bring cheer and hope to human souls. All are puzzled with the problems of their own being and happiness. This is philosophy, and all men are philosophers; but largely without method, and with poor logic, and no first principles. Hence, there is little agreement; and what is called "Reason and Common Sense" is, in a great degree, nonsense. In the chaos of opinions, we try to find the line and system of plain truth.

The beginning of wisdom is knowledge of man, the knower, in himself, his powers and limitations. So we first try to discover our Self, and to portray a man. In consciousness is found a selfhood and positiveness, and a consistent, self-proving philosophy of personal life. This describes beings by their doings.

It develops the conception of causation into a connected line and system of the whole philosophy of the nature, relations, and destinies of persons. It gathers to itself, and conserves, all known truth; and from it all the errors, follies, and "Isms," philosophical and religious, fall, of their own weight, discredited.

This conductive philosophy rejects many, and conserves many, of the old beliefs of men. It confirms itself by rigid logic, lays itself parallel with all other philosophies and sciences, and courts the attacks of all logic that does not use consciousness and activity for its premises. We believe, not only, that it is self-proving, but that the mutually destructive clashes of the thought-systems of the nineteenth century have left this the only possible reputable philosophy, and a sufficient one. This line and system of assured truth we try to trace; and it leads us into glorious realms, and to magnificent vistas.

Then, along this line of conductive philosophy, the human person finds himself related to a Divine Person, who is his Cause, and to a realm of moral relations that grow out of that philosophy of causation and personal activity. So we study that Divine Person, to find in him a light on the glories, rights, and destinies, of the human person.

Tracing this line of philosophy in history, we survey it in The Bible. We find that book a treatise on philosophy, the foremost teacher of first principles, the earliest teacher of the philosophy of personal doing, and of causation, and even the introducer of the modern words, phrases, and principles that are now most approved as rational and philosophical.

We, however, ask our readers to abandon many old methods of argument and forms of expression, to accept some novel conclusions, and even to modify in some respects their interpretation of The Bible. But we find the reasons for such modification by the authority of The Bible itself. And The Bible, and the Christian theology, issue from the testing, glorified.

So this book follows one chain of philosophy, which is a golden line, or a stairway of light, from the child of God to his Father's home.

CONTENTS

CHAPTER I

THE ENIGMA OF LIFE · · · · · 13

CHAPTER II

CONSCIOUSNESS · · · · · · 15

There is no such thing as proof; Logical proof is not proof; Consciousness.

CHAPTER III

SELF-CONSCIOUSNESS · · · · · · 18

Consciousness is not single; It reveals the person.

CHAPTER IV

HUMAN PERSON · · · · · · 20

§ 1. *Self-expression;* Person, active; Pleasure and pain; Character; Self-defense; Love; Taste; Will; Continuity.

§ 2. *Intellect;* Doing does; What we know; Plato; Aristotle; Kant; Words describing intelligence; Reason; Lego; Logos; Categories; Kant's categories; Experimental knowledge; Sensation and sense-perception; All knowledge is of concretes; All knoweldge is of activities; Being; Consciousness is an action; Knowledge relative; Personal equation; Sense-perception; Faculties; Attention; Association of ideas—memory; Symbolization and correlation; Ideas of time, space, quantity; Consciousness plural; Idea of causation; Quadruple consciousness; Idea of purpose; Skill, wisdom, common sense; Obedience; Multiple consciousness.

§ 3. *Moral science;* Causation, purpose, obedience; Ownership and rights; Value, ends, quality; The first cause;

System; Moral right; Beneficence in the universal
system; Rights of men; Conscience; Cultivable.

§ 4. *Soul, mind, and spirit;* Human personality plural;
Soul; Mind; Spirit; Spirits children of God; Moral
argument for immortality.

§ 5. *Categories of human person;* Kant's principles of the
pure understanding; The Categories.

CHAPTER V

THE DIVINE PERSON - · · · · 74

§ 1. *A physical and psychical argument.* Universal belief
of the eternal uncreated existence of matter; Argument from design; Argument from causation; The
cause of complexity and correlation; Relations are
mutual and reciprocal; The Creator of atoms is the
Creator of the world; Materialism; Deification of law;
Natural systematization; Evolution; Involution; Pantheism.

§ 2. *An intellectual argument;* Idealism; Skepticism and
agnosticism; Anthropomorphism; Infinite Being and
infinity; Monism, unitism; True infinity and unit.

§ 3. *A moral argument;* Theology precedes philosophy;
Suneidesis; Moral design and relations; God rules as
Creator; A maker is analogous to his work; Creation
by will; Kant quoted; Plurality in the Divine Unity;
God our Father and a spirit.

CHAPTER VI

THE RELATIONS OF THE DIVINE AND HUMAN PERSONS 97

The Creator and the universe are always connected; Providence, prayer and supernature; Moral relations; Moral
character; God's right to create men with freedom of
will; The laws of God are His loves; They are also
His indignations; Laws alternative, vindicatory and
punitive; Theodicy; Past life is persistent moral relation to God; Salvation; Natural religion has no remedy for sin; Conscience knows no pardon; Conductive
philosophy hopeful; Requisites in human salvation;
Through revelations; Through spiritual agency.

CHAPTER VII

PHILOSOPHY IN THE OLD TESTAMENT · · · 108

§ 1. *The Trilogy of Genesis;* Creation of the world; Creation of matter; Names of God; Elohim; The first sec-

tion of Genesis; God's Word; The second section of
Genesis; Creation of moral persons; Jehovah Elohim;
Installation of moral relations; Two trees; Sin is moral
death; The first moral law; The first sin; Its results;
Cherubs and flaming sword; The third section of
Genesis; Jehovah; Enlarged society; The first crime.

§ 2. *General tenor of the Old Testament;* Patriarchal theology; The Mosaic education; God's person and rights;
God's holiness; Sin; Types; The tabernacle and the
temple; Priests; Sacrifices; Purifications; Atonement;
The breastplate of judgment; Urim and Thummim.

§ 3. *Divine Spirit.*

§ 4. *Immortality;* Sheol; Necromancy.

§ 5. *Salvation;* Spirit's help; Mediator and sacrifice.

CHAPTER VIII

PHILO THE ALEXANDRIAN JEW · · · - 143

§ 1. *Philo introduced.*

§ 2. *Philo's Doctrine of Deity;* Causation; Origin of matter; Supreme Being not knowable; Supreme God has
no gender; Supreme God a person; God our Father;
His creating and ruling faculties; God known in His
doings; Foundations of moral law are in God's person;
God's Word; God's Word a person; God's Word His
Son; God's Word an idea; God's Word is God's
image; The Divine Word; God's Word always active;
Many words of God, Angels; Philo's logos doctrine is
Jewish; Right reason (logos) of Nature; Two Words,
two Sons of God; The Word is law; Spirit of God;
Divine Spirit; Spirit was created; The Spirit a power;
Two Spirits of God.

§ 3. *Philo's Man;* Child of God, and in God's likeness;
Bodies made of water; Water and spirit as emblems
of birth; Blood; Soul; Two souls; Spirit; Spirit is
from above, *ánothen;* Mind; Mind is from above; Intellect and reason; Intellect immortal; Speech; Faculties; Freewill; Consciousness and conscience; Conviction; The Advocate, Paraklete; The breastplate of
judgment; Summary of psychology; Salvation.

CHAPTER IX

SYRIA AT THE CHRISTIAN ERA · · · - 184

Central crossroads of ancient world; Synagog cult; Sects;
Essenes; Pharisees; Sect names from the breastplate
of judgment; Therapeutæ; Sadducees; Fruitage of
the Hebrew training; Gnostics.

CHAPTER X

JOHN THE BAPTIST · · · · · · 195

A pupil of Jesus; His doctrine; Baptism a symbol of the
creation of man; Baptism of Jesus; Spirit's presence;
A philosophy of salvation.

CHAPTER XI

PHILOSOPHY IN THE NEW TESTAMENT · · · 203

§ 1. *Its Metaphysics;* Consciousness; Authority; Supernatural philosophy; Revelation of God and of His
will; Inspiration.

§ 2. *The Divine Person;* Jewish doctrine continued; An
advance in the doctrine of personality of God; The
Word of God; Jesus; He claimed to be God; He was
believed to be God; Jesus, the light; Names of Jesus;
Lord, Jehovah; Jesus in prophecy; Prophecies of
Daniel; The Messiah, and Son of God; The Son of
Man; The kingdom of heaven; The fullness of time;
Advent of the Anointed; The Lamb of God; Saint
John's trilogy; The Book of the Revelation; Outline
of the Apocalypse; Keys to its interpretation; Chap-
ter I; Chapters IV, V; Chapter VI; Chapter VII; The
first parallel; Chapter VIII; Chapters IX, X; The
second parallel; Chapter XII; Chapter XIII; The
number of the beast; Chapter XIV; The third parallel;
Chapter XV; Chapters XVI, XVII, XVIII; Chapter
XX; Chapters XXI, XXII; The last four parallels;
Prelude and peroration; Apocalyptic ideas elsewhere.

§ 3. *Miracles of Jesus;* Use and value of miracles; Authen-
tication of miracles; Scientific objection; Philosophical objection; First practical objection; Second and
Third practical objection.

§ 4. *Spirit of God;* Ontological principles; Spiritual, or
moral, relations; God a spirit; The Holy Spirit; The
Trinity; The Holy Spirit, as influence; Birth of Jesus
from Holy Spirit; Baptism with Holy Spirit; The
gift of the Holy Spirit; Blasphemy against the Holy
Spirit; The Paraklete, Spirit of Truth.

§ 5. *Human Person;* ·New Testament is philosophical;
Human bodies; Birth from water; Blood, soul; Birth
from above, from God, from spirit; Spirit in *John III,
3-9;* Sayings of Jesus about spirit; Superiority of the
New Testament's doctrine about spirit; God's Spirit
the definition and source of spirit; God the Father of
spirits; Immortality.

Contents

§ 6. *Human Rightness;* The aim; The principles; God's will the law of action; Personal nobility; Morality; Bodily and spiritual sin; Rightness in and towards one's self; Rightness towards God; Rightness towards men.

§ 7. *Salvation of men;* Freewill is the disturber; Outline of the plan of salvation; Atonement; Began before creation; Vicariousness; Atonement in time; It required some performances; These must be subsequent to the beginning of sin; Vicarious atonement by Jesus; The blood of Jesus; Vicariousness in blood; Atonement in the life of Jesus; In death; Priestly atonement; Vicarious atonement not in any single act; Elements of personal relations and influence; Atonement is grace.

§ 8. *Adoption, or Installation, of Children of God;* New birth; Agency of God's Spirit; Glory and bliss of the children; Holiness; Christian experience and living.

APPENDIX

Comparison of the Apocalypse and the Prophets · 345

The Beasts of Daniel and the Apocalypse · 349

Saint Paul's Apocalypse · 352

The Apocalypse of John the Baptist · 353

Index to Topics · 359

CHAPTER I

THE ENIGMA OF LIFE

What is a man? Who shall or can answer? Who even tries to describe the Living Being that pulses in the blood, and springs in the force of muscles, and thrills in the ardor of nerves, and that thinks, wills, loves, enjoys, suffers, hopes and fears? What is his substance and form? Where is his seat? What is his force? And, above all, what is his destiny?

Neither Science nor Philosophy have answered these questions, although there can be no beginning of Philosophy, nor completion of Science, without some knowledge of what a man is in himself. Science and Philosophy now so far recognize this dependence, that Science is become an eager quest of the nature of a soul, and Philosophy more and more puts forward Psychology as its chief study and aim; and yet, under the name of Psychology there is studied, not the nature or being of the soul, but only knowledge and thoughts, and their connections and behavior.

Every religion is a philosophy resting on some theory of the nature and being and destiny of souls. And so every soul sometimes, perhaps always, cries out, What am I? Am I Master, Guest, or Slave in this body? What are my forces of safety and danger in this whirl of earthly life; and what will be my nature and resources in the possible life hereafter?

In the following pages an answer, rational and philosophical, to some of these questions is attempted. First, we find a reasonable beginning, or basis, of knowledge of ourself; and on that we try to build and develop one coherent and symmetrical theory of the nature of a Person. On this, or around this, arrange themselves all the facts and problems of life, truth and happiness. The field of survey is all the magnificence of glory and good in life. The line of study is one continuous thread, starting in the simplicity of the consciousness of every person, learned, simple or child, and ending in an assurance of the reality of all the wealth and splendor that are garnered in the grandest philosophy, or cherished in the loftiest aspirations of children of The Author of All Things.

Then we make some study, in history and literature, of the recognition and utterance of these facts and of the principles of the nature and relations and destiny of human persons.

If this study appears abstruse, the questions, facts and thoughts are those of the daily common life, and of the most familiar interests and experiences of all persons. All thought is mysterious, and all intelligence is profound. Only a fool has no enigmas and puzzles. Fortunate is he who is alive to the necessity of gathering into his view all the facts of his knowledge and experience, and of linking them by an honest logic into one intelligent system that, at every point, shall be true to reason and to life.

CHAPTER II

CONSCIOUSNESS

To live is to believe something. The assertion and defense of beliefs is the universal passion. The cessation of belief is insanity or death. The hosts are pressing forward with a cry for truth, and often with ardor and sacrifice not less honorable, nor even less superb, than the heroism of a soldier.

Philosophy is a war between beliefs and doubts. Its first question is, What is truth? A man's first step in philosophy brings him to a doubt of facts. His second leads him to a doubt of himself. To doubt well is magnificent. To doubt ill is contemptible, and a crime against nature. In the last steps of philosophy a man returns to a disciplined and wiser faith in himself, and, through this, to faith in a blessed truth and a cheerful world.

In this world, and for human beings, there is no such thing as proof absolute. That which is commonly called Proof is only a demonstration that one belief is as reliable as some other one. But the column of evidence rests at last on some unexplored ground. *There is no such thing as proof.*

Logic does not pretend to discover original principles or primal truths. It is only an arrangement of words and sentences by which one of them is so laid open as to reveal whether *Logical proof is not proof.*

or not another is contained in it. Logic is a process, not an intelligence. It can be performed by machinery. In the trickster's hand, logic is a device for veiling premises, assumptions and sophistries. It has been the weapon by which truth has been murdered.

But it may be asked, Have we not Reason which discovers truths, or furnishes fundamental principles? It would be easy to fill pages with mere names of men gifted with supreme acumen and learning, leaders in psychology, philosophy and theology for the millions; and all of these have affirmed what they called first principles of truth; and yet no two of these men have agreed as to these principles or the inferences from them.

Do we, then, know nothing? Are there no assured facts, no reliable grounds of belief, no trusty principles of Reason? Assuredly there are these; but, because they are first principles they cannot be anything else. They cannot be deduced, argued, proven, analyzed, pierced, surrounded, shrunken, nor enlarged.

There is something that we call Consciousness. It is the first, deepest, fundamental sense, feeling, perception, or whatever else you choose to call it, of the
Conscious-
ness. mind, soul, reason, spirit, or whatever else you choose to call yourself. This is not proof; but it is that which occupies the point at which that which is called Proof aims. It is not evidence, but conviction. It is the last link in the chain, and the first. It is not logic, but premises. It is the self-assertion of the Living Being. This alone is knowledge; and this is the only conceivable knowledge. It is not logic, but premises. It is that from which Logic and Reason derive all their facts. It is the beginning and the end of reasoning. Whatever is not known in consciousness,

or is not fairly deducible from something in consciousness, is not provable, nor really knowable. Wherever beliefs may originate, or however they may be received or declared, they are believed only on some ground of consciousness, some inward compulsion that brooks no denials.

But philosophers have never been honest with their consciousness; because it is next to impossible to be so. Philosophy has always been consciousness plus theories, plus logic, and plus innumerable follies. Philosophers have derided the Common Sense of Man as gush, and have forgotten that there is a philosophical gush that is death-dealing. Ice water from mountain tops is more of a gush than is the life-laden spring in the valley.

Logic begins where consciousness has preceded. Logic is an army, and consciousness is its commander; and together they are invincible and dominant.

CHAPTER III

SELF-CONSCIOUSNESS

Consciousness never is, and never could be single. It is a consciousness of a feeling, a desire, an experience, a belief, etc., but with this it is a consciousness of Self. Even as a consciousness of Being, it is a sense of being of some special sort. It is a unit; but, like all other units, it has two sides, or an in and an out, a to and from, a beginning and an end. We are always trying to do the impossible with consciousness; for we try to isolate it as a simple thing, and at the same time to bring it into a description in language which has only compound terms. In language there are no nouns which can be defined without adjectives, because in Nature there are no beings, substances, actions or events apart from relations which, to any intelligent Being, are qualities. In language, as in Nature, there are no verbs without subjects, but we are always hunting for the noun that has no adjective, and the verb that has no subject, and the subject that has no verb.

Consciousness not single.

Consciousness is necessarily a consciousness of Self. Idealism and monism would like to see all verbs solid with their subjects, and to write "I do," or "I feel," in the mazes of a monogram; but consciousness refuses, and before it says "Do," or "Feel," it finishes saying "I."

Consciousness reveals the Person who is conscious.

Self-consciousness is inscrutable, partly because in one

18

aspect it is single, and partly because in another aspect it is complex. It is single because it is the one fact of knowing. It is complex because the knower is more than a knower, and cannot separate himself from his relativities, his needs, capacities, experiences and sentiments.

But it is said by some that consciousness is at once the witness, instrument and substance of knowledge, and the judge, jury and advocate in the trial court, and hence there is no assurance that there is anything more than consciousness. But that is sophistry; for consciousness is never on trial as to its existence. A supposed case of consciousness may be on trial, but only because self-consciousness is confessed and made a first principle of fact. If the case is on trial in a court where you cannot throw out the witness without expelling the Judge, and can only impeach the Judge by denying the law of impeachment, and the Judge refuses to expel himself, you cannot throw the case out of court.

But there are those who say that consciousness is not self-consciousness, because it is not consciousness of what self is. This is a sophistical attempt to forestall self-examination by assuming for each of the words, *What*, *Self* and *Is*, an unwarranted meaning. Knowledge can be real without being complete. An infinite knowledge would be only a sum of many knowledges, each of which was real but narrow. It is the aim of this little book to show that our knowledge of our Selves is enormous; but it is knowledge more of actions than of being. Action does not beg for recognition, but enforces it.

That which knows is He, She, You or I. Names are only conveniences, or garments. And so, for our convenience, we say "Self" and "Person;" and the name Person means no more nor less than Self; and Self is that which knows by consciousness.

CHAPTER IV

HUMAN PERSON

§ 1. SELF-EXPRESSION

We now set before us the task of discovering this Person of our Self. It is a chase as difficult, perhaps, as the pursuit of a moccasined man over the stony ridges of pathless crags. But, as trained trailers follow and discover fugitives, and as keen-scented nostrils hang on invisible tracks to their end, so we enter on the search, hopeful and eager; for it is a pursuit of all that is best in knowledge and in hopes.

To discover and describe what is meant by the names Self and Person, one must explore consciousness, and systematize all that is found therein. To do this perfectly would be to gather all actual and possible biographies, to collect all possible experiences and conceptions of all souls, to catch all possible enjoyment of art, music, and poetry, to drone with the dullard, and kindle with the fire of the patriot, the statesman and the enthusiast, or to patiently dissect nerves with the Scientist and souls with the Philosopher; in short, to be in touch with humanity in every thought and feeling.

In this pursuit of our Self, we propose to survey first, not what we are, but what we do, or rather to describe our Selves only as doers. If there is a possibility of finding out what a Person is " In himself," or out of all relations with other things, we neglect that pursuit at this point. We follow the trail of the personality that is a self-conscious activity. We describe the Being whose life is an active self-expression: for, whatever a Person may be in his Being, he has adaptations to activity and to relations with his world.

In the pursuit of our Self, we must notice and describe all the kinds of action of a Person. But this will not be a mere writing of a list. It will rather be like a picture of a busy world of people. And it will be a chart of a battle-field, for, to say that " A Person acts," is to raise the battle-flag of philosophy. Around this assertion the battle of the giants has raged, with consummate skill, and keenest and heaviest weapons. It is the ceaseless war between skepticism and consciousness, in which consciousness comes into the field an incorporate, irresistible positiveness. Personality knows itself as acting, and as quivering and springing with active vital force, in response to touches that are the impact of other actors and motions. Consciousness of personal doing is a protest against idealism, monism, and agnosticism. The thing or Being that does act, and can act, is a thing or Being that is.

We will first observe the simplest forms in which the life or being of a Person expresses itself, and then come to the study of the highest Reason, and then ask if Philosophy can be constructed on anything but Psychology, and if Psychology can be constructed on anything but personal activities of minds, and if such Psychology is imbecile or glorious.

Call up, then, this something that is named a Person. If you cannot weigh him nor fetter him, you can observe his doings.

See him first in pleasure or pain. He who enjoys or aches lives. When he thrills with delicious joys, can you persuade him that delight is unreal, or that he who is so happy is nothing? When he is torn with pain, and when, perhaps, almost all his sense is one concentrated agony, can you convince him that torment is nothing, or that he who suffers is nothing?

Pleasure and pain.

This Person comes to us certifying his real-being by his character, or the persistent self-expression of a disposition. He wants something, wants desperately, passionately, wants always. And he wants to do, to do always, to do fully, perhaps violently. All his sense of being condenses into one sense of adaptations and relations and suitableness. He who has these has attitudes towards them, and this is character, and that which has such character is a Person.

Character.

See him, next, in the passion of self-defense against invasion, or dismemberment, or robbery, or humiliation, or dishonor. He fights for life, rights, happiness, or honor; and this battle-passion is the vital forceful springing of a living Person. The recoil from a lie, or a meanness, or a breach of fidelity, or an insult, is the life-expression of a Self, a personality.

Passion of self-defense.

See him, next, as the Being that loves, whether with the gregariousness that may be a timid clinging, or that "enthusiasm of humanity" which to some minds is a synonym for religion; or whether it be with that liking which results from being like, and is an expression of character, and makes the harmony of life, its sunshine, its wealth; or whether with that devotion which is the paradox of self-expression, that mystery which word-logic declares to be impossible, and which is

Love.

the most real of realities, the potent factor in all noble life.

See him as a Being that has æsthetic taste, or a sense of excellence, beauty, agreeableness, in Nature, art, or music. What is this but an adjustment *Æsthetic taste.* of a living noble Being to his environment? Excellences are not in things, but in the Persons. They are revelations of the presence and nature of the Persons.

See him as the Being that wills. But shall we here define Will? It is the concentrated essence of the self-expression of a personality. It is his Self, *Will.* moving its Self. It is the freeness of a self-mover. It is the sovereignty of the soul. It is the Royal force of a living Being, a force that may be defeated or misguided, but cannot be else than free. Logic cannot define it. Some logicians have said that a Will determines itself. But this is to say that Will is some separate element in a Person, and is not the Person's Will, and therefore is not a Will at all. Some logicians have said that it is determined by motives, and the strongest motive. But this is to say that the Man is ruled by some parts of his Self, and that his Will is one part of him. Logic fails to define Will; but self-conscious Will explains itself as self-moving of the compound Person who is the real unit of living Being. Will is the living Person's declaration that he is a Person, a Being of many parts and multiple relations and wants, and of manifold powers. It is the province of a Will to choose according to the actual, not the ideal, circumstances. A choice of ideals is distinct from a choice of actions. A Will that can take counsel of intelligence, experience, policy and everything else in personality and relations, is a Person's Will, and anything else is no Will. A Will that can change with circumstances is a Person's Will, and anything else is no Will. Will is good or bad, not because something else in the Man, or out of the Man, makes it so; but because it is the self-expression of the Man's Self, and is the Man's freeness, and cannot be anything else than free.

See this Person also as the life that has continuousness and memory. He clings to the glory and riches of his past; and the shame of his past, and its evil, will not leave him. His past is the affluence of his present. He is what he has been. Neither Science nor Logic can explain this continuity of being. Logic is bewildered when it attempts to explain how a being that was can be the being that is. And Science that, in despair, abandons all effort to explain how atoms of matter hold together, is still less able to tell how the life or being of a soul runs in one line through its yesterday and its to-morrow. But, what Science and Logic cannot do, Consciousness does; for the soul that is to-day knows itself as having been long ago. In the science of conscious life, perpetuated identity with one's past experiences and history is the glory of personal being, and is its garnered treasure.

Self-continuity.

§ 2. INTELLECT

We have, in the preceding pages, noted the simplest elements of the life of a human Person. But we have not seized the man, nor seen his Self. We have only noticed his experiences and his doings, and, in these, have felt the presence and the quality of the man's Self. The experiences in ourselves, which our consciousness, on its most solemn oath, will swear are real, have been like the tokens of the experiences around us; and in ourselves we know our fellows. But we have not found and grasped a man. We have, however, been conducted near to his presence. We have felt in ourselves, and noted in the world, the principle that he who does is.

We may pass on now to view a man in his grandest performances and noblest experiences. We must view him as rational or intellectual. But we shall not find the man in his selfness. We shall find him only in his doings; yet we are in these conducted where the spiritual air is tempered with his presence, and his voice is heard and his touch felt. And by these experiences and doings of our own Self we recognize our own noblest vitality, and are conscious that our body homes not unworthily an heir of Heaven and a child of God.

Students of human life, Philosophers we call them, have assumed that study of what a man is, and of what he knows, is one study. We, too, shall proceed to observe what a man knows, and hope from this to be conducted to a clear view of his nature and his destiny.

We may, however, profitably first glance at the theories of the three greatest leaders in philosophy, Plato, Aristotle and Kant.

Plato taught that a human person is an organized real being. He is a growth not of Earth but of Heaven. He has, in a previous existence, been in sight of, and in touch with, ideas which originated Plato. in God's mind and are eternal entities. He took in the knowledge of these ideas once, because he is of stuff like them, and is an individualized idea. He tried to establish philosophy by distinguishing between the two Greek verbs *einai*, (*to be*) and *gignesthai* (*to become*). He said that only God and ideas *are*, and that other things only become. In this he made philosophy a mere dialectical quibble about the verb *to be* and the noun *being* (*ousia*), while he really recognized nothing as existing except God and forms conceived by God.

*Hence the teaching of Plato, which on his lips fascinated the world, and inspired in men a sense of living as Children of God, in view of eternal verities, became, in the mouthings of Plato's successors, a cold skepticism and an agnostic despair.

Plato almost alone, perhaps we should say quite alone, among all the philosophers of the world, attempted to formulate a Psychology, or theory of what a human person is, and made this to some extent a basis of his theory as to human Reason. He figured a man as having in his head another man, who is his rational (*logistikón*) part, wise, incorruptible, and immortal. This knows so much of divine truth as it has seen in a previous existence. It is its right and duty to dominate the whole Person. Then he has in his breast a second part, which is instinctive (*thumoeidés*) and spirited. This is like a lion, impulsive and heroic. Then he has a third part, which is greedy (*epithumetikón*) and beastlike. This is like a hydra monster, and occupies the lower body, and is earthly, sensual and perishable, or, if not perishable, punishable.

Plato's most celebrated and influential, but in genius far inferior, successor was Aristotle. Plato had

Aristotle. explained everything through his consciousness of manhood as childship of God. Aristotle and

---

*Plato's men did not really live either in substance or with vital power. Perception also was discredited. Man and consciousness were minimized by the very effort to glorify them. There was left no criterion for ideas except their harmony with each other in the universal system of ideas; and that harmony had to be judged by discredited human minds.

his men were machines for analyzing, enumerating, and classifying thoughts. But the machine never verified itself; and although this machine did its own thinking, its ideas neither originated in God nor in the thinker, but were in the material things that he saw. Aristotle was an incarnation of logic—cold, bare, and spiritless. He is the World's Master in formal logic; but his logic has no psychology. He had much to say about *energy*, but nevertheless he could not rise above futile verbiage about *being* and the verb *to be*, and his philosophy was but a machine moving itself from nowhere to nowhere, and halting at last in an arid desert of doubts and empty words.

*The words used by Aristotle for names of intelligence implied, or ought to have implied, the agency of a man in his knowledge; but under Aristotle's pen they became merely names of forms of objective knowledge. His consciousness never asserted its authority.

Among modern philosophers, no one has been so influential as Immanuel Kant. He is wonderful in his dialectical acumen, and minuteness and subtlety of logic. He is sometimes full of quickening fire in the expression of great thoughts. He is a synonym for glorification of Reason. And yet he is the disseminator of despair and deadliness.

Kant.

Kant used all the power of his great abilities in push-

Nous (*mind*) was to him a form of wisdom, but not a part of a Person. Although, in a vague way, he discusses inconclusively the question whether or not mind is conscious of itself (See Metaphysics, Book XI, ch. 9), or is the same entity as its perceptions and its objects of perception, yet as to the question, What is a mind? he was "all at sea." (See also Ethics, I, ch. vi, 3, and Book VI, 2 and 11.)

Under his pen, *gnosis, sunesis, episteme, gnome, dianoia, logismos, phronesis*, and *aesthesis* meant objective knowledge. Even to *logistikon* he discusses rather as to its usefulness than as to its essence.

ing forward the already universal and destructive conception, or theory, that truth is to be attained only by
logic, and in its harmony of ideas with ideas. We have
to thank him for having pushed that line of theory so far
that its refutation and self-destruction could not help
following him.

Kant glorified Reason; but it was not *a man's* Reason.
Kant ignored human Mind as a factor in intelligence,
but he did not deny it, because consciousness and conscience were quick in him. But his successors have
dared to deny what he only said was not proven, and
have scorned consciousness, and have made skepticism
and disbelief the premises for their logic.

Kant saw truth as something existing *a priori.* He
assumed that for his starting point, and gave all his
attention to an examination of that. But he did not
escape from himself and his consciousness, nor from his
sense of the operation of causation, which, as we hope
hereafter to show, is the dominant fact and principle in
philosophy. Hence, as he did not wish to say, like
Leibnitz, that ideas are innate in men, and did wish, in
some vague way, to confess the power of intellect, he
does affirm that " Reason is a faculty of principles," and
that there is a " Causal relation of Reason." But if we
ask, What is a faculty? and, Of what is Reason a faculty?
we get no satisfaction from Kant.

Kant tried to mark out the lines within which the
truth must be found, if there is any truth, and according
to which our knowledge, if we have any knowledge,
must arrange its ideas. He made logic a study of forms
of thinking that does not think of actual things. He
studied knowledge as something for men's minds, but

refused to admit the minds of men as agents of their own activity.

Kant's system of Reason is like a geographical globe prepared for a map of human knowledge. The poles, equator, parallels and meridians are exactly drawn, but there are no lands nor living beings. It is not an Earth, but a dead moon. It is a map of thoughts, but ignores the thinker. And yet this chart, as he left it, appears as if drawn on transparent paper, having under it, in strong colors, a picture of a world crowded with living men. The followers of Kant have, as it were, withdrawn that lower sheet. Kant had only said that Reason does not know that there is any real being; but his successors have said, There is no being. They have thrown away the globe, and have made their chart a shadow on the changeful surface of a cloud. But they have not explained the source of the light and shadow, nor the nature of the cloud. That which Kant called "Transcendental Logic" has wrecked what he called "The Transcendental Æsthetic."

Before we proceed to our study of Reason, we notice some of the names which have been given to Reason and the performances of intellects. These are as flags on the battlefields of philosophy; Names of intelligence. for, although the power of a mind to construct names as symbols of conceptions is one of men's grandest faculties, and is indispensable to the evolution of intelligence, it is nevertheless true that the fixing of such names has always caused a stagnation of thought, followed by intellectual bigotry and fanaticism.

Every word that is used to describe or name any kind of human knowledge is a word designating an action of the person who knows. *Know* is the same as Greek *gignosko* and Latin *gnosco*, and means as they do, *I think.* *Apprehend* means *seize.* *Perceive* means *take thoroughly.* *Conceive* means *take together*, or *take in myself.**

No word has performed a more important part in modern philosophy than the word *reason*; and scarcely any other word has been used so irrationally. It

Reason.

comes to us through the French language, from the Latin, in which it (*ratio*) meant a *relation*, or a perception of a relation, or a reckoning, or a ratio, or a reasonableness. But it did not mean either a *part*, or a *faculty* of a Person. It has come to mean, in different mouths, four different ideas, viz.: *First*, universal impersonal truth; *second*, reasonableness; *third*, a faculty of mind; *fourth*, the exercise of mind in reasoning. But, while many use the name *Reason* often, and arrogantly, and with very positive language, almost nobody has made a pretense of defining it. It has been more convenient for everybody to assume that his favorite idea of it was the right one, and the one in which to deny its trustiness and glory would be the act of a fool. It is a word which nobody has a right to use without declaring in which of the four meanings he uses it. If the use of the word could be restricted to one meaning, it might be of great value; but the history of philosophy shows the word and its equivalent to have been used for little purpose except ambiguity, shuffling, and tricks, and largely to obscure truth, and to hide the person of God.

Another word which has exercised an enormous power to the present time is the verb *lego* in Greek and Latin.

---

*The other Greek words are these: *Oida, I know*, means *I have seen.* *Epistamai*, is *I stand on*, and means *I understand.* *Noeo, I think*, means *I use mind.* *Dianoia, intelligence*, means *minding* distributively.

It is impossible to study philosophy without examining and using this word; because from it are made the Greek equivalent for *ratio,* and our words *logic, intellect,* and *intelligence.*

Lego's.
Logo
Logic.
Intellect.
Intelligence.

The verb *lego* meant *I lay,* in Latin and in Greek. *Intelligence* means *knowledge of relations,* and *the faculty of knowing relations.* *Intellect* means *laid in relations,* and *the faculty of knowing relations.* From *lego,* the Greeks made the noun *logos,* the first meanings of which are *ratio, proportion, relation, degree,* and *division.* Later it came to mean *word, saying, speech, statement, account, argument, explanation, definition, proposition, theory.* Later it had a place in philosophy.

Logos will often be found translated into English by the word *reason.* But it never, in Greek, meant *reason* as a part of the being of a person, or an equivalent of the word *intellect.* It had in philosophy three general meanings: First, the truth in universal Nature; second, the apprehension of that truth in (not by) the minds of men; third, the right expression of that truth in logical thought and in speech. In these three significations it did important service, alike in the common and the metaphysical language of the Greeks.* We shall have occasion to observe its place in the writings of Philo Judæus and the Apostle John. Here we may well ask with much interest, What did Greek master-workmen in philosophy conceive to be the nature of

*See Plato: Theaetetus, 200 to 210; Sophist, 259 to 264; Republic, 510 and 511.
Aristotle: Ethics, Book I, ch. vii, 13, 14; ch. xiii, 15, 18; Book VI, ch. ii, 2; iv, 4; v, 3; Book VI, ch. i; ch. v; ch. vii, 7; ch. xi, 4; ch. xiii, 3 and 4; Book VII, ch. i, to Book VII, ch. ii, 7. Metaphysics, Book I, ch. i; Book II, ch. i; Book VIII, ch. v.

reason, or *logos*, and what was their idea of the reasoning faculty in a man?

Unfortunately, while they did not use the word *logos* as ambiguously as we now use the word *reason*, they did conceive that Reason (*logos*) is something existent in itself,* possibly originating in the Supreme Deity, but existent in the nature of things, and a law to all truth. And they never, except in Plato's and Aristotle's theories of *eide* and *ideas*, carefully studied the problem how this universal truth becomes a possession of a man.

Earnest efforts were made by the Greeks to describe, scientifically and systematically, human knowledge of

the things of the world. All the different ideas, or kinds of knowledge of material things, were classified, and these classes were named. The names given were called "Categories," i. e., names, or predicables. We cannot help admiring the acumen of the Greeks, as men of our western race, who, alone of all men, saw the importance of such logical steps in philosophy. The earliest schedule of categories, made by the so-called Pythagoreans, divided knowledge about things into four general classes. It said that we know things in, or as, *ousia* (being, or essence, or substance), *posón* (quantity), *poión* (quality), and *prós ti* (relation).

What we know.

Categories of intelligence.

Evidently here was an admirable beginning for a rational and scientific philosophy; but it was gravely imperfect.

It was made from no fixed philosophical point of

---

*The word *logos* was commonly used only in such terms as "*to have logos*," i. e., to have the universal wisdom, and in phrases with the prepositions *with, through, on account of, according to*. Logos was commonly spoken of as *the right reason of nature*.

view, and therefore the categories crossed and overlapped each other. The first category, *being*, might include everything, or it might be merely a conception, or a name for a mere logical inference about what is a prerequisite for any and all knowledge. The other three categories each had at least two viewing points—one in the things observed, and the other in their observer. The whole schedule was imperfect, because it made no recognition of knowledge of activities, events, conceptions, and organized beings, or of life.

Aristotle added to the four categories six others, viz.: *chrónos* (time), *tópos* (place), *keisthai* (situation), *échein* (possession), *poiein* (action), and *páschein* (suffering). Later he added others. But, wonderful Master of thought and logic as he was, he only introduced new confusion; for the first four of these later categories are only itemized categories of relation, and the other two are categories of active or vital beings. Later, some of the Greeks used the word *hypostasis* (*substance*) instead of *ousia*, and made other unimportant variations of the schedule. It must be observed that whether they used the name *ousia* or *hypostasis*, or any other term, to express such ideas as have been rendered into Latinized forms, as *essence, existence, substance*, or *entity*, these words never meant to them the verbal idea of *to be* or *to have being*, but always meant a material something at the basis of substance.

Kant brought to the study of categories rare powers of analysis and logic, but he attempted a new, a different, and an impossible performance. He sought to schedule the categories of The Understanding while he excluded consciousness, experience, and all the other elements of psycho- Kant's categories.

e more numerous than
ing, intertwining lot of
persuade a person that
when he is only talking
ment such that there is
recognition of a unit of
phases of *reality* and
ion that *a priori* ideas
fact, all idea of *being* is
deduced belief. Such
's contain nothing but
ed to describe either
ually philosophical, but
d by itemizing in three
and Quantity, all the
king the Latin words
nd prefixing the prepo-
etc.

t, drop all thought of
owledge as   Experi-
Self in our   mental
ent persons.   knowledge.

ion, a very simple thing

ced and unnatural. Im-
hers are named twice, as
s. Some items are only
eal recognition of actual
e itemized categories of
ality, but is a quality or
longs equally in all four
Limitation, as used in this

s. It has a specious ap-
ge of real things; but is in
sentences about anything

logical science. He designed that his categories should be names for the varieties of knowledge as purely theoretical. He said, They are the *a priori* conceptions of the understanding, answering to all the logical functions in all possible judgments. The inevitable result was that his categories were, in one aspect, attributes of objective substance, and, in another aspect, they were only formulas of logical processes in a thinking mind, and there was no way for bringing these antipodes into oneness. They are words in the air, which implied the real existence of matter and mind, but confessed neither, and prepared the way for denying and insulting both. They are categories of matter that is not matter, and of mind that is not mind. While making a magnificent struggle to attain superhuman intelligence, Kant is like an eagle tossed with broken wings on the division line of air and sea.

Kant's schedule of the categories is as follows:

I. *Of Quantity.*
Unity.
Plurality.
Totality.

II. *Of Quality.*
Reality.
Negation.
Limitation.

III. *Of Relation.*
Of inherence and subsistence (substance and accident).
Of causality and dependence (cause and effect).
Of community (reciprocity between the agent and the patient).

IV. *Of Modality.*
Possibility, Impossibility.
Existence, Non-existence.
Necessity, Contingence.

The faults* in this schedule are more numerous than its words.   It is a kind of revolving, intertwining lot of colors.   It is a cute invention to persuade a person that he is talking or thinking of things, when he is only talking of words.   There is a deft arrangement such that there is an appearance of starting with a recognition of a unit of being, passing through all the phases of *reality* and *existence,* and reaching a conclusion that *a priori* ideas have existence in necessity.   In fact, all idea of *being* is excluded, either as an *a priori* or a deduced belief.   Such schedules of categories as Kant's contain nothing but empty words, not really designed to describe either things or ideas.   A schedule equally philosophical, but utterly worthless, can be produced by itemizing in three groups, called Relation, Quality and Quantity, all the words that can be made by taking the Latin words *herence, tension, ence* and *sistance,* and prefixing the prepositions *ab, ad, con, de, ex, in, sub,* etc.

Let us, then, for the present, drop all thought of scheduling the categories of knowledge as pure reason, and let us study our Self in our experiences as rational or intelligent persons. *Experimental knowledge.*

Intelligence begins in a sensation, a very simple thing

---

*The arrangement in trios is forced and unnatural. Important categories are omitted and others are named twice, as if seen from different viewing-points. Some items are only negations of others. There is no real recognition of actual quality and modality. Of the three itemized categories of quality, *reality* does not mean actuality, but is a quality or manner *in assertions; Negation* belongs equally in all four groups of the categories or in none; *Limitation,* as used in this group, is limitation only in assertions.

The whole scheme is full of tricks. It has a specious appearance of giving names to knowledge of real things; but is in fact only a list of possible forms of sentences about anything or nothing.

as long as the man does not think about it. But if he reflects, the sensation resolves itself into at least two,

Sensation and sense-perception.

if not three, elements. It becomes a consciousness of his Self, and a consciousness that something else has come into relations with his Self, and a consciousness of an idea of a cause of his sensation. Then if he asks about causation, and asks how he knows even what he sees or touches, and asks how much is true, there he is bewildered. Alas for him if he asks, Do I know in my brain or at my fingers' tip? or asks, How does a thing out of me become a knowledge in me? He is told, and truly, that he never saw or touched anything. What he has seen was only light as it reflected; and light is waves of an unknown something that, for describing, has to be hunted by mathematics, and never is described or known. He is told that what he thinks he sees has only sent light into his eye, but even there he has not seen the picture that is there of the object, but it has done something to one of his nerves, and that has done something to or in his brain. He learns that compound or shaded colors, and appearances of solidity, and perception of distances, are all operations by himself.

He is told, too, that when he thinks that he touches something, he is mistaken; for no atom touches another in the world.

Blessed is he now if he does not despair, nor cease to think. He has only been taught that he does not know so simply and immediately as he supposed that he did. It does not follow that he knows nothing, nor that he is deceived. His consciousness has not been invalidated; for what he is conscious of is a true consciousness. He has only learned that there are many media between things and his sense of them, but he can become conscious of many of these media and of their exact laws.

What the man is conscious of in sense-perception (as we call perception by the senses) is that he has received some information. Information must always remain information; but there can be conveyed to any being just so much information as his faculties are adapted to receive.

By touch, there arises in a man's mind a conviction (which is consciousness, or very like it) that something has touched him; and he has a very definite conception of the nature of that thing. This consciousness we must re-examine. Right here we must classify the facts of consciousness, and here we must formulate some principles of philosophy.

The first principle coming out of an examination of consciousness is this, viz.: All human conceptions are of concrete things. General, universal, abstract, nominal, and conceptional ideas we have in abundance, but there is not one which is in our consciousness until it has been observed in some actual concrete thing. There are no abstract facts, such as goodness, badness, right, wrong, truth, or falseness, except in substantial things. Imaginations of non-existent and impossible combinations and organizations may be in our thoughts, but no conception of a primal elementary idea can be in our mind that has not been observed in a fact or thing. A man has not many perceptions before he compares and classifies what he perceives, and gives names to the classes of ideas. These he calls abstract conceptions. Then he makes abstractions of abstractions, and principles of principles, true and false; but the basis of all these is his perceptions

All our knowledge and ideas are of concrete things.

of concrete actual things. Indeed, the most of our abstract conceptions are but a notion of some single thing, or of a few things. An unlearned man cannot argue or reason without appealing to his few experiences and facts; and a philosopher does little better.

The second principle coming out of our examination of consciousness is this, viz.: All our conceptions are ideas of things as active. We know nothing whatever except actions. Science has demonstrated that solidity, form, weight, cohesion, gravity, temperature, color, taste, smell, and chemical and mechanical properties of matter are forms of motion of its atoms. In these words there is outlined not only the whole world of Science, but also the battlefield of Philosophy. Philosophy has only two armies and two battle-flags, although there are divisions and factions within the armies. The one army proclaims that the noblest, or most perfect, knowledge is of *being*. The other declares that all knowledge is of *doings*. Very early the Greeks recognized that motion and energy (*kinesis* and *energeia*) could not be disregarded in philosophy; but when the methods and logic of Aristotle became generally used, Philosophy turned away from Science and devoted itself chiefly to a search for what is called *being*. Science impelled this search only by its weariness in the effort to find order in the mass and multitude of facts, and by its confirmation of the truth that every fact has its cause. The chief impulse to the search for *being* was the natural love of men for skill in logic. Under this impulse they pursue the ultimate, or first, principle in all things, and in all lines of study. This ultimate object of pursuit is *being*, or that which *is*. We pursue it under the various names of

All our knowledge and ideas are of the activities of things.

essence, substance, entity, the thing in itself, the unit, unity, the first cause, etc.; but whatever may be the name given, the object pursued has been one, viz., that which is under the substance, and before action, and simpler than any known unit. This aim is chimerical. It is even absurd. Men still pursue it with arts of logic, but Philosophy despairs in the pursuit. Men cherish in their consciousness and their logic the conviction that there is *being;* but they despair of knowing it as *being* or as *unity;* * for we know and think of nothing but concrete things; and we know, and can think of these, only by and in their activities. This is not to say that we know only material things, and that we know only by sense-perception. It is to say that we know an enormous amount, and know gloriously, in consciousness, and that our knowledge is of the real and the actual, and of the moving things, and of the living and forceful things, in their doings and their products.

The logical complement to the facts just stated is that knowing is itself an action. But this truth does not depend on logic. It is a declaration of consciousness itself. The dogma that consciousness is an action is, however, the doctrine about which the hottest fight of philosophy will perhaps always rage; for if in consciousness a man does something, surely the man exists; but then arises the momentous question, How, if consciousness is an action, can we know that it is right action, and that its product is truth?

Men have always, by the very names that they give to

Consciousness is an action.

---

*It is profitable to see how the master mind of Aristotle tries to define *being* by various turns of the verb *to be,* and by tricks with the prepositions. See his Metaphysics, Book I, chs, ii and iii, and Book VI.

primal intelligence, implied that it was an action. *Perceive* means *seize thoroughly*. *Conceive* is *seize together*. *Apprehend* is *catch on*. You cannot turn consciousness into an inactive merely recipient faculty, by saying that knowledge is information received; for to receive is *to seize*.

A further part of the answer to the question, How do we know? is this. Knowledge, as known in conscious-

Knowledge of things is always relative to human faculties. ness, is a seizing, by the Self, of some relation of a thing to the man's Self, or a seizing of some *doing* (action) of the thing, in which it is relative to the *doing* of the man. No matter what may be the outcome of this declaration, we must assert it, both as logic and as consciousness. As surely as, in a mathematical equation, one member equals the sum of the elements

Personal equation. in the other, so surely there is in all knowing a "Personal Equation," or formula of elements and factors, a part of which are the faculties and activities of the man.

But it does not follow that beliefs can be invalidated on the ground that they are personal. To prove that human knowledge resting on consciousness is false, or even doubtful, it must first be proved that The Cause or Creator of men is not able to bring true information to men, or that he could not make men capable of receiving or conceiving truthfully. Is consciousness a lie because *receive* means *seize?* or because a Human Person is something more than an open-mouthed sack? Why, then, should negative theories have preference of right on the roads of philosophy? Why should we applaud him who compares man to a shining drop in a miry pool, rather than him who recognizes in man a protegé and favorite, if not a child and image, of God? Why should consciousness, which no science nor logic can impeach, be insulted on its imperial throne? And yet there will always be philosophical doubters; for knowledge is information; and if The First Cause had endowed men with ten thousand senses, and their evidence furnished an almost infinite description of substances and of their doings, and if The Creator, with an audible voice and in a visible form, declared the truth of the information, even then this certification would be relative to the powers and activities of men, and susceptible of rejection as not proven; but alas for him who should reject it!

Theories as to the nature and means of conscious knowledge of things by perception through the senses have been many. Some declare that it is only a combination of material sensations. Others call it a representation to the central nervous seat of intelligence, communicated by the nerves. Others say that it is a pre-established harmony between sensations and the mind. Others imagine that there is a medium between sensations and the mind, transforming feelings into ideas. Others declare that consciousness is immediate knowledge of things. Others say that things are only ideas, perhaps created in the mind itself, or perhaps suggested by some arrangement of inexplicable Nature. But is there really any reason why our bodies, which are the assistants of our joys, the mediums of our self-display, and the instruments of our great performances, should be in the courts of Philosophy scouted vagabonds?

When we observe and consider the intellectual acts and the noblest conceptions of Reason, and we ask how they arise in human minds, we are directed away from the trickery of logic, which only turns a kaleidoscope of words, and plays with the ins and outs of phrases, and we discover in a human person powers and functions exalted and glorious. As we survey each of these, we observe that they are not only helps to our highest wisdom, but each is the essential, and almost the beginning, of all intelligence; and, without each of them, men would be idiots, and truth unknowable.

Faculties and acts of the personal mind.

Foremost among these faculties is that which we call Attention. It is Directed consciousness. It is consciousness knowing itself as an activity, and controlling itself. It is consciousness governing its own direction, quickness, grasp and tenacity. It is not merely an occasional exercise of the mind, but is ever active in the waking man. It is the faculty that opens the doors of the treasury of the mind and commands a delivery of its affluence. And if Man is to know himself in consciousness, it is attention which is to make the study with spiritual scalpels and lenses, and is to count the respirations, pulses and vibrations of the soul.

Attention.

Next we notice in human intelligence something that all persons observe as being curious, and that logicians and philosophers speculate about, but which, as a study, is a part of psychology, and is of utmost importance. We observe that ideas have a connection together, a connection by classification, and a persistent union in our minds. This is not merely an occasional occurrence, nor a rare phenomenon. It is an essential element in all intelligence; and just in the measure of its perfect operation Man has wisdom, reason, genius and personal intellectual power.

Association of ideas. Memory.

Without it intelligence would vanish as it dawns, and thought would be no chain, no conception even, but a sequence of fugitive unrelated glimpses. The association of ideas is thought correlated, adjusted to its relations with other thoughts and with the personal life of the thinker, and then reeled up in the Being that is behind and below consciousness. It is the persistence of mental life, bearing constant evidence of the under working of a persistent living personality. It stores away thoughts with a history of their origin in circumstances, and also with intelligence of their likenesses, connections and relativities; and therefore when the thoughts mount again into consciousness they come in linked chains, or broad pictures, or in troops. Sometimes it seems to be a Master of our thoughts; but it is so only as a man's past always dominates his present.

This association of ideas is not essentially different in the greater conceptions in our minds from what it is in our lesser experiences; for it is not a connection of impersonal reason, but is a connection of each thought with the Being of the man himself. He is the link and tie of ideas, and they are the witnesses to his existence. And the measure of their quantity and quality is the measure of the mental nobility of the man. The persistent connection of thoughts, and the power of giving attention to parts of that connection, are the two phases of memory; and memory is the *sine qua non* of personal nobility, and makes both the present and the past experiences of a soul a persistent wealth. Woe to him if it is only a persistence of separate sights and sounds and touches, and not a correlation of ideas which The Creator has designed for eternal union.

Next there come into our notice two faculties and functions of mind, which work with the attention and the memory to perfect their work. One is a faculty of making in the mind such symbols and representatives of knowledge, that ideas remain when the things and experiences are forgotten. It makes words and language, art and harmonies, logic and its premises. It raises a soul out of its sordid and gross associations into the intellectual and spiritual life. The other is a faculty of multiplying attention and memory and association of ideas, and of correlating the many experiences and the plural ideas of the intellect, so that out of them come ideas of ideas, and principles of principles. These two personal faculties exalt the man from the condition of a mere receiver of impressions into that of a Being to whom great principles of Nature, and wide-reaching purposes and ideas of The Creator are revealed.

Faculty of symbolizing. Faculty of correlating ideas.

After we have recognized that grand personal powers and actions in men are the means which furnish an inestimable wealth of intelligence to them, we find that we have in them an explanation of a large group of conceptions which are always present in our ideas and experiences, and without which there can be neither experience nor thought. And yet these ideas are unsolved puzzles in every philosophy which rests more on logic and analysis of objective thought than on recognition of the nature of consciousness and on the personal active functions of men. These conceptions are our ideas of quantity, time and space, which Aristotle classed as *categories*, and Kant called *a priori conceptions*. A rational examination of them will show that they are products of personal actions and experience, and that, in a greater measure than any other conceptions, they are assisted

Ideas of time, space, quantity, plurality, division, dimension.

by, and dependent on, that human body which so many rationalists disparage.

Kant specially mentioned as *a priori* conceptions the principles of mathematics, and the categories time and space. He could not have selected any that are more evidently physical and experimental; for, all the processes of mathematics are either mere variations of methods of counting, or mere equivalent definitions. Kant often cites, as *a priori* conceptions, the fact that $5+2=7$, and the fact that two sides of an angle, or two parallel lines, cannot enclose space. But, in fact, no sum in addition, nor any multiplication table, was ever learned by anybody except through counting or memory of hearsay. And that "Angles and parallels do not enclose space," is only an equivalent definition of angles and parallels; for "enclose" means "surround by continuous lines," and angles and parallels are not continuous lines.

If we scrutinize our perceptions of things, we soon perceive a consciousness of directed attention; or, in other words, a consciousness of direction of our Self, and that this directed consciousness Space. fixes itself on various points of the observed objects, and that we perceive these points in their relations to each other and to our Self, and that we perceive our Self, or are conscious of our Self, in relations to them. And this is Space, a consciousness of measurable reach of direction of our Self, in respect to attention and perception. This is the simplest aspect of the conception of space. But we are, in our bodies, constantly conscious of perception of different objects, or different impacts, at different parts of our organism, or at different angles

from our center of personal consciousness. These rela·
tions and separations of parts of objects, we learn to
measure only by experience; and this experience is
gained in its first steps by some sense of measure, extension, or reach, in our own person, or by some sense of
time occupied in the process of measuring. Space is
therefore a conception of plurality in the relations of
physical objects to each other and to our Self, and is
measured by our consciousness of different parts of our
own physical organism, or by the angles and reach of
directed attention, or by time.

If we scrutinize further our self-consciousness, we perceive always a consciousness of self-continuance, gauged
Time. or measured by something that is in consciousness itself, and inseparable from it.
This is time; or, in other words, time is consciousness of
continuance of our Self. This, by experience, assisted
by our personal power of making general conceptions
and symbols, and of perpetuating them by memory
as laws of our thought, becomes a general conception
of time, applicable in all our experiences, and in all
conceptions of actions or events. Who shall say that it
may not be a regulated vibration or oscillation of our
personal being? Science has demonstrated that all the
so-called qualities and accidents of matter are measurable motions of particles, and Science is demonstrating
that the vital functions of our bodies are performed in
pulses or vibrations. There are in our physical life,
direct and reflex action, flux and reflux, stroke and relax-
ation, which in our health compromise and harmonize
with each other, but by their conflicts produce disease,
dementia and death. Analogy of Science may indicate
that there is a pulse and vibration of the soul, or of that

subtlest, most hidden part of our physical being, at which mind seizes matter, and takes control. Time is primarily a consciousness of successive exercises of vital action. Secondarily, it is a consciousness that the oscillation of our attention is associated with a sequence in the vital experiences of our bodies, and in the activities of the material world.

The discussions in the preceding pages have been steadily illustrating and confirming, on many lines of survey, our doctrines that personal conscious- Conscious- ness is an activity, and is of plural facts, con- ness is nected with one another. Pursuing the study plural. of intellect further, we are brought, by both logic and self-examination, to a perception that consciousness is itself plural, and that in this truth there is a conductive philosophy reliable and glorious, a philosophy of personal being.

It has been the popular fashion to declare that consciousness is an unit, and that it cannot be consciousness of anything but just *being*, or Self, and that all the rest of our wisdom is uncertain and unreliable. Against such doctrine, derived from inferences from false premises, we affirm that consciousness is multiplex or plural, and that this fact is the reason why philosophers have recognized quantity, quality, modality and relation as necessary categories of knowledge.

In one aspect consciousness is single. It is consciousness of the unity of its possessor. This is the last vanishing glimpse of Self as seen by One's Self. Single con Really this unity or singleness is a result of sciousness. confining One's Self to a single viewing-point. It is seeing One's Self through only one window.

Philosophers have felt compelled to find assurance of

the reality of existence or life.   They have thought to
find it by tricks with the verb *to be,* and they have made
infinitives and nouns and participles out of it, as if it
meant something, and yet, all the time there was no idea
in it; for *to be* is not really a verb.   It is only a copula.
It is only an equation mark of equality, like ＝.   Hence
the Greeks were so confused in their words that they
named the first category sometimes *being, ousia* (really
this is *essence* or *substance*), and sometimes *quantity.*   But
almost all the world has approved Aristotle's dictum
" Unity (*to hen*) is entity " (*to on*).   In one view of the
matter they were right ; for consciousness of quantity is, in
its beginning, a person's consciousness of his own being,
his independence, oneness, selfhood and wholeness.

But no experience of a person's consciousness ever
was, or ever can be, single.   A person is always conscious, not only that he exists, but that he is
of a certain sort, and that his "suchness," or
quality, consists in faculties for activity.   He
knows that he *is,* but more than that, he knows that he
has something, and that which he has he knows only as
powers of action.

But, no person ever had a thought that was not about
some action, real or imaginary.   The knowledge of the
outer world begins, for all persons, in the
third category of the person's Self; that is
to say, in his *exercise* of his faculties; and this
is his category of *modality.*   Hence *quantity* of substance
is, in our knowledge of it, a perception of many contacts
that the person has with its many parts (or atoms), which
are joined in oneness by the intelligent faculties of the
person.   He looks at himself, when he wishes to, through
a single window, and finds his selfhood, but he always

*Double con-
sciousness.*

*Triple con-
sciousness.*

looks at other things, and often at himself, through many windows, and he discovers himself by his many doings.

In this triplicity of consciousness arises that conception which is the chief principle of philosophy, the central fact in all the system of truths, the basis of all reasoning. This fact or principle is named Causation. In every perception we are conscious that something does something. Philosophers have recognized a great importance in the idea of "Cause and effect." It has been discussed as a law, and as a deduced conception, and as a formula of an equation: but, in fact, it is the simple truth that "Doing does," although in philosophy there is no greater fact.

The idea of causation.

All life of intelligent persons gets its constant illumination from exercise in the consciousness of causation. We act, or do, *to ourselves*, moving and receiving motion. We are at both ends of these acts, and know cause and effect as one action in ourselves.

We may now proceed to say further that every conception in consciousness is so far plural that it is at least quadruple. In every perception of things, the knower knows the thing as doing something, both to the perceiver and to other things. That is to say, he knows it in its relations. He knows it as a cause actively related, or connected, with many other things. By this knowledge, the man comes up into all the wealth and splendor of mental endowment. Here he finds the affluent material of his logic. He, in every one of his conceptions, knows himself as being, as having faculties, as using those faculties, and as correlating the relations (or relativities) of perceived things, until he sees widened out an universe

Quadruple consciousness.

of conceptions and principles glorious beyond measure. In the quadruple consciousness, the single perceptions become multiplex conceptions, and the individual facts become the interwoven systematization of a magnificent universe. And in this conceived universe there are principles of principles, and generalized facts of facts; but not one of these is an inferential product of Logic, or a creation of Reason; for man knows nothing that has not been brought to his consciousness by the relation of his trebly conscious person to the multiplex relations of the concrete things, or the events, or the living beings of the world. In the quadruple consciousness, sound ennobles itself into music; and lines and surfaces become the beauties of painting and sculpture and architecture; the activities of matter develop into the grandeur and ministrations of Science and Art: and causation expands into conceptions of possession, ownership, rights, skill and moral law.

That which the quadruple consciousness of a man knows, constitutes his grand endowments and wealth. This raises him above the brutes. This ushers him, a Prince, into an universe which ever unfolds to him new glories, and invites him into an inexhaustible field of ministering resources. And this unmeasurable treasure is not a creation of the Reason of men; but has come to them in their perception of the relations in the facts, beings, and activities of the world. Are we humiliated by this? Not unless it is a shame to be second to The Creator. If we were the makers of the grandest conceptions, then the facts of the universe would also be imaginary and its things unreal.

We must note here, that probably the loftiest conception that arises in the human mind is, at least as to its chief element, a conception of purpose. Even brutes know themselves as doers, and know their wishes and aims; but they probably know these as indi- vidual aims to exercise instinctive activities. *The idea of purpose.* But man, in his quadruple consciousness, knows himself as aiming at intelligent action, and knows intelligent action as purpose: for this is the definition of purpose, just this and no more. Intelligent action is directed aim. It is the personality and will of intelligent Person acting. It is not an inductive conception, a cre- ation by thought; but is a consciousness of what intelli- gent action, in relation to things and circumstances, is. Aimless action is idiocy or insanity. Intelligent action, known in consciousness as purpose or aim, is the crown- ing glory of the splendor of personal being in men or Gods, and, as we shall observe further on, is the core and essence of that consummate excellence in personal beings to which we give the name Morality.

In what we have said of quadruple consciousness, we have used the language of philosophy, but we have only interpreted the thoughts and consciousness of all men. The common sense, or general *Skill, Wisdom,* consciousness of normal men, fairly devel- *Common sense.* oped, is an acceptance of truths that have been brought to us in facts. Wisdom is not invented conceptions, or harmony of theories with theories; but is humble obedience of mind to the reception of facts that are found in things. What are skill, and science, and art, but submission to the truth which The Creator brings, in things, within the compass and vision of the mind, that is to say, into the quadruple consciousness of a man? After all our boasting about our Reason, our progress, our inventions and conceptions, we find our

glory and our happiness in our conformity to the laws
and facts that are in things, as we discover these laws

Obedience.   and facts, not in ourselves alone, but in
Nature as relative to ourselves. This is obedience to The Creator; and perfect obedience is consummate wisdom and complete virtue.

We might now attempt here to write in a schedule of
categories, a scientific and philosophical portrayal of the

Multiple con-   powers, blessedness, and glory that inhere in
sciousness.   the personality of a human being. But the
plural consciousness brings forward so vast an
array of intelligence, and displays such a system of the
relations of men to things, and of each man to all men,
and of principles to principles, that we must linger in
contemplation of some of these facts and principles.

The plural consciousness finds its greatness and glory
in the fact that it makes intellect itself the subject of its
study. The lesser animals can, like men, have consciousness of being, and of having powers, and of using faculties, and of perceiving some of the relations of things.
But a man can make his Self, and all the stored treasures
of his complex being, the object of his reflections.

§3. MORAL SCIENCE

Chief among all these glories that are in men, or that
come to them, through the consciousness of the affluent

Moral   wealth in the endowments of Man's personal
science.   being, and through the performances of his
personal powers, and through his perception
of the facts and principles of the countless relations in
the things and activities of the world, is that one which,
as a philosophy of the well-being of Man, and of the

highest happiness of human persons, and of the direct-
ing aims and the motive springs of action in human
lives, is called Moral Science.

Nothing in the realm of human conceptions is
accorded more unanimous and enthusiastic eulogy than
theoretical morality. About nothing is there more complete consensus of opinion than there is about the general principles of practical morality. But when we look
for agreement among men in the application of these
principles, or for a prevalent regard for that part of
moral science which relates to what we call right and
wrong, or when we attempt the study of the fundamental
principles of morals, the unanimity breaks up like the
surface of water under a wind, and the ideas which as
theories are adored, are in practice despised and hated.

Moral Science is not a system of religion, nor of virtue, in any narrow sense. It is the whole broad system
of all that is highest and wisest in wisdom, all that is
noblest in performance, and all that enters into the happiness or the misery of men. It is the science of the
perfection of the human person, not only in all those
elements of physical and mental life which we have
enumerated, but also in many more which rise far above
them in the plane of excellence, and indeed fill the
whole horizon of that field in which are the forces and
values of personal being. This field is so vast that for
the purposes of this little book, as a study of the philosophy of human personality, we must content ourselves
with a contemplation of the essential and fundamental
principles that come to us in the crowded intelligence,
or plural consciousness, of men.

In our survey of the conceptions which arise in human
minds, and are correlated and joined in our plural con-

sciousness, we found three which are always present in a person awake and sane, and are connected with almost

Basis in conceptions of causation, purpose, and obedience.

every thought. These three conceptions are of causation, purpose, and obedience. When these three conceptions are viewed in their relations, and in the conclusions to which they conduct us, there opens to us a magnificent prospect of the splendor and wealth of human personality, and of the possible destiny of men.

The consciousness of causation, beginning in our knowing ourselves as causes, or causers, then becoming

Causation.

a perception that all knowledge is of activities, and that all action is causation, and that causation is inherent in all existence and all vitality, is the basis and the constructive principle in Moral Science.

In the consciousness of causation there inheres, or is born, the idea of ownership, an idea dominant and

Idea of ownership or rights.

blessed in all the lines of human life, and furnishing the impulses to all the ardor of human pursuits. The consciousness of causation is a feeling that the caused thing is forever joined to its cause. An entire separation of an effect and its cause is inconceivable. There is a connection of relation that is eternal. The idea that you own your creations, and that in them you have added to the sum of your own possessions, becomes the first element of the idea of what we call Rights. Then the spirit of the man inflates with a sense of the rightness of self-defense, and with a sense that an assault on his ownership is an attack on the nobility, and on the value, of life itself. And so, from very childhood, the consciousness of acting becomes a beginning of the sense of exaltation and dignity inhering in the ideas that we call Rights and Jus-

tice. These ideas of ownership, rights and justice,
become in us general principles that spread a halo of
what we call "Sacredness," over all the relations of
Society, and that become on one side a passion of assertion of ownership, and on the other an equal authority
of restraint. But each single perception of rights or
justice is a recognition of ownership based either on
some causing action of the owner, or on some rights
imparted and transferred by the first causer of the right.

Viewed from another point, the idea of causation
appears inseparably joined to a perception that all intelligent action is a movement towards the production or causing of something. In other
words, intelligent action is purpose. This
idea of purpose is interpreted and illustrated

Ideas of purpose, value, ends, and quality.

to us by all our consciousness of our own nature, by all
our wants, by all our passion for self-expression. It
becomes a sense of value, or rather, it is a sense of the
value of the ends not yet grasped. A person cannot
conceive of himself as not, at every moment and in
every action, pursuing ends that have value to his living
being. This sense of value is the sense of what we call
quality. It never comes to us except in a perception of
the way in which the ends of things or of actions express
the purposes of living persons, or bear on the welfare of
living beings.

The combined conceptions of causation, ends, purposes and values, so pervade all our consciousness of our life and of the relations of things,
that they become a perception that we are
free actors, pursuing with intelligence valuable ends. It develops also into a conception

Idea of a First Cause of men and the world. System.

and conviction that the same principles prevail every-

where, and that we are ourselves parts of a system that
has one First Cause; and that, in this system of things,
its Cause, or Creator, has the rights of ownership that
are inherent in causation, and is pursuing, with intelligence, ends that to him have value, or quality and excellence.   It becomes a conception and conviction that the
Cause of the Universe has the right to obtain the ends
or values for which he has created the World.   In this
conception The Creator does not stand before our minds
as a power, but only as The Cause of a universe, which
in many respects and relations can never be separated
from him, and in which he has a right to attain his ends
and values.

Later this conception of The Creator's rights may be
reënforced and illuminated by our perception of the
value of the ends pursued by The Creator,
Ideas of
moral right,   and by our personal sympathy with the ex-
duty, obliga-   cellence of those ends; but the conscious-
tion.
ness of the ownership that inheres in causation is itself the foundation and authority of what we
call the law of rightness in the universe, or Moral Law.
The Nature which The Cause of an Universe incorpo-
rates into it, cannot be anything but right, no matter
what it may be; for there is no other standard of right
practicable or conceivable.   If The Creator had purposed and caused an Universe very different, in its things
and forces and operations, from this one in which we
live, it would have settled itself into a system, would
have worked out its ends, and would have evolved a
harmony in its activities, or at least a peace in which the
forces intended for mastership would exercise the control designed for them, and this mastership would be
their right, because, at the last, it is the right of The

First Cause. Then, because every idea that a man has, except those of consciousness of his Self, comes to him in the perception of the relations of concrete things, these master forces of the Universe, but especially those that are masterful in the social and political life of personal beings, become to men as voices that declare the ends, or values and purposes, which The Cause has ordained, and which, therefore, are The Creator's rights.

Then, when a free-willed person, like a man, in whom the ends of The Creator can be reached only by his voluntary conformity to the purposes and methods of his Cause, inwrought in Nature, sees the designed ends of creation and of life, as having value in the system of being, and as part of the rights of the Cause of himself and Nature, his consciousness responds with those conceptions which we call Duty and Obligation. Then he makes the verbs " I ought," " You ought," and the word *ought* means to him the authority and rights of The Creator as The First Cause. Books innumerable—books eloquent and forceful, books that are magnificent defenses of virtue and right and excellence—have been written to maintain that the first principle in moral science is the immediate consciousness of obligation, and that the conception which forces us to say *ought* is intuitive, primal, and unexplainable. That it is immediate in consciousness is true, but it is not there as an abstract idea. Life and experience are made up of individual momentary activities and relations, which teach to us the principles that they illustrate, and in each of these facts and relations where the sense of obligation is present, the consciousness is a sense of the rights which inhere in the ownership of The Cause. Moral law, right, duty, are words that would have no meaning, or rather could never arise, in an Universe that had no single, or universal, intelligent Cause or Creator. In a system that has an intelligent Cause they are words authoritative and inflexible. The system, however, which our Creator has instituted, is so immense in its provision for human good and happiness, and so affluent in excellences, that it adds to our conception of The Creator's control of his rights another conception of beauties, harmonies and beneficence; so that, in our plural consciousness, our conception of moral law is a conception of an infinite righteousness exercising everywhere an authority that aims at universal bliss in harmony.

In this Universe, a human Person knows himself as a part of both the means and the ends of The Creator, and then with consciousness of his own freeness, and with a sense of the value or quality of his own being as compared with The Creator's design, he cherishes in himself a conception of duty that explains and glorifies itself, and glorifies its possessor as being very near to The Creator.

We must believe that there is no such thing as value, or right, or moral law, except in personal beings, and in their relations to their Cause and to each other. In nonvital Nature all things are of equal value and rightness; and nothing can be wrong. In the relations of men to each other, and to their common Cause, everything is a moral relation, because it has a relation to the ends designed by The Creator for personal beings. These moral relations are of three classes, and include, *first*, everything that a person does to himself as affecting what The Creator designs him to be or to do; *second*, what the person does or gives to his Creator in recognition, worship or service; and, *third*, what the person does to or for other persons.

Moral duty calls first to sanctity of the body. It presents an ideal of normal health and action. It suggests purity and chastity and a loathing of self-degradation. It raises and expands the sense of self-value and personal honor, as a Child of God, till it becomes a dignity, and a passion of self-defense, that abhors ignorance and self-deception, and scorns a lie, and loathes a breach of trust. Then it glows with a sense of the value of great thoughts, noble sentiments, pure loves, and earnest Will, all measured by a divine conception, which has not grown out of mere experience, nor had its origin in the soil or on Earth.

Secondly, the Moral Consciousness erects a conception of the nature, character, purposes, beneficence and rightness of The Cause of the Universe, until ideas of his Will fill the soul as a presence of a holy law. It expands until the soul glows with a sense that obedience to the Author of life is self-exaltation, and that praise, adoration and service belong of right to The Creator from men.

Thirdly, the Moral Consciousness, instinctive with a sense of the value of The Creator's purposes for the whole host of his children, asserts its authority in all the broad field of political and social science. It draws together the family, and gives all the significance there is in the names, Parent, Husband, Wife, Son, Daughter, Brother and Sister. Then it broadens its compass, till it engenders and illuminates the conceptions of neighborism, of race, of nation, of the solidarity of Society, and finally of that love, justice and ministry which are

comprehended under the name " Enthusiasm of humanity."

We are sorely tempted to linger here for a disquisition
on the rights of men; but we must content ourselves with
a recognition of the general principles.

Rights of
men.

In its first bearings, the Will and purpose
of The Cause of the Universe relate to the
individual person. He stands in some relations to his
Creator as if no other soul existed on the Earth. The
Divine Will has made him, and has endowed him with
capacities, and needs, and ends, and duties. So far as
these are contained in, or related to, the soul's sentiments and acts towards his Creator, that is to say his
beliefs, his loves, his obedience, his private worship, the
Creator has delegated to no other man or society any
right of control or interference by force. And the Creator has given him a home on the Earth, and a share in
its stores and resources. Somewhere, somehow, as long
as his life continues, he has the right of home and of sustenance, and a right of ownership in what he produces.

But the Creator has made a host of persons, all of
them objects of his love and ministry, and subjects of his
moral law. Hence the stores and resources of the world
must be partitioned and shared. More than this: The
Creator has made Society to be more serving than
served. The stores and resources of the world are much
more in Society than in Nature. The accumulated wisdom, experience, philosophy, science and inventions of
the men of the past, gathered into history, literature,
culture, arts and civilization, are the world into which
the man is born a citizen, on which he may justly make
demands for justice, protection and love, for good laws,
education and help; and which gives to him, even at its

worst, almost all that he has, and more than he can repay. If he makes discoveries or inventions, or new ideas, or wealth, he has done it with what the past men have supplied to him. They have pushed him forward a thousand steps before he made the final one. Hence his right of ownership of even his own productions has some limits, and he owes more than he ever pays.

Duties and rights are joined together. Ideal Society is incarnate reciprocity. This fact is the inspiration of patriotism. It gives meaning to words like *country*, *nation*, *fatherland*, that have analogies with the meaning of *home*, and even with the fatherhood of God. The words *justice* and *love* would have no meaning if there had been no divine constitution of Society. And these two words are woven together as one. Blessed is the world only because the Creator has not left its system to evolve itself merely through the passions of men, nor under the guidance of intellect alone; but has made moral forces and ideas persuasive and dominant, and has established as moral agencies the consciousness of his purposes and values and Will, with the sympathies and forces of love like his own.

To the moral consciousness, there has, in English, perhaps unfortunately, been given the special name *conscience*, which is the French name for both consciousness and conscience, and is derived *Conscience.* from the Latin *conscientia*, which also has the double meaning. The special word *conscience* has caused most harmful misconceptions. It has been considered something different from consciousness. It has been regarded as a tribunal to which the soul is responsible. It has displaced The Creator from his judgment throne. Men declare themselves justified if they think themselves so.

They go further, and say, that they are justified if they are conscientious, and sincere in this, even if their sincerity has only been a cherishing of some notion or passion which they have fostered in themselves by grossness, prejudice, follies and lies. Conscientiousness is not conscience, but disposition towards One's conscience. It may displace the perception of The Creator's Will and ends, and may erect Selfwill into a standard of rightness; and it may become imperious and masterful, just in the proportion that it is narrow, ignorant, passionate and perverted.

Conscience cannot be understood, nor set in its right position in Moral Science, unless its relation to the *sentiments* and *emotions* of personal beings is fully recognized. The ends and Will of The Creator cannot be conceived, nor even believed to exist, except as dear to his sentiments, emotions, loves, or whatever other name we may give to the idea of having interest in the lives of personal beings. The values, goodness and rightness of the aims of The Creator in human society can only be understood or conceived by, or through, sympathy, or fellow feeling, with the living experience and happiness and misery that teem in the loves, emotions and sympathies of the people. Pure intellect cannot compass it, nor even touch it. Pure intellect may perceive many of the relations of things, or of beings, or of truths; but it makes no estimates of worth. It tells facts, but not values. The sentimental, or vital, moral consciousness can understand that there are in men capacities nobler than the instinctive, sordid and sensual appetites, and can understand that The Creator has aimed at the happiness of personal beings through their chastity, service, justice,

Conscience is sentimental and emotional.

loves and unsensual tastes. Pure intellectual consciousness takes note of facts and of their relations. It perceives that they are causes and effects; but it has no conception of the meaning of the phrase "For the sake of."
Consciousness could not be moral, moral law would have
no meaning, and conscience would be unknown, if we
had no sentimental experience of the worth, good and
rightness, that are possible in personal lives, and that
are the ends aimed at by the Will of The Creator.

Conscience, or moral consciousness, is then, *first*, a
perception of the relation of the lives of personal beings
to ends designed by The Creator's Will; *second*, a perception of the value of these ends, and also a perception
of valuable ends that are unappreciable by pure intellect;
third, a consciousness that we ought to stand in personal
harmony with these ends and aims; *fourth*, a consciousness of our actual disposition and performance towards
The Creator and his aims; *fifth*, a judgment as to the
moral quality of dispositions and performances.

This is not saying that rightness is utility, or is to be
gauged by utility. Nothing is, in fact, useful that has
not been aimed at, to that end, by The Cause of the
Universe; and righteousness, or virtue, is sympathy with
the Will of The Creator, and is action for the sake of The
Creator.

It follows, from what we have observed, that moral
consciousness, or conscience, is susceptible of culture
and perversion. Like all plural consciousness it depends for its intelligence and cor- Conscience
rectness on the nature and number of the cultivable.
facts that it notices, and on the wisdom with which they
are correlated. As consciousness, its ultimate and fundamental facts are immediate or direct perceptions, and

its conception of causation, and of the rights involved in it, are included in its primal intelligence; but the application of these conceptions, as principles, in the relations of living beings, depends on the intelligent observation of those relations.

That the sentimental moral nature can be cultivated is the grandest fact in human life, and is one of the most precious evidences of the beneficence of The Creator. Alas, for the matured person whose tastes and sentiments are not purer, richer, and stronger than an infant's!

§4. SOUL, MIND, AND SPIRIT

In our observation of the nature of a human person, we have recognized in him force, intelligence, and sentiment. Each of these is an activity, but they are so diverse in their methods, instruments, results and productions, that, if consciousness did not know them as one unity of person, Reason could not conceive them as one life. We are compelled to make and use distinct names for these three parts of our personality, when we speak of them as living or acting. Names are arbitrary inventions for our service; but the ideas of which they are symbols may give to them enormous importance in philosophy. The great never-to-be-forgotten question in this connection is, What are the vital differences of nature in the three elements of personal being? For on the answer to this question depends the transcendent question, How, and how much, are we higher than the brutes?

Human person is complex or plural.

Force, the first form of manifestation of life, is known only in connection with a material body and physical organs; but neither Consciousness, Reason nor Logic has been able to demonstrate that it is a product of matter. The forceful kind of being has quantity, quality, modality and relation; and may have them in great diversity. It may have consciousness, Soul. selfness and faculties. It may perceive facts, and actions, and their effects. It may even correlate some relations of things, and perceive some causation, and many adaptations. But it cannot make abstract ideas, nor principles of principles. To this kind of vital being we may give the name Soul, and there is no serious objection to giving, (as the Greeks did with *psyché*), the same name to the essence of all living beings. The giving of a common name does not imply that all souls have the same nature, endowments and destiny. It only implies that the highest faculties of the inferior creatures, and the lowest faculties of human persons, have some analogies. It merely designates a limit, behind which Reason, and even Consciousness, cannot explore. It is that part of the living being which is forceful, instinctive and self-moving. In using this name we must leave out of view any original meaning of the word *soul*, and its equivalents, *psyché, anima, âme, alma, seele*, etc.

For that part of a living being, or that vital energy, which supplements soul by, if we may so speak, handling ideas, abstracting and generalizing conceptions, correlating the relations of Mind. things, formulating truths and principles, and making symbols and names for ideas, the word *mind* is a good enough name. The great fact is that this is not an improvement of soul life, but is apparently a distinct, and radically different, addition to it. It is something which is connected with soul life, but imparts to it a kind of life which, in its powers and its sympathies, comes near to that *being* which is causative, immaterial, and eternal.

When we come to a contemplation of the third part, or kind of human life, we hesitate for a name. A

Spirit.

satisfactory name, descriptive of either its essence, form, powers, or quality, seems not possible. Hence, naturally, all the names that have been given to it have been words that meant *breath;* because air is the least gross of substances, and breathing is the subtlest of physical acts. Men have never been able, and no one except Plato has ever tried, to conceive the personality of the human being as immaterial, pure power and character in pure form. We know ourselves and others only as bodies, or in bodies; and the life below consciousness eludes our sight and touch. Hence the Hebrews, and even Philo, the most philosophical of Jews, thought that spirit was substance. Even now the most haughty kinds of philosophy (if we except Agnosticism, which is really a negation of philosophy) occupy themselves chiefly with discussions of substance, and confound substance and being.

The name *spirit* (and Hebrew *ruach*, Greek *pneuma*, Latin *spiritus, anima* and *animus*) is very faulty, but we have no better word available. For ages it has stood as a symbol of the highest truth in the consciousness of men, alike in their science and their philosophy; for it has signified their conviction that men's bodies are but vehicles of the true Man; that personality is immortal, and that character or moral nature inheres only in that part of Man which has disposition and sentiment.

We need a word for a name of that part of a human person which is moral. That part is neither the body nor the intellect; for acts of bodies take their character from the will and sentiments of the person, and intellect is concerned only with ideas, and at its best it is only intelligent of *facts* as known in *things*. There is a part of men which has a sense of divine ends, and has sympathies, loves, character, disposition and will, and through these knows the value, rightness, beauty and holiness of the divine ends. Therein also are courage and its inspirations, and therein are the hates and awful passions. Therein is everything that makes the right and wrong between men and men, and between a man and his Creator. For this part of a man, the word *spirit* may well enough serve as a name, for want of a better.

If, using this name, we wrestle with the problem of the difference between Man and the animals and meaner creatures, and ask how much of man is spirit, and how much of mind and soul joins with it to make one person, and where the man ceases to be animal, perhaps we cannot do better than to say, that human consciousness begins at the top. Nobility and glory, or passion and perversion, invest the triple person made of spirit, mind and soul, and the greater question is, not where man leaves the brutes, but where human being laps upon the animal, and how much of common soul inheres in the nobler being. And if there is an ascending scale of words and ideas, and it ends at the side of God, why should the subtler and nobler consciousness be less believed than the gross senses of the cold and coarse or seething flesh?

In the consciousness of spirit-being there is a line of conviction, which may not have the authority of a demonstration, but is a strong persuasion, strongest in the best and wisest souls. This is the conviction that the souls of human persons are in a true sense children

Childship. Human spirits. Children of God.

of their Creator. When a human spirit interprets to itself the depths of meaning that there are in loves, and in values of life, and in ends of being, and in purposes, and in duty, and in right and wrong, it does more, and declares that moral principles, relations and laws, have their origin in connections of personality. The moral relations are personally ontological, as well as statutory. We have shown principles which imply that a being is under the moral laws, and in the moral relations of the system, of which he is a part, only so far as he is personally ontologically related in that system.

Moral argument for spiritual kinship.

This does not mean that moral relations exist only between beings that are of like personality; for a moral being is made moral by his personally ontological relation to his Creator; and through him he is in moral relations to every kind of being that has its values of life ordered by the same Creator, in the same system. There is no moral relation where there is no community and reciprocity in life. If these do not much exist directly between human beings and lower creatures, they do largely exist through the relations of persons to the personality of Him who created the system. Then, moral law does not exist for any beings who are not, in some sense, Children of the Creator.

As moral principles founded in personally ontological relationships reach back to their source, so they reach forward to an ontological result. Moral relativity cannot conceivably be compressed into the time limits of an earthly life. Conscience demands for it a futurity, and philosophy conducts to a conviction that moral law is an effect and evidence of a life that has no cessation. Conscience has no condemnations for a being who is not a free personality in the vital

Moral argument for the immortality of men.

moral system, and in perpetual relations, as a person, to its laws of mutuality and reciprocity, and its loves.

This moral argument for immortality is the verdict of true psychology, and the climax of the philosophy which we may call conductive. It is the cry of conscience against that pantheism, and that monism, which pretend that, if there is spirit, there is but one universal substance. Universal, intelligent, impersonal spirit is either gross matter or universal emptiness. It is an unmeaning phrase. The pantheism that means universal identity, or impersonal unity, can have no relativities, no systematization, no moralities. Only such pantheism as there may be in a system of the relations of individual free personal spirits can be moral, or philosophically conceivable, or have the applause of conscience. This is replete with life and glory, and with assurance of endless personal vitality. There is an ascending scale of words and of ideas, and it ends at the side of God.* Loves, right, will, spirit, Child of God—these are as steps of the staircase rising to the better world. "Glory to God in the highest places, and on Earth peace! Good will towards men!" is only heard and understood by human spirits because it is the language of the family, and because the human spirit can respond, "Hallowed be Thy name, Our Father."

§ 5. DESCRIPTION OF MAN IN CATEGORIES

If, in the preceding discussions, we have been true to facts, we ought now to be able, scientifically, logically and philosophically, to describe in outline, by exact

*In this discussion we have, as far as possible, omitted discussion of the personality of The Creator, and of guilt, punishment, and their related topics.

categories (i. e., predicables), our knowledge of men's person as it begins in consciousness and evolves into all the glory of moral life. A schedule of categories may reasonably be demanded of us by those readers to whom the discussions shall seem faulty. "The Personal Equation" must be formulated, in order that it may be defended, and that Psychology may become a science.

A few further explanations of principles and methods must precede the schedule.

1. The words *quantity*, *quality*, *modality* and *relation* must be recognized as naturally serviceable names for the kinds of conceptions in which we may be known to ourselves or to others.

2. In a person's self-consciousness his knowledge of himself will not be a comparative measure, but will be his fundamental *being*. His quantity will be his unity, and will be the same as identity, independence, totality, selfness, or whatever else we may call his personal oneness, when we observe it from different points of view. But while self-consciousness is knowledge of individuality, it is not an abstract notion of oneness; for personal identity is complex, organic and vital.

3. A schedule conforming to self-consciousness must put relativity after modality.

4. In a complete table of the categories of personal being, there must be three schedules, the first containing the predicables of psychical, or vital, being, the second containing the predicables of the faculties that are concerned with the relations which are correlated in knowledge by the intellect, and the third description of the relations of a Person with his Creator.

Inasmuch as intellect is a certain quality of the personality, and in its activities it deals with, and exhibits, an advanced range of conceptions, by correlating the simple perceptions known in the psychical life, it follows that intellectual quantity includes vital quality, intellectual quality includes vital modality, and intellectual modality includes vital relativity. And, inasmuch as what we may call Moral Life is a certain modality and relation of the intellectual life, and exhibits an advanced range of correlated conceptions based on those of the intellectual life, it follows that in the third schedule there must be observed a similar precession, so that moral quantity, quality and modality include, respectively, intellectual quality, modality and relation.

5. The verbs which help to describe personal being must not be the verb *to be* only but the verbs *have*, *exercise*, and *correlate*.

6. We can profitably use some suggestions of Kant, in his discussion of what he calls "The Principles of The Pure Understanding." These he classifies as:

Kant's Principles of the Pure Understanding.

 I. Axioms of Intuition.

 II. Anticipations of Perception.

III. Analogies of Experience.

IV. Postulates of Empirical Thought in general.

These are the four classes of the conceptions that are in consciousness; that is to say, they are the forms of the intelligence of a self-conscious and rational person; and while they could have no place in a philosophy of pure reason, they take a great importance in a conductive philosophy based on self-consciousness; for they are, in fact, *quantity*, *quality*, *modality* and *relation* as known in consciousness. The second and third items may better, perhaps, be named Adaptations to Relations, and Adaptations to Experience.

CATEGORIES OF A HUMAN PERSON (as in consciousness).

OF STRUCTURAL BEING.

	Of Quantity.	*Of Quality.*
Vital or Psychical.	THEY ARE "AXIOMS OF IN-TUITION." THEIR VERB IS, "I AM." Inherent, Introherent, Self, Subsistent, Existent, Real, Identical (One, Total), Free, Complex, Finite, Whole, Vital, Propulsive, Organic, Conscious, Sensitive.	THEY ARE ADAPTATIONS TO RELATIONS. THEIR VERB IS, "I HAVE." Consciousness, Senses, Selfhood, Power, Energy, Selfness, Nature, Disposition, Affinities, Coherence, Continuity, Reach, Needs, Receptivity, Aggressiveness, Form, Constitution, Conservatism.
Mental or Intellectual.	The categories of Vital Quantity. The categories of Vital Quality (the latter converted into their nouns or adjectives).	The categories of Vital Modality. Experience (Habits, Education, Bias, Prejudices). Æs e ic association of ideas. th t
Teleological, or Moral, or Spiritual.	The categories of Vital and Intellectual Quantity and Quality (as adjectives). Consciousness of value (i. e., ends). Associated ideas of personal relation. Will, Loves.*	The categories of Intellectual Modality. Conscience of comparison with normal personality and the Will of The Creator. Sense of self-value, or excellence. Impulses to optimism in Self (rightness, chastity, purity, worth, honor, nobility, integrity, continence, and self-employment).

*There is Will in every vital act of intelligent Person. Hence in Psychical Modality and in Mental Quality it is not to be specially named. But there is a propriety in the universal custom of naming the structural and active moral self-expression by different words—viz., Loves and Will.

CATEGORIES OF A HUMAN PERSON (as in consciousness).

OF ACTIVE BEING.

Of Modality.

THEY ARE ADAPTATIONS TO EX-PERIENCE. THEIR VERB IS, "I EXERCISE."

Attention (Alertness, Concentration). Self-expression. Address, Direction. Association of ideas, Memory. Instinct, Hope, Fear. Intention, Force, Causation. Sensation.

Of Relativity.

THEY ARE "POSTULATES OF EMPIRICAL THOUGHT." THEIR VERB IS, "I PERCEIVE IN CORRELATION."

Impact, Contact, Affinity Pleasure, Pain, Danger. Sequence, Time, Space, Motion, Extension, Divisibility, Plurality, Shape. Assistance, Resistance, Combination, Effect, Possession, Sense-perception, Tone, Color.

Categories of Vital Relativity. Invention (Symbolization, Language), Qualitation (Abstraction), Contemplation, Reflection, Æsthetic Taste.

Causation and Effect, Ownership, Personality, Enumeration, Mathematics, Value, Generalization, Logic, Judgment, Science, Philosophy, Reason, Harmony, Beauty, Music, Art.

Categories of Intellectual Relativity. Conscience as to duties to the Creator, in respect of rightness, or excellence in Sentiments (love, reverence, gratitude); Obedience (loyalty, service, humility); Faith (in his Will and Word); Worship (recognition, adoration, prayer, praise, thanks, penitence).

Conscience as to duties to Society because of relation to the Creator, in respect of value (or rightness) in Truthfulness, Fidelity, Justice, Love, Family sentiments and acts, Friendship Altruism, Solidarity, Socialism, Philanthropy, Kindness, Liberality, Patriotism, Neighborism, Statesmanship, Government, Punishment, War, Protection and Service, Education, Beneficence, Influence for virtue, "Enthusiasm of humanity," Influence for God and religion.

CHAPTER V

THE DIVINE PERSON

§ 1. A PHYSICAL AND PSYCHICAL ARGUMENT

In the preceding survey of the personal nature, powers, and destiny of our Self, we have, at several points, seen that our philosophy includes, and depends on, the existence and actions of a personal First Cause of all things. This, however, is only like opening the door of a palace, when immediately visions of splendor, and evidences of wealth and power, invite us to enter the halls, and reach the presence of the King himself. We must attain assurance of the existence and activity of a Sovereign personal Creator, or all our convictions and our hopes are involved in obscurity.

Nevertheless, an examination of the religions, theologies and philosophies of the World reveals the fact that almost nowhere, at any time, has the existence of an absolutely first cause of all things been affirmed. All men have Gods; but very few men have thought that their Gods were either Creators of men, or makers and defenders of moral law. Everywhere, except to a limited extent among Hebrews and Christians, the eternal uncreated existence of matter has been assumed. The mystery of the cause of firstness has so dazed theologians and philosophers that they have hardly tried to define or find the First Cause, and have halted

74

far short of it. Hence, with beliefs in some kind of God universal, unity of theologies and philosophies has not been even approached; and we may come to the study of the existence and nature of the Creator almost as if it were a new subject.

The argument for the existence of God, from the evidences of intelligent and beneficent design in Nature, is so familiar to us, who are accustomed to the Hebrew Scriptures, that we do not notice how little part it has in the World's beliefs, nor how dexterously it is evaded by those who may wish to do so. No person has more fully or more eloquently than Immanuel Kant stated how the evidences of intelligent and benevolent aims in Nature bear us irresistibly to the acknowledgment of a Creator, and yet Kant denies that Reason reaches or justifies that conclusion. In fact, unless the argument from the evidence of intelligent and moral ends in Nature can be maintained by philosophical facts and principles more radically fundamental and ontological than those usually advanced, it may be weakened by many lines of attack. But these attacks cannot harmonize together, and no two of them can be right at the same time. There are too many of them, and they are mutually destructive. Fortunately for the truth, the radical philosophical facts are attainable; and the attacks, being inspired more by destructive purposes than by a self-sustaining and constructive philosophy, shatter their forces on these facts which are intrenched in consciousness and conscience.

Attacks have been made on the argument from design by assaulting the word *design* with shrewd logical tricks. And if we use the word *design* carelessly, so that we assume in it the personal agency that needs to be proven,

The argument from design.

we lay our argument open to the keen weapons and subtle
onslaughts of the Humes and Voltaires, and all the Skeptics and Deists. But in some of the preceding pages,
when we were analyzing and defining human ideas, with
no object except to accurately describe human intelligence, we recognized that intelligent action and design
are synonymous terms. If we perceive intelligence in the
universe, there is no intermediary between intelligence
and design. But we have perceived this intelligence.
We have perceived it directly and immediately, in our
consciousness and our conscience, as one of the first
principles of intelligent philosophy. And it is universal
wherever there is intelligent activity; and its cogency,
as evidence of design, cannot be lessened by tricks of
phrases, such as the assertion that creation is something
unique for which we have no analogies in experience.

We have also recognized in preceding pages that all
things are forces in action, and that all knowledge is per-
Argument   ception or conception of actions, and that the
from   perception of an action is one and the same
causation.   thing as the perception of causation. This
principle, or rather this fact, is an essential and universal
one in all perceptions, and in all things. There is no
intermediary argument, or inference, between perception
of things and perception of causation. Per-
Cause of   ception of the World is perception that it had
complexity   a cause. Perception of the World is really a
and correla-
tion.   multitude of perceptions of a multitude of
atoms, things, organs, actions, relations, influences and
correlations; and, in each of them, causation and design
(intelligent action) are obvious. Skeptical philosophy
pleads that we cannot argue about this as we do about other
causation and design. But, in fact, causation and design

are more directly perceptible in the correlation of forces
and in harmonized complexity, than in anything else. It
is possible to doubt, in a certain way, the causation of a
single atom of matter; but doubt of causation and design
in the harmonies, complexity, and correlations of the
elements of the World, is irrational and impossible. But
a willing, not to say a determined, skepticism has inge-
niously devised many objections to a recognition of a
Creator. Kant, who has made an eloquent statement of
the evidences of design in Nature, and the cosmological
argument for practical faith in a Creator, says after all,
that this is only evidence of an Arranger of Nature
rather than of an Author. Others have adduced as hindrances to faith in a Creator, metaphysical theories like
Idealism, psychological theories like Monism, materialistic theories like Evolution, and a deification of the
word *Law*. Against all of these we may adduce the
principles which inhere in our primal conceptions of
being, and come to us in our plural consciousness, being
the common sense of our daily experiences, classified and
formulated by science and correlated by philosophy.

A leader in these facts and principles is the axiom that
all *relations are mutual and reciprocal actions*. There can
be no one-sided relativity knowable or effective. Hence, there can be no relations between
Relations
are mutual
things, or between things and persons, unless
and recip-
rocal.
provisions for the mutuality of the relations
have been made by The First Cause, in the constituted
relativities of things. If there could be several, or
many, self-existent Gods, they would be to each other
as nothing and unknown; and any universes created by
different Gods would be to the other Gods, and to each
other, entirely devoid of relations and unknowable; and

even ideas could not be alike in any two universes that had not the same First Cause. On the other hand, the Creator of a universe could not divest himself of relation to it except by annihilating it; but he could change his works, or his ways, or his plans. Hence no Deity except the Creator of the universe could be its organizer or arranger, or stand in any relation to it, or even know of its existence. Of course, it follows that, even if self-existence is something uniform, we can never know any God but the one who made the universe; and we can know him only in the mutual relations which he has constituted.

If we would pursue to the end the search for firstness in Nature, we must take up, scientifically and philosoph-

The Cause of atoms is the Creator of the World.
ically, the study of atoms of matter; for science knows no forces or activities of Nature that are not atomic. Atoms are not nuclei or vehicles floating in or carrying portions of some general world-force. An atom is known to us only as a set of motions co-ordinated together. Each motion is invariable in its quantity; and the character of the atom is constituted by the nature and number of the motions in the set; and it is effective, and perhaps measurable, according to the number, direction, speed, and length of its waves and revolutions, and the number and force of its collisions. If to our external observations we add our personal consciousness of the nature of force, action, and causation, we conceive an atom of matter to be a set of movements started by a volition of a Creator, and limited, invariable, sphered, commissioned, and localized by co-ordination in a narrow range of action, adjusted to a larger external range of relations. As uncaused co-ordinations and harmonies

are impossible, the further back science, philosophy, and logic press their search towards the ultimate atoms of matter, the nearer they come to the recognition that there is one Cause of the universe and its atoms, and of all its activities and relativities.

But, however evident the existence of an intelligent First Cause may be to many, or even if to most persons, it is not strange that it should be denied by multitudes of learned, intelligent, and well- Materialism. disposed people. Therefore, while we may pass without discussion the coarse and brutal forms of ignorance, apathy, sensualism, and passion, which only make the pretense of belief in materialism an excuse for grossness, we must here give a respectful and rational consideration to three forms of materialistic philosophy which are somewhat prevalent among intelligent and learned men. These forms are deification of law, evolutionism, and materialistic pantheism, all of which gain a specious appearance of a scientific basis, but are in fact more theoretical and dogmatic than the most speculative philosophies, stop far short of first principles, suppress consciousness, and override Reason and philosophy. Professing to be rational, they demand of us unbounded credulity; for they require us to believe that matter is intelligence, or that Nature is governed by a Necessity that has no cause, and for the existence and power of which no explanation is conceivable.

To some persons the evidence of the continuous operation of wisdom in the forces of Nature is convincing. They rightly believe that the atomic forces of matter are in the matter; but they Deification of law. try to rise to a higher level by affirming that there is a vague power controlling matter. They do not define it, because definitions are troublesome things to defend. They call it Law, but they do not mean anything that in any other connection is called law. They do not make it an idea. It is an unfinished phrase.

Law is not force; nor does a conception of a law of Nature explain the source of a force, but only its behavior and regularity. If any vast number of atoms were together, but separated absolutely from all others, they would act on each other according as the conditions favored or hindered their mutual approaches. But eventually they would assume the character of a system, would exhibit everywhere the pursuit and attainment of intelligent aims, and would present that aspect which we call the effect of laws; the interworkings, harmonies and results of the highest and most complicated exhibitions, being traceable to the atomic forces intelligently correlated at the creation. In our universe-system, these workings are of such vast numbers, and the harmonies and victories display such immeasurable intelligence, and the results are so beneficial to human beings, that the higher and subtler laws and workings become more conspicuous than the less and gross ones. But whether the system be large or small, since the intelligent co-ordination of magnificent results was initiated in the creation of the atoms, we are compelled by Reason and personal consciousness to believe that force and intelligent aims are effects of a personal Being's Will.

Of all the forms of materialistic theology, none comes to men more seductively than that one which is called
Evolution. Evolutionism. It appeals to that pride and that natural and proper self-gratulation of scientific observers, which accompany great attainments and surprising discoveries. It is approved, as a prob-

able theory of the methods through which life has improved, even by eminent believers in a personal First Cause. As a science, or rather in science, it has a noble sphere. But, so far as it is a theory of causation, it is naked materialism of the crudest kind. It does not offer any theory of a First Cause, nor even any facts that guide in that direction. If evolutionism could, as very probably it may eventually, array ten thousand times as many facts as it has gathered, it would not touch the problem of first causation of matter. As a philosophy it abandons all first principles, and teaches that effects are greater than their causes.

We do not care to antagonize here those eminent observers whose science has added glory to our age, made our world seem larger and fuller, alike of beauty, uses and intelligence, and has sent thrills of enthusiasm through all circles of intelligent people. But for the petty and superficial scholarship, which takes note only of the forms of things, while it overlooks all the facts of animal chemistry and the dependence of life on organizations, and co-ordinations and vital functions, and ignores multitudes of facts where it adduces one, how can we entertain any respect? How can we respect the evolutionism which is chiefly an arithmetical audacity? —which is not appalled by the obvious necessity for infinite time for the infinite multitude of the processes which it affirms—an audacity which is ever able to say, Take more time. Figures are inexhaustible.

Reason and true Science bid the student of evolution to look both ways along the line of study. They note that the agencies, processes and results are in Involution. the system of things from the beginning. They turn our admiration towards, rather than from, a plan of creation. They set before us the science of Typical Forms, as the most wonderful thing in Nature, and demand our admiration of the divine prescience, which, devising a moderate number of perfect ideals of type, could modify these in infinite variety, and could produce with exact adjustment to their necessary environment and their circumstances, alike the minute and simple forms, and those enormous saurians, batrachians, mammals and birds, whose antecedents are undiscovered, and apparently are undiscoverable. They set up involution as a companion study to evolution. They teach us that seeds and germs produce what has been put into them, and that whatever involution there is goes on in an adjustment to an intelligent co-ordination of the whole system of Nature. Nature is a science of ideals, which are intelligently devised plans carried into effect with perfect skill by unlimited power.

There is a materialism that arrogates to itself dignity and an appearance of moral character, by associating Pantheism.   an acknowledgment of Deity with its adoration of matter. It calls itself Pantheism, with emphasis on the first or the second syllable, according as it desires to deny a Creator or to confess a Cause. It is an empty name. It aims to divert attention from the inadequacy of its ideas of The Cause, by dilating on the splendor of effects. It attempts to make zero enormous. When it, in a weak and halting way, confesses a Divinity in the greatness, the relations and interworkings of the universe, but declares still that the intelligent and vital force is that of matter, it retains all the weakness, narrowness, and irrationality of materialism. So long as it affirms that Deity is immanent in matter, inherent in and identical with it, it is irrational, and has no adequate recognition of the Cause of intelligence, order, beauty and beneficence. When, on the other hand, it affirms that Deity is pervasive of matter, inherent in it, but not identical with it, it has only debased its ideas of The Creator unnecessarily and irrationally.

If, in the preceding pages, we have kept on the true lines of science, philosophy and reasoning, we have found, in causation, consciousness and ontology, assurances of the creation and control of the substance of the universe by a First Cause that is superior to it, absolute Master, intelligent, aiming at great ends, and securing *Summary of the reasoning on causation of matter.* those ends, not by himself working in matter, and being its force and vitality, but by constituting its relativities through and in the act of causation of its elements. The reasoning must proceed much further before it demonstrates in this Creator the most and the greatest of those attributes to the sum, or the possessor, of which we give the name God, and bring our adoration. But even so much understanding of him, as we gain in this reasoning, exhibits him as having character, wisdom, purposes and power that can inhere only in a Person, and that Person, One who is sole Sovereign, and glorious and mighty beyond our power to measure in our conceptions.

§ 2. AN INTELLECTUAL ARGUMENT

By the same consciousness and reasoning which demonstrate that matter and all material things are coördinations of activities, and therefore have a First Cause, or Creator, it is also demonstrated that intelligence and intellect have a Creator. A man is of a higher order of being than other earthly creatures, because he can make

his Self and his actions the objects of his study.   But
it is yet true that all his ideas are conceptions of things
and of their relations.   Even his highest, general and
abstract, ideas and principles, are in their essence conceptions of material things, or of living active beings, or of
their relations.   Even if it were possible that there could
be truth which was not in such connections and relations, whether it were self-existent, or were created by
The Creator of the universe, it would be to us as nothing.   Hence, as a coördination of movements makes
matter, and living beings, and the universe, and its relativities, and therefore it has a personal Creator, so the
coördination and correlations of matter and mind make
intelligence, and these mutual and reciprocal relations
must have had an intelligent personal First Cause, or
Creator, who made both matter and mind.   This reasoning is, however, denied and attacked in several ways.

First, it is said that knowledge is only conceptions,
of which no explanation can be given, and of which no
defense can be made.   This is idealism, not
Idealism.
objective and plausible like Plato's, but subjective.   It can only acquire plausibility by claiming
that all ideas are results of immediate consciousness.
Such idealism ridicules the logic of common sense, bur-
lesques consciousness, and denies causation.   It ignores
the fact that our consciousness not only exhibits ideas,
but affirms judgments, and declares truth and untruth.
As primal consciousness affirms that material things are
real, so our intellectual consciousness affirms that our
generalizations, correlations, and classifications of facts
are true or correct.   Ignoring these facts of consciousness, idealism denies causation, subverts all beliefs, and
leaves its victim no stay against skepticism, and no res-

cue from despair. It is only a deification of puzzles; but the World will not accept a philosophy that calls a man a corporate vacuum, worships Zero as Creator, installs negations in place of truths, and uses Reason for its own degradation. The World cannot honor a theory that destroys every good belief, and builds no structures, and that delights in casting shadows over all human paths, and in embroidering the drapery of an universal coffin.

Secondly, our confidence in the existence of a Cause of intelligence is assaulted with an attack aimed at the foundations of all beliefs, and at the existence of all assurance; but only as aimed against faith in a personal God does it exhibit any earnestness, or much motive. In its milder form it is reasoning, but only to certain points of interrogation and suspense. It graciously tolerates our beliefs as amiable weaknesses; but it asks us to honor it because it cannot see its way through the labyrinths of truth. This is not a philosophy, but a surrender. Doubt is noble so long as it fairly weighs reasoning, refuses to be credulous, and has some principles that are touchstones and gauges. But when it is a stagnation of thought, an atrophy of Reason, an indolent habit, a contempt of conservatism, or a disregard of consciousness, it is contemptible. Skepticism that is a vitalized interrogation, an organized feebleness, a chronic perplexity, has no claims to respect.

Skepticism. Agnosticism.

In its stronger and more aggressive forms, with the name Agnosticism, it is neither puerile nor ineffective. Denying the authority of consciousness, it urges its own logic of negations, and denies everything. Of course, its logic lacks premises, and can have no confirmations; but the passion of denial, a zeal of war, like the enchantment of love, is its own reason and defense, or at least

is all that itself desires. Agnosticism that does not go
to the extent of a denial of all intelligence, but only
denies that we can know God, presents plausible arguments, and must have respectful, logical, and philosophical answers.

First, it is said that a man's conceptions must necessarily be mannish, imperfect and erroneous in respect to
Beings that are superior to himself, and to
Anthropo-
morphism.
things that he cannot himself make. This is
plausible, but irrational. We cannot know,
and do not need to know, all about God; but neither
science, reason nor philosophy tends towards showing
that God could not make men so that they can receive
true information from him, or so that their leading conceptions of him, in consciousness and conscience, are.
incorrect. We may even say that if any of our conceptions are untrue because they are mannish, it is the
scientific conceptions of the material things that are
doubtful; and it is vital principles of causation and
moral relations (interpreted to us by our vital consciousness) that must be trusted. We may admit that, on the
principles of Agnosticism, if there were two Gods the
one could not communicate to the other any thought in
his mind nor any fact that originated by his own will;
and yet a man may know what such a God could not
know; the philosophical principle being that knowledge
of facts does not wholly depend on greatness of the
knower, but does depend, for its very beginning, on provisions for intelligence made by the Creator of minds
and of things in one system, and adjusted by mutual
and reciprocal relations. In other words, the relativity
of knowledge, which skeptics take as a basis for their
unbelief, does really limit the extent of our knowledge;

but it is the one condition that makes knowledge possible, and by it some, and even sufficient, knowledge of The Creator may be attained by men.

Secondly, the dogma that a man cannot know God takes the form of an assertion that a finite being cannot know an infinite one—a most seductive phrase, but an irrational and even an unmeaning one. Sometimes an attempt is made to make the phrase philosophical by making it read, "The finite cannot know the infinite." This, however, strips it of whatever appearance of meaning it had in its other form; for there can be no "The infinite," except "The Infinite Being" or infinity, and of neither of these is it designed to speak.

Infinite Being. Infinity.

The word *infinite* is either a negative word, or an instrument for tricks. It means incomplete or unfinished. In this sense it cannot describe a perfect Being; but it might describe our idea of him; in which case it would not mean that he is unlimited, but that our conception is incomplete. In fact, if we say Man cannot know the Infinite Being, we only mean that a man cannot circumscribe his own uncircumscribed idea. *Infinite* is a negative word, and the attempt to make it a positive conception is an effort to turn nothing into something. The attempt to make *infinite* a definite word is only the effort of a man to outrun himself. We can always say *More, After,* and *Before.* If all space were filled with machines multiplying figures for ages, we could still say *more:* but it would not mean anything except what the noun might mean which we write after the figures.

Infinite is not a proper term to apply to God. An unfinished, incomplete God, who cannot reach the compass of his own being, is an absurdity. In ontology there are no infinites. All things, and all Beings, even The Creator himself among them, are just what they are, no more nor less. A Deity can be perfect, supreme, and unlimited by anything except himself, but he is a very definite and positive Being. There can be no infinite attributes of Deity; for perfect ones are not infinite. Infinite wisdom would be unfinished wisdom; but perfect wisdom knows all that there is to know, and there it ends. Infinite power and possibility are, in ontological philosophy, absurd; for ontology knows nothing but actual *being*, and that is the one thing that is fixed and definite. In ontology, that is to say in *being*, there are no possibilities (i. e., uncertainties or contingencies) except those of the will and actions of free personal Beings. Infinite possibility is impossible finiteness. Our uncertainty of the Creator's plans and will is not ontological possibility. There is no infinity even of space; for space is only known to us as direction of our attention, limited by reach. But direction has no quantity, and reach is limitation.

The conceptions of unity and relativity will contend with each other in our minds so long as we study *being* with only the verb *to be*, and the nouns *essence, being* and *substance*, and so long as we think that relativity is unworthy of Deity.

There are many acute and learned persons on whose minds the conception of personal unity, and the mysteries of *being*, exercise such potent control that Monism. Unitism. they affirm that all *being* is one unit, in such sense that all substance or essence is one. This may be pantheism, if it emphasizes the conception of God; or idealism, if it extols ideas; or it may go to such an extreme of monism as to declare that mind and its ideas, Deity and matter, cause and effect, are all one. But one what? That, it cannot tell. In obliterating all relations it obliterates all quality, character and name; and its *one* cannot be being, essence, substance nor person, nor anything else than zero. A Monism that has no monad, a Unitism that has no unit, abolishes all conceptions, and becomes a mere trickery of words, a turn of a kaleidoscope. It is born dead, and its friends can do little more than invent names for a coffin-plate. When it becomes an enthusiasm for elimination, a frenzy for subtraction, a passion for denials, shrinkage and emptiness, it is a surrender of psychology and a flight of philosophy. With a pretense of service, it dethrones Reason. Under a show of homage, it buries its King. It claims a right to throw all philosophy and intelligence into its bottomless pit. And yet it grasps for rescue the names *being* and *substance;* but its *being* cannot *be*, and its substance neither *stands*, nor is *under* anything. Unitism, however, rarely attempts to be pure and unadulterated monism. It must use some pantheism, idealism or materialism, if it will be anything more than mere phrases. Even so, if it calls all intelligence a wave of the All-Mind, or all second causes vibrations of the All-Power, or all operations changes of state of the All-Substance, its First Cause is impotence, and its All-Being is zero in a vacuum.

There is a true infinity and a true unit. The Universe, in its coördination by and with one First Cause, has unity and totality, which are the categories of the quantity of a unit that is not a Person. The unit is the unity of a system. In it all things, all force, all life, all relations, *consist*, or stand

The true infinity and unit.

together. And this is infinite, because there is nothing but itself that can limit its Self. All its relativities are combined in the causal relation of the will of the Creator.*

§ 3. A MORAL ARGUMENT

We have now recognized that the coördinations of forces, and the correlations of intelligence, demonstrate the creation of Nature by an intelligent First Cause. When we advance further, to the study of moral life, with its ends and aims of creation, its values of life, its relations to the happiness of personal Beings, its conceptions of rightness and duty, and we find these to have their whole essence and character in conceptions of relation to a First Cause of the universe, the demonstration of the existence and rule of a Creator becomes an irresistible conviction.

The conviction of this relation is so innate in consciousness that, always and everywhere, theology has preceded philosophy, and apparently there would nowhere have been a philosophy if there had not first been a Moral Science. There

Theology precedes philosophy.

*Plato closely approached this conception of the Universe-System. He declared that the universe contains all being. Aristotle said the same of *the aión.* Neither Plato nor Aristotle completed the conception by seeing the causal relation of The Creator. Both believed matter uncaused and eternal; but Plato said that the only things worthy to be called existent are ideas (*eide, appearances*) and this makes one system of all that is truly *being.* Aristotle excluded finite things from God's *aión,* and discussed infinity only as limitation of human knowledge. He does not use the word *infinite* in reference to God.

The *infinite* is *apeiron* (non-experimental) and *aïdion* (i. e., not individual, *idion*). *Ho aion* is "the bound outside of which there is nothing according to Nature." *To on* (*the being*) and *to hen* (*the one*) are impersonal universal being. All of these words are in the neuter gender except *aión,* and that is only masculine because it belongs to a class of words (ending in accented *on,* and signifying a container) which are always masculine.

would have been no Aristotelianism if there had been
no Platonism. There would have been no occidental
modern philosophy without both of these assisted by
Hebrew theology. Even the recognition of conscience
in philosophy preceded the recognition of the authority
of consciousness, and the word *consciousness*.* All the
history of modern philosophy, beginning with Socrates,
has been a history of moral ideas, beginning in conscience of men's relation to a governing Creator.

Nature is a ministry for human Persons. Its whole
teaching in physical science is a display of aims at intelligent ends. Its whole teaching in social sci- Moral
ence is a demonstration that these ends are Design, and
the good and happiness of human Persons. relations.
Its chief teaching in psychological science is, that consciousness is a sense of a relation to the will, ends, and
rights of a First Cause. Its great lesson in Moral science
is, that intelligent and sentimental human life is in relation to the desires and sentiments of that First Cause.
The long course of philosophical, scientific, and logical
study, proceeds steadily towards the full recognition of a
creating and governing Cause, who, through the relations
which he has established, displays his nature and character. But if the way of philosophy and science is long
and tardy, that of conscience is early and quick, and lies
at the very beginning of the pursuit of the truth that has
value for human Beings, and for their Creator. Conscience makes a short path across the fields of philosophy to its God.

*Although the Greeks used the verb *sunoida* (I know by
myself) to signify positive assurance, the noun *suneidesis* was
scarcely, if at all, used before the Christian era. See pages
173 and 206.

The formal moral argument for the existence of a personal Creator and Ruler is neither long nor obscure. It begins with the principles of causation. It recognizes values in life, which are inwrought in the plan of creation. It recognizes these as being dependent for their attainment on sympathies, tastes, affections, and all else that we call moral character, in human Beings. It sees all these as relations that, like all relations, must have had a cause; but it also sees in these the elements that we call rightness and good and justice and holiness, and which can have no explanation or authority except as the Will of The Cause of the universe. The principles of

Only as a creator can God rule.

ontology affirm that only as a Cause has God a right to govern. No God, however good, wise, or mighty, in his sphere, would have either right or power to rule a World that he did not make; and if conceivably we could know such an alien God, we might adore and love him perhaps, but to serve him would be a crime against our Creator.

The principles of ontology go on to affirm that a Creator whose Will ordained a World which sought val-

A maker is analogous to his work.

ues for human Beings in their purity, affections, sympathies with goodness, and mutual loves and ministries, must himself be ardent with like holiness, love, and personal character, and be a Person in the best and highest sense of the word.

The nature of personality, as known by us in consciousness and conscience, is such a conception as permits to us no idea of creation, and especially

Creation by will.

of moral order and law, except as the act of a Will. Philosophy, psychology, and logic, all indeed lead us to a recognition of a necessary unity in all *being*, but it is not a monism justifying an affirmation that there is but one *substance* in the universe, and that material and vital activities are only changes of state of the monad substance. In all such language the word *substance* must be either empty of all meaning, or describe some divine matter or body. It cannot be made to have a meaning by any logic about unity or being; and if God's works, intellectual and sentimental, are performed by a sort of physical performance of his spiritual substance, the fact is unknowable and inconceivable to us, and the idea of it is abhorrent to all our vital and moral consciousness. Moreover, a change of state of a Being that is unity and immaterial is impossible, and if it were possible, no change of state could be a cause of anything. There is a moral monism; but it is the unity of a moral *system* held together by relation to one Will that is replete with personal sympathies, character, and aims. Only once can the paradox of self-existence be possible, and it cannot be a paradox of anything but glory and honor in itself. Self-existence is the unit which philosophy declares, but it is a self-existence of a Cause, a Will, glorious and infinite in its creative work. Consciousness and conscience are the windows through which souls look on the ways in which one perfect Person has exercised magnificent purposes for loving ends. And when they have looked, the language of souls speaks infinite volumes of happiness, and intelligence, and love, and hope, in one thought and name, "OUR FATHER."

Even Kant says, "Teleological unity is so important a condition of the application of my Reason to Nature, that it is impossible for me to ignore it. But the sole condition, so far as my knowledge extends, under which this unity can be my guide, is the assumption that a supreme Intelligence has ordered all things according to the wisest ends. * * * The conception of this Cause must contain certain determinate qualities; and it must, therefore, be regarded as the conception of a Being possessing all power, wisdom, etc., in one bond." Again he says, "In the sphere of moral belief I must act in obedience to the moral law, * * * I am irresistibly constrained to believe in the existence of God, and in a future life. * * * My belief in God is so interwoven with my moral nature that I am under as little apprehension of having the former torn from me as of losing the latter."

When we have declared that our Creator is a person, have we said all that we know of him, or do the principles of ontology, and the analogies of existence in personal relations, furnish the means for yet more conception and description? We know him in activities and power as a Cause, and in wisdom as a Mind, and in aims and loves as such as that which in ourselves we call Spirit. But shall we say that he *is* each of these, or that he *has* them? Human language is unable to define the distinction, either in ourselves or in God. We must say both *is* and *has*, according to our viewing-point and the relations of our phrases; but the three natures must be one Person as they are in men. And yet, is it not possible that, in the profundities of the nature of the self-existent Person, who correlates in his Self his power, mind and spirit, there may be distinctions, with powers of intercourse and relation, making a glorious plurality of personality?

Plurality in the Divine Unity. Spirit.

If, with our logic, we declare God to be self-sufficient, our personal sense of the nature and naturalness of love so joins with our conviction that his longings of love have made him a Creator, as to make it rational for us to believe that love in God is something that has demanded, and has had eternally, the satisfaction of personal plural intercourse of spirit with spirit in himself. Philosophy and ontology demand oneness in The Creator in respect to self-existence, and demand that The Cause of everything that is not the Person of God shall be the One God, and demand absolute harmony of coöperation between all Persons of Deity.

But philosophy and ontology have not learned to describe personality, except by its doings. The doer is not seen, weighed, measured nor grasped. Human life below consciousness is inscrutable; and is only knowable as power, intelligence and spirituality, in oneness of personal being. Still less is the person of God describable, either positively or negatively. But so long as we maintain his self-existent unity, and his unity as Cause of all that is not his Person, we may believe that the perfection and bliss of God rather imply than discredit plurality in himself. Upon what else could the intelligence and the moral nature of Deity be exercised before his creation of inferior persons, if there were not in his Self capacities of intercourse and relation?

Our conceptions of God sink into blankness if we try to think of his wisdom as having nothing to know except his own oneness, or if we try to think of his moral nature as having none of the relativities that are the essence of morality and its loves. Self-sufficiency of a Person without relations, is to us a phrase without significance, or else it is shocking to our moral sense.

In two ways, however, we may name The Creator with names which, if not perfectly explicable, are yet replete with precious meaning to us. We may not unreservedly say that he is power or wisdom; but, on the principle that the greater contains the less, we may say that he is spirit, or a spirit.   We look on power as the servant of

God our mind, and we see no worthy field for the ex-
Father and ercise of mind except for moral relations of
a spirit. persons; and we see these only in the exer-
cises of the loves of personal beings pursuing what to them and to their Cause are the values of life; and we recognize these as inhering in that personal nature which we call spirit.   On the principle that a Cause must be greater than its effects, we must believe our Creator to be immeasurably better than our conceptions; but on the principle that a Cause must construct his designs according to his own nature, we must believe that our Creator is a spirit, in some analogy to our own spiritual being, and that he acts, as is the nature of spirits, by personal Will, like a King upon his throne.   So in the truest and best meaning, in the deepest vital meaning, in the sweetest and most soul-filling meaning, Man can say of and to his Creator, " OUR FATHER."

CHAPTER VI

THE RELATIONS OF THE DIVINE AND HUMAN PERSONS

In the preceding pages we have recognized relations between men and their Creator which are of transcendent importance; but we have not stated all the principles involved, nor all of the logical deductions from them. Some of these other principles we must notice here, in order that we may see the momentous interests that depend on our attitude towards God, and on his attitude towards us.

1. The Creator of a system of physical things and vital beings cannot cease to have relation to that system, except by annihilating it; but he can annihilate it, if he has not made it on moral principles that require eternity for their effect. It would perhaps be impossible for us to conceive philosophically an annihilation of matter, if we really knew it as substance. But we only know it as motions; and if counter motions should be set against these, the forces or motions on both sides might be reduced to absolute zero. As we know them, all effects are perpetual, whether they be effects of will or of motions of a substance. Hence, as we know substance, we can see how it can be balanced in its forces, and be bound by another force; but this leaves it still existent. How far its existence may be dependent on the continued will of

The Creator and the universe always connected.

the Cause, we, perhaps, can never know; nor have we much interest in knowing. What we are interested in knowing is, that effects are persistent, and that they have their free identity, but are constantly related to their Creator in a relation analogous to ownership. He cannot discard .them, and they cannot escape from him, unless he annihilates them. But, for aught that we know, he may create new elements, and institute new operations, and so greatly change the course of Nature. And, inasmuch as moral facts and moral law are wholly made of relations between The Creator and his creatures, and these moral relations are, in this World, bound up in the material constitution of things, The Creator is always in the relation of a Moral Governor to human beings, and to the World that is their home.

2. In The Personal First Cause of such an universe, whose creative act is by will, and who remains in persistent governmental relation to his creation, there are possibilities of additions and modifications to his work. An universe-system which includes free-willed persons, and is made for adaptation to that freedom, has, for its natural complement, free personal action by The Creator, to meet such otherwise uncontrollable action of the created persons. It is impossible for our moral sense to justify God for creating, if there is no supplemental power of ministry, providence, instruction and help from The Creator. Without a belief of this, all moral ideas are vitiated, and all evidence of harmony in the universe is invalidated. With our belief of a personal Creator and moral Ruler, a divine providence and supernatural help are reasonable expectations. Such a conception, while it

Providence.
Prayer.
Supernature.

glorifies God, invites and even commands the spirits of men to come to the Spirit of God, in communion of love and faith, to ask in prayer what their souls desire and need, and to receive answers and beneficence by his personal performance.

3. While the relations of The Creator to men are analogous to those of ownership, he has voluntarily modified them, by giving to men moral en- *Moral rela-* dowments, and adapting them to moral order *tions of Cre-* and rule. Neither moral ill nor moral good *ator and cre-* can come to us without the exercise of the *ated persons.* free-will of persons; for moral good and ill are exercises of freedom of personal life. Moral relations, like all other relations, are reciprocal and mutual. The attitude of God is that of a Cause, Owner, Ruler and Father, the attitude of a spirit towards spirits. The relation of men to God is that of duty and responsibility or obligation; for with such names moral consciousness describes its sense of the normal subjection of a free-willed person to his Cause and Holy Ruler and loving Father. An abnormal attitude, disposition or will towards The Creator is sin. Violations of God's desires, or of his Will, as shown in Nature, Reason, Conscience, or otherwise, whether the violation be in our dealing with our Self, or with him, or with our fellows, are sins so far as they are performances of our spirits, or result from failure of our spirits to perform their duties. Acts that are only muscular, and thoughts that are only perceptions, memories, or imaginations, cannot be said to be moral except as they are results of neglects or of wickedness. But acts of Will, or those that arise from tastes or habits, and those that are held by our attention, and

cherished in our tastes, have a relation to God's Will
and have moral character.*

Many sweet and saintly spirits torment themselves
with a fear that fugitive thoughts, and bodily suggestions
to which they do not yield, are sins.   Other persons persuade themselves that they are innocent while performing
acts criminal, violent, or beastly.   The moral principle
by which all cases may be judged, seems to be this, viz.:
Sin is wrong relation to God's Will respecting One's
personal being, or his attitude towards God, or One's
relations and acts to One's fellow-men.   Hence, acts,
thoughts and desires that in themselves have no wrong,
become wrong in such relations of men as cross God's
Will.   And acts that are against God's Will under their
circumstances, are not moral wrong, if they do not result
from a wrong spirit towards God, or from previous neglect or self-corruption.   There is sin when the personal
Spirit loves and desires to do; or does recklessly, anything which does, or might do violence to the Will of
God in the universe, however innocent the same things
might be in other relations.

Character is one of our imperfect names for the Being
of a spirit.   It is his Self, as having quality and disposition.   A man in cultivating his loves, chang-
Moral character. ing his disposition, informing himself. of
moral order and good and evil, and in train-
ing his spirit, is making himself lovable or unlovable
to God.   Sin is a wrong disposition of spirit; but inasmuch as all of our acts have a relation to God's Will for
ourselves or our fellow-men, they all somewhere are con-

*Discussion of the importance of free-will seems to have
begun with Philo Judæus.   See page 170.

trolled by our moral character, and must be judged as moral acts.

4. Although it is impossible for us to attain to such a comprehensive view of God's rule and plan, that we can understand how, in his love and his justice, he could create a World for so much evil and suffering, growing out of men's free-will, yet it is apparent that only with and by free-will can men be moral beings, or be God's children, or attain the chief good and values of life. Without it men would be either fools or beasts, without virtue, loveliness or exalted happiness. As we can discover in the universe no higher end than the glory and blessedness of The Creator in the moral excellence and happiness of his children, as free Persons, we may believe that the awful power to sin and suffer is in some way consistent with his perfect benevolence. We can see that endowment with personal freedom is of vastly more value to a man, and to the universe, than constitutional or enforced innocence would be.

God's right to create men with freedom of will.

5. Moral law is the personal attitude of God towards persons. It is his wisdom joined with his desire, in an expression of his Will concerning free-willed persons, respecting the values and ends of personal existence. It is his wish, animate with the infinite earnestness of his supreme and perfect life, as operative in the universe. In its first aspect it is that for which, so far as Men can know God, he lives. The awful momentum of his Being is behind it. It is his self-expression moving his beneficent, but also terrible arm. It is his self-love, and his out-going love. And, because it is his love, it is the most absolute and fixed element in his revelation of himself to men.

The laws of God. They are his loves.

6. As a love is a personal expression of a sense of the value of an object, so it is also a dislike of the opposite.

They are also his indignations. In the sentiments of a spirit—those surges of life-action which refer us only to consciousness and conscience for their explanation and justification—the undercurrent of love is abhorrence. In one passion subjective love and hate meet objective good and evil; to embrace the one, to fight the other. Love dreads, and clashes, and hates. Only a Being who loves strongly can know indignation and detestation. A notion that God can act, or ought to act, alike towards good and bad is at variance with every intuition of moral sense, and would infuse a tinge of contempt into our conception of divine amiableness. Hard as it may be for us to conceive that God is animated by abhorrence of a wicked human spirit, the opposite conception would be irrational and immoral.

7. Divine law, or The Creator's self-expression, in aiming at or loving certain ends, and in making their attainment dependent on certain lines of

Laws are alternative, vindicatory and punitive. action, causes opposite results of opposite actions, and thus appears to satisfy itself with these results. In physical things that satisfaction may be real; but in moral things it cannot be true, so long as words have meanings, and sentiments are expressions of personal being and character. All moral philosophy and intuitions affirm that God is not satisfied with his punitive and alternative law. There is love in it; but it is love for the system which is upheld, and for the good which is sought, and for the persons who are in harmony with the good ends pursued.

While we are convinced that in some ways punitive

law may produce good for even the punished persons, this conviction rests on spiritual rather than visible grounds; for moral judgment affirms that an offender when punished receives not only the natural, but the deserved results of his life-action. In the intuitions of conscience, punishment has a meaning which cannot be described as chastisement, correction, or discipline. There is a meaning in *ill desert* which is not good, although it carries the view of our spirits to the verge of a rayless abyss. But what it is the desert of one person to receive, it is the duty of some other person to administer; for there is no ill desert where there is not some mutual relation of persons. Chief among the persons who have a duty, even if it is self-imposed, towards offenders, is he who is the Guardian and Cause of all good.

The belief that God stands in an attitude of indignation and antipathy to a spirit who is rebellious against good, is part of our conception of holiness and justice in God. The intuition that God loves good spirits, and is averse to bad ones, is one belief.

The justification of God for the creation of men to be wicked and miserable is not one special and side-problem in philosophy. It is the general in- Theodicy. scrutable problem of the origin of creation. It involves to their utmost depths the problems of God's self-existence, and of his nature and purposes. Reason is blind and impotent before these problems. But Man and life and moral law are here for facts; and the more exact and imperative the law is, so much the more is the evidence conspicuous that in it is the vital stress of an infinitely adorable and loving God.

8. The act that is performed has become eternal. Life

is not destroyed as it passes, but becomes in moral judgment the real life and fact.   Life is self-mak-

Past life,
persistent   ing for eternity, and carries forward the crea-
moral rela-   tion by God, who works for persistent effects.
tion to God.   This is the grand and awful mystery of spiritual life.   In his consciousness and his conscience, a man
knows the thread of his personal identity, and that his
past is his persistent Self.   The history of a soul must
always be a part of that for which he is perpetually under
judgment before himself and his fellows and the infinite
Creator.

In view of the principles before stated, nothing can
surpass in momentous interest the questions, Can
wrecked souls be rescued, and how? Can God

Salvation.
change?   Can a free-will be made to have a
new disposition?   Can a heart reform its loves?   Can
an ignorant mind be made intelligent?   Can a gross
taste be made delicate and pure?   Can character be
radically changed?   Can a soul be emptied of its deceptions and wrong prejudices?   Can a spirit that is foul
and violent be made sweet and reasonable?

The philosophy which argues that there is a Creator
and a moral law, but goes no further, we call Natural
Religion.   It is a small part of true Conduct-

Natural
religion has   ive Philosophy; yet many persons compla-
no remedy   cently regard their ideas of this as if they
for sin.
were a virtue and even a salvation.   But
Natural Religion, even while it sees beneficence in the
universe, is a religion of condemnation and despair, a
dread of a God terrible in the severity of an inflexible
Judge. Natural Religion exalts law that demands
righteousness, but has neither mercy nor pity, and can
only command and demand.   Even when Natural

Religion acknowledges that God is a loving Person, it yet sees him as pushing forward for goodness a law in inflexible hostility to its opposites.

Conscience, that knows sin as a personal matter between souls and God, discovers no possibility of pardons. It quakes as in the grasp of an infinite arm, and as hearing the voice of an insulted, outraged and indignant personal Sovereign. It cannot conceive that wicked spirits can deserve salvation, and it cannot discover how holy God can give to men what they do not deserve, or withhold what they do deserve.

Conscience knows no pardon nor Savior.

Conductive Philosophy finds principles which encourage a conviction that, when the whole history of the World is made up, there will be brought to a triumphant finish a perfect scheme for the greatest possible blessedness of the whole family of God. Reason sees that the enormity and terribleness of sin inhere in the fact that it is a personal matter between The Creator and finite spirits. Reason cannot discover how The Creator can forgive, love, and help a spirit against whom he is arrayed by his diversity of character, his personal indignation, his justice, and his devotion to that moral excellence for the production of which the universe is created. And yet, Reason finds ground for hope in the fact that God is a Person; for in his personal nature there may be a reserve of resources and of principles which can remedy every evil except the determinate will of a free Person. And when Reason admits that in God there may be plural personality, it sees, in the relations of the Divine Persons to each other, possibilities of personal considerations, personal influences, and personal performances, that encourage a

Conductive philosophy hopeful.

hope that, through spiritual and moral agencies, the loving Father may effect a salvation of men consistently both with his own character and the freedom of men's Wills. Reason believes that The Creator never would have given life to men if there had not been, before creation, ample security of blessedness to an innumerable host of the errant, tempted, and wretched children of God.

Reason cannot forecast the methods and acts by which The Creator would effect the rescue of men, but it can indicate some of the principles that would be operative, and some of the lines along which the methods would act.

Requisites in human salvation.

Salvation from sin cannot be effected by force. It must indeed begin in God, because men have to be saved from themselves. Somehow, some time, somewhere, there must appear in God something that harmonizes justice with mercy, honors the broken laws, allays the righteous indignation of the outraged personal Creator, and covers the dishonored man with some other personality, holy, innocent, and excellent.

It must change the man's mind, and convert his heart to a love of God, and his spirit to a willing obedience. It cannot narcotize the man, but must master him in his full pride of intellect, and in the dominant career of his self-will.

It is rational and reasonable that salvation should come through a revelation, by which men can be taught God's rights and character as Ruler, at the same time that he is displayed in a personality that wins love.

Through revelations.

It is rational and reasonable that salvation should come through spiritual operations of God. In the preceding pages we have analyzed human nature and moral science till we have recognized that moral life, for good or evil, is spiritual life of men in relation to the personal life of God as a Spirit. There, where sin meets its condemnation, the remedial agencies must be set in action.

Through spiritual agency.

It is rational and reasonable to expect the salvatory help to come both by divine control of general lines of men's social conditions and personal circumstances, in long processes, with many relapses and wrecks of society, and by immediate presentation to, and influence on, the spirits of men. Spirit is Sovereign in men; and so, salvation must come in ways that turn hearts towards God, install moral habits in men's souls, and establish God as LORD AND FATHER OF SPIRITS.

CHAPTER VII

PHILOSOPHY IN THE OLD TESTAMENT

Every theology and every religion must be based on, and be true to, science and philosophy, or it will be either short-lived or immoral. A religion based on truth can carry much dead weight of ignorance and misconceptions, and yet be spiritual, worthy, and useful.

Many ancient great races have had their theologies and religions beautiful in some ideas, and excellent in some moral precepts ; but all lost their moral beneficence because their science and philosophy were untrue. It is in the nature of things that no theology can be perpetual or universal, that does not declare the creation of matter by its God, and does not found its moral principles on the authority and character of The First Cause, as personal Creator of all things, and Father of spirits. No religion and theology except the Hebrew has made such declarations. Not only is it unique in this one feature, but just in this inheres all its power.

Religion and theology must be based on science and philosophy.

§ 1.   THE TRILOGY OF GENESIS

Before this present century, any scientist who should have attempted to describe creation would have failed. One who should to-day attempt much detail might incur the ridicule of the next generation. But scientists are agreed in belief that

Hebrew story of creation.

the probable progress of the arrangement of the World, after the creation of a nebulous universe, was in general as follows :

First.   After some condensation, the Earth was covered by a hot atmosphere and dense vapors.   The first visible light came through unbroken clouds.

Second.   Islands and continents rose above the seas, and the clouds rose, but were still dense.

Third.   The Earth clothed itself with the verdure of a hot, moist climate.

Fourth.   Condensation advanced until the clouds broke, and the sun and moon could be seen.

Fifth.   Animal life first appeared in the seas.   Early, as we reckon geological history, there came enormous birds and monstrous amphibious and swimming animals.

Sixth.   The Earth became very much like what it is now, and the animals of the present time appeared.   And last came Man.

This is exactly the sequence as detailed in the Hebrew Bible.   Who can account for its correctness ?   Did the ancients attain the geological science of the nineteenth century, and lose it all again, except this fragment ?

Whether The Bible begins with the creation of atoms, or at a somewhat advanced stage of the evolution of order, is not clear.   The latter has been believed by learned men among Hebrews and *Creation of matter.* Christians to a considerable extent ; but, when we consider that " The heavens and the Earth " include everything, and that the word* used for *create* in the first verse of *Genesis* is more nearly expressive of first pro-

* The word is *bará* and means to *build, make,* or *cause,* precisely as we use all these English words.   But it seems to be connected with the Shemitic word *bar* meaning *son,* and the Indo-European root *bear.*

duction than the other word in that chapter which is translated *make*, and that the word translated *firmament* means a closed expanse, and is equivalent to the Greek word *ouranos* and the Greek idea of an *infinite self-sphered system of all things*, we find that the first verse of *Genesis* is best understood as a declaration that the Deity who organized the universe created its matter. Here alone, in all the literature in the World, is causation put forward as the basic principle of science, philosophy, theology, and religion. Here is not merely a recognition of a Deity, but an affirmation that he to whom the Hebrews gave their adoration, and declared their allegiance, he who was their Ruler and Moral Governor, created the universe. And his name is Elohim.

Names may be trifles; but when a significance has become attached to them, when they, like flags, are set as rallying symbols of a nation's faith, they become of immeasurable importance. In the first chapter of *Genesis*, and in the first three verses of the second chapter, the Hebrew name of God is Elohim. This is not a personal name, like Isis or Jupiter. It is a general title, and is plural in form, and corresponds to *Deities* or *Gods*. In parts of the most ancient Hebrew Scriptures the usual name of God is El. This occurs fifty times in the book of Job, and sixteen times in *Genesis*, and often in compound names. Moses was told (*Exodus* vi, 3) that this was Abraham's name for God. Apparently the oldest title was El. Then, in analogy with Babylonian and Assyrian usages, *u* or *o* was added. Later the letter *h*, of which Hebrews were fond, was added making *Elo'h*. The plural of this is *Elohim*. It is common habit to call this plural form a sign of dignity; but there is little ground for such an

Names of the Creator. Elohim.

assertion. The reasonable supposition is that the plural word was intentionally adopted, because of its suitableness, and that its use in this chapter set a fashion for common later use.

Although the title Elohim is plural, the verbs that are used with it are in form of the singular number, except in verse 26, where God says, " Let us make man in our image, after our likeness." If the first section of *Genesis* is taken at its *prima facie* reading, it represents the Creating Deity as a plural Being in unity, who made Man in some similarity, even double similarity, to himself, and especially in the relations of a Master and Owner over all other living creatures.

Verse 2 says, " Spirit of Elohim hovering above the face of the waters." The word which has been translated in English Bibles *moved*, means *hovering* or *brooding*. It is a participle converted into a feminine noun, and does not agree in gender with *spirit*, which is neuter, nor in number with *Elohim*. In the analogies of Hebrew usages, it may picturesquely represent metaphorically a bird, or abstractly a maternal power.

This first section of *Genesis* has been declared by many modern critics to be one fragment of some ancient legends. Certainly it constitutes one complete chapter, having a single theme. It is by Hebrew standards of composition, a masterpiece. It is picturesque throughout. It has a good deal of that double statement (or parallelism) which is characteristic of Hebrew poetry. This fact must be largely taken into account in interpreting its repetitions and synonyms. If it is old it bears much the appearance of being a revision, carefully adapted to some specific purposes. Its use of the plural title *Gods*, is an evidence

The first section of Genesis.

rather of recent than of antique origin ; but is not de-
monstrative of either; for it may be designed to declare
plurality in God.   The phrases in reference to the days
have especially the appearance of final touches, designed,
perhaps, to perfect the whole conception, by bringing in
a suggestion of God's rest and the law of the Sabbath.
These verses are counting-phrases, having poetic parallelism ; for day, in the second member, means light, and
evening and morning, in the first member, mean obscuring (or obscurity) and dawning.

The first section of *Genesis* gives no explanation of
creative processes.   How could it ?   Its silence is its
wisdom.   It only says, "God said, Let," etc.   But in this
phrase language and philosophy have done their utmost.

"God said."
God's Word.

Language can do no more for itself than to
trace back creative processes to an origin in
language.   Or, if we take words as symbols
of philosophy and reason, we can do no more than to
trace origins back to an initiation in reason ; for here we
have reached a personal cause acting with wisdom and
will.

We will not here say much about this "Word of
God," because its significance is not conspicuous in the
Old Testament.

These two words " God said," did, in fact, give a tone
to all of the Old Testament, and became a chief element
in Hebrew philosophy.   The Hebrews knew God, first as
The Deity, whose word was power, and second as the Com-
manding God, whose word was law, and then as the
revealing God, whose word is truth and instruction and
cheer.   We shall take a later occasion to note how this
finds expression in the nineteenth psalm.

Later, when the use of the Greek language by the Jews

had made familiar to them the philosophy involved in the word *logos*, the "Word of God" took its place as one of the foremost elements in wisdom, philosophy, and theology, and we shall have much occasion to take notice of it.

While this first section of *Genesis* is picturesque, rhetorical, and poetical, as a philosophical outline of creation it is ideally perfect. If it does not specifically declare all the chief principles of the philosophy of creation, it at least suggests them, and is in harmony with them. Here is personal God, acting by intelligence and will and in spirit, making in one system the physical universe and men; and these men are in similarity to God, who himself is plural.

And these men are dual, constituted for moral relations to each other, and invested with delegated authority from God for moral dominion. The foundations of a real science, a true psychology, and a rational philosophy are laid down in perfect harmony, and without a flaw. And this section includes just what belongs to the philosophy of creation, and there it stops.

A second section of the Book of *Genesis* begins at chapter ii, verse 4, and ends with the close of the third chapter. Superficially viewed, this section Second may seem to be chiefly another story of cre- section of ation, with more details about God and men, Genesis. and with a new name of God. More carefully read, it is a philosophical epitome of the story of the installation of mankind as moral Beings.

An epitome of moral science must portray The Creator of Nature and of men, the education of men as to God's rights and Will respecting individuals and society, the natural and punitive effects of rebellion, and the possibilities and principles of forgiveness and restoration. This is just what this section does; no more, no less.

First, it gives a name to the God who is Moral Ruler. This name is *Jahoh Elohim*, except in iii, 1 to 5, where

Jehovah Elohim.

it is *Elohim*. Whether it is a double title, *Lord God*, or a partitive name, *Iahoh of Gods* (just as in the first chapter *ruah elohim* may mean Spirit God, or Spirit of Gods), is disputable. The antiquity and significance of the name Iahoh, or Jehovah, are also doubtful. Its proper pronunciation is unknown. The Greeks and Romans wrote it *Iao, Iaou* and *Ieuo*. The Hebrews reverenced it so much that they ceased to pronounce it, and said other words, meaning Lord, or God, wherever *Iahoh* was written.

At the era of Christ, this name was treated as if *Lord* was its true and only known meaning. Philo bases arguments on its use with this meaning, and Greeks, Syrians, and Romans always wrote it *Kurios, Mar*, and *Dominus*, all of which mean *Lord*. It is always *Kurios* in the Septuagint Greek version of The Old Testament (even in *Ex.* vi., 3), and always *Mar* in the Syrian version. It occurs many thousands of times in the Hebrew Old Testament, but only four times in the English version, being in all other instances translated "Lord," although that is also the translation of the word *Adona*.

It has been conjectured by eminent scholars that the name *Iahoh* is derived from the Hebrew verb *haïah, to be*, that its pronunciation is *Iaveh*, and that it means *He is* or *He shall be;* but the conjecture is very doubtful. The name seems to have been originally *Iah*, which occurs in early compound names and in poetry. It occurs in *Ex.* xv, 2; xvii, 16. It is joined with the name *El*, as in Psalm cl, and appears in the ancient acclaim *Hallelu*

Iah. It appears to have been lengthened into *Iahoh* precisely as *El* into *Eloh*. *Exodus* vi, 3 seems to indicate that this change was made in the time of Moses, and that then *Iahoh* was substituted for *Iah, El* and *Elohim* in older histories.

If now we read *prima facie* the second section of *Genesis*, it presents to us Iahoh God, or Iahoh of God (Gods) or The Lord One of Gods, as the doer of all that in this section is related. A part of the section recapitulates what has been previously related as done by Elohim. The harmony of narratives is preserved by continuing the name Elohim for The Creator, and even for the Law Giver (iii, 1 to 5). But there is joined to Elohim the name Iahoh, for a specific purpose which is clearly definite.

When creatorship is to be made prominent, and causation and likeness to God are to be observed, as the basis of moral government, The Creator is Elohim, for the Hebrews. When the installation of moral government is to be related, and the personality of The Creator is to be emphasized, and the unity of the revealed and revealing God and The Creator is to be made the basis of a comprehensive exhibition of philosophical principles, then the name is made Iahoh God, or the Lord One of Gods.

The second section of *Genesis* relates the beginning of moral relations in human society, and the installation of moral law. It makes an ideally perfect exhibition, by a picturesque and poetic (Hebraic) rhetorical form of statement. It makes it philosophically complete by reiterating that the Lord is Creator, Cause, and Father. It makes an introduction to the revelation and reign of the personal

Installation of moral relations.

Deity, whom we know as Jehovah, or Lord. It helps to bridge over, for human minds, the expanse between the inconceivable Cause of the universe and the Deity who has, if we may so speak, assumed the responsibility and the task of control of human life. It turns one side towards the ineffable God of infinity, and the other towards the Lord who reigns, alike in law and in providence, beneficence, and love. And it says that these two are one. Then it exhibits the Lord God as teaching to men the laws and principles of moral government and of human welfare.

Moral relations to God could not be on a normal footing until the personal Creator and his will were made known to the intellects of men; for morality and goodness are not vague sentiments, but are disposition towards the known person of God, and are practically efficient only in specific acts in relations towards his known and, we may say, itemized will, as to his Self, and as to our fellows. Beneficent moral government also required revelation and warning of the personal attitude of God towards rebellious and wicked souls. This section of *Genesis* declares the entrance of mankind into life with the vantage of clearly definite instruction in moral law.

Human moral nature is in two parts, and conscience is double. We may call the two parts knowing and living. One is intellect, the other is spirit. One is consciousness, the other is conscience. One is mental, the other is vital. And God's displays of Himself to men are also twofold. One gives truth, and the other gives life. One appeals to mind, the other to heart and will. Each of the twain of God corresponds to one of the twain in men: so that a symbol of one is largely a fitting sym-

bol of the other.   An ideal conception of moral government must display the truth and will of personal God to
human minds, and through them touch and enter the
spiritual living of men.

This section of *Genesis*, being only a moral history,
represents moral truth (which in one aspect is God's
law) and moral life as two trees.*   One is in its divine
aspect revelation, and in its human aspect is knowing.
The other divinely is ministry, and humanly is living.

We cannot conceive symbols more appropriate and
complete of the moral life.   We may follow them out
into emblemism of all that is best in divine beneficence, and of all the facts of human moral life, rooted
in the Earth for its present home, but spread in the air
and light of God, and under Heaven, for fruitage of
worth, beauty, and delight.

But here the display of God was not all in symbols.
"The Tree of Knowledge of Good and Evil" was made
significant by specific verbal statements of Divine Will.
Man was instructed that the one moral test is in obedience or disobedience to the personal Will of The Creator.   Then he was instructed that knowing and living
are bound together, and that sin known in experience
and performance is moral death.

"In the day that Thou eatest thereof, Thou shalt
die," is something more than a metaphor.   In a moral
argument for immortality of men, it appears   Sin is
that we are moral beings because we are im-   moral
mortal, and we only, in the best sense, live   death.
when we are right with God.   Jesus was uttering the

*See *Dan.* ix, 24, 27, and *Rev.* xi, 3 to 12, for a suggestion
of the symbolism of "Vision and Prophecy" here.

profoundest truths when he said, "This is eternal life, to know Thee, the only true God." Death begins when health is broken. The tree that has lost its natural supplies, or clogged its vital channels, may continue to be wood, but as a tree it is dead.

The first section of *Genesis* displayed the Creator, and also man in his personal relation to the personal Author of his being. The second section ex-
The first Moral Law.
hibits the beginning of moral relations between human persons; which is almost the whole range in which a man can obey or disobey the Will of his Creator. These began in the instant that here were two free human Beings. The family was instituted with its laws, laws of mutual love and help, laws of personal independence with moral union. Jahoh Elohim is exhibited as the law maker; but he is first Creator and Father. He specially gives life to the human spirit, and law to the human family.

In the course of events the woman is alone. A thought, and then a wish, slip into her mind and heart. The Creator had made two self-sphered lives
The first Sin.
unite. The mysteries of independence and of union, untried in experience, balance in the woman's soul. An ambition rises in her soul, a strong, magnificent ambition. Has not she equal rights with Adam, or even móre? Was not she, by maternity, most like Elohim, and Adam like Jahoh? Shall she not test this sovereignty of the Divine Lord, and the supremacy of the human Lord; and in the testing establish the law of Nature against the statute of The Lord?

The essay is made. Is it by an imperious assertion, or by sweet persuasion? Is it a stroke for dominion, or a restless enticement to a joint rebellion? In either case it will do violence to both God and Man. It will break on one side the innocence and peace of childship, and on the other the union of confidence, and love, and mutual respect. It will bring in the law of Nature, but at its worst, in humiliation, shame, and self-reproach. It will awaken conscience that discovers God's rights, and crushes self-respect, and smirches mutual regard.

The fearful step is made. The defiance is ventured. The sin becomes a joint one. The man is not wise enough, or not strong, and good, and magnanimous enough, to set the errant mind and heart of Eve aright. And the woe breaks in as a flood, with fear of the Lord God, who cannot be escaped, and with mutual discovery and shame for the companions in guilt. The discovered truth was death.

Then (iii, 22) "The Lord God said, Behold Mankind is become as one of us, to know good and evil." As in Deity the principles of moral life all lay in the relations of persons to persons, so now Adam and Eve, even in their shame, had passed out of self-hood into the discovery of duties, and of divine law, and of that wide realm of moral life which lies in the relations of society. They who had failed towards each other and towards Jahoh, when they were but two, learned that a broader range, a harder task, a more awful responsibility, lay before them; for their children must enter into the struggle of moral life, with the burden on them of the parents' faults and weaknesses.

Results of the first sin.

The meaning of the remainder of verse 22 is doubtful. Our English version says, "The Lord said, *Lest* he put forth his hand and take also of the tree of life and live forever; so [and therefore] he drove out," etc.

But the Hebrew says *and* instead of *so*, and it reads
"That he may not put," etc. The word translated *lest*,
does not mean *in order that not*, but simply *that not*. In
Prov. v, 6, a similar phrase means "(She is determined)
that she will not," etc. The Syriac version makes this
phrase of the The Lord a question, and the Greek version may (or at least with a slight change it may) be
read in the same way. This phrase may mean, I fear
that he will not; or, he is decided that he will not; or,
it is doubtful whether he will or will not, etc.

The last part of iii, 24 is also of doubtful meaning.
"He placed at the east of the garden of Eden the
cherubs and a flame [as] of a flashing sword, for guarding
[or preserving] the path [or approach] of the tree of
life." It is now known that cherubs among Shemitic
people were composite figures, usually of a man, a lion,
an ox, and an eagle, used for religious emblems, and
probably signifying the consecration of all the elements
of human life and personality to God's worship. Later,
in the Mosaic ordinances, such symbols were placed in
the sanctuary, and over the ark of testimony.

We must therefore understand either that Adam
established and continued a sanctuary for religious
service and the advantage of spiritual living, or that
God established such a sanctuary, and invested it with
emblems and evidences of his favor and of the continuance of his grace under the changed circumstances. But
the way that had been open and free, by the nature of
normal life of God's children, had become a way of law
and labor, of study and striving, of conscience and service.

And so, as a picturesque recital of the necessary
principles and general facts of the beginnings of moral
history, this second section of *Genesis* is ideally perfect.

The fourth chapter of *Genesis* is a third distinct section, which in philosophical significance falls behind neither of the others. It outlines the installation of moral law in the relations of multiplied Society. This, also, is in its style poetic, with parallelisms.

The third section of Genesis.

With the birth of the first child came the momentous questions of the parents: Is this new soul ours or God's? Are we to it as God is to us? If Jehovah is our Creator and Lord, what is he to this one? Eve cannot see the whole mystery; but she has learned much, and Jehovah's rights are clear to her, and she says, "I have gotten a man to Jehovah."

In this section the name Elohim is not used. Creation is not here emphasized; but Jahoh in his rule as Lord has been recognized, and this section only deals with his taking moral rule over the coming hosts. So, in this section the name of God is only Jahoh.

Soon another man is born. The circle of moral relation is enlarged: but selfness has not fitted itself to the Will of God, nor to a spirit of love. A brother is ajar with his brother, and with God. Divine lessons mediate for righteousness and peace. Cain is told: "If thou doest well, is not that exaltation? But if thou doest not well, sin is brought home to you [croucheth at the door]. Also to thee shall be his desire, and thou (I say) shalt protect him." An ideal formula of moral law for Society.

But reason and religion did not avert the sin. The first crime against society was committed; and, in this, Man came again face to face with The Lord. The cry of Abel's blood was a voice for Jehovah to hear, and he heard it, and made it the occasion for a statement of Divine Law over and in

The first crime.

Society, and of the limitations of private vengeance. This section of *Genesis* continues till it includes the multiplication of people, the beginning of polygamy, the three parallel couplets of Lamech telling the prevailing ideas of morality, and ends with the saying, "Then Enosh hoped to call [by] the name of Jahoh." The last sentence is obscure in its meaning; but at least it ends the story of human crime and fears, with an expression of human faith calling, calling not like Abel's blood, but with hope, in the name of The Lord.*

The first four chapters of *Genesis* thus constitute a trilogy of conductive philosophy, matchless as philosophy, and unequaled as literature, except by the thirteenth chapter of Matthew. It evolves from its first verse, as a song that is true to its first bar. Causation and fatherhood on the

First four chapters of Genesis a trilogy.

divine side, knowledge and response on the human side, blending lives in the unfathomable and glorious relations of personal beings, these are the truths of Reason and of Moral Science, and the World has learned them from this ancient book of the Hebrews.

§ 2.   THE GENERAL TENOR OF THE OLD TESTAMENT

The Old Testament, more than any other book of the World, is a treatise on philosophy. Not, indeed, speculative or argumentative, but declarative of fundamental

---

*Philo Judæus four times explains this sentence in his way. He treats it somewhat like the moral argument for immortality in our preceding pages. "Enosh [Man] is the intellect." "The only real man who is established in good hopes." "They do not look on the man devoid of hope as a man at all." Man, according to Moses, is a disposition of the soul hoping in the living God." "Irrational animals are devoid of hope; but hope is a presage of joy." See *The Worse Against the Better*, ch. 38; *On Abraham*, ch. 2; *On Rewards and Punishments*, ch. 2; *Questions and Solutions*, 79.

principles. And the bearing of these on human life it illustrates by the history of individuals and of society, and chiefly by the story of their errors, failures, sins, and crimes. It lays bare, as no other book does, the motive forces of sin. With its principles, warnings and appeals, it shows the long road strewn with wrecks.

Passing all questions about authorship and inspiration, and omitting details of the individual books and local circumstances, we find in the Old Testament one unbroken thread of principles, one core of invariable faith. The principle is the reign of The Creator in Person. The faith is trust in the universal Father.

Until the time of Moses, men lived in the strength and arrogance of life as now, and in the fascinations and resources of the World. Most men cared for no past and looked for no future. Gods were only names to fear, or to use as mottoes for national pomp. Morality was not religion nor theology, but maxims of utility, taste, or compromise. But in some unknown way a line of truth was preserved. In some part of one family, Jahoh, or we will say, Jehovah, is remembered and worshiped. The family sins, much like others, and is punished when it is wicked; but the faith in The Divine Father, The Lord, continues in some souls.

Patriarchal theology.

By most persons, however, the Creating Father was forgotten, or remembered as a character in an unimportant tale. Even the true theology dropped to one idea, held in narrow view, in misconceptions, with sins and vices, but occasionally with love and service. This creed when written was like Abraham's. "Abraham believed Jehovah, and he reckoned that to him as righteousness."

How the record of this faith was brought to us,

by whom recorded and when, by whom preserved, by whom edited, we do not know. But there are gleams of glorious light in the darkness, which we cherish because they display the harmonious doctrine and dealing of the personal Father.

The World came to the fifteenth century before Christ with its old institutions crumbling, and no indications of its future. The power and the civilization of Egypt, with its outward elegance and inward foulness, were breaking fast. The arts and science of Babylon were decaying in the sloth of luxury and vice. Assyria was attacking the heart of Babylonia. The Persians were crude and fierce in their highland homes. The Phœnicians were worshiping their coarse and savage ideals of God; but had not yet carried them to the western parts of the sea. Greece had not thought of literature, nor even of an alphabet.

The Mosaic education.

Europe was then dotted with camps of petty states or wandering tribes. Syria, covered with forests, vineyards and grasses, where now are bare rocks, was crowded with towns and villages, and peopled by many tribes that had little union together, and whose idolatry was gross and cruel.

Into such a people there was brought a theology, or a philosophy, or a religion, which had no counterparts or analogies anywhere in the World. It came through the ministry of the Hebrew leader, Moses, and we know it through his words and books, and we call it " The Mosaic revelations and institutions." Separating this from the pages of the history of the people among whom it was introduced, mostly an intractable and wicked people, it bears the character of a wonderful system of education in the facts and principles of Moral Science.

That morality and the training of conscience must be attained through education, is an axiom everywhere and always.   But no people needed this education more than the Hebrews.   They had grown to be a nation in serfdom among idolators.   They had had no teachers of truth; for there were none in the World.   They had little or no literature, and few traditions.   They had no religious teachers, leaders, priests or sanctuary.   They seem to have forgotten the Sabbath, if they had ever observed it.

Saving truth for men is knowledge of their Creator, and of His plan and will.   But if it were not this, and if it were moral maxims and correct life, two things are requisite for the institution of right moral life.   One is truth; the other is habit.   First the facts of creation by a God, and of the character of that God, and of His plan and will and personal reign must be known.

But maxims of morality cannot be learned in formulas alone.   Not until they have been learned in experience and practice can they become natural.   Souls learn in living, and spirits evolve character by obedience.   But religion, or morality, is not moral maxims nor formal living.   It is worship and service of Him who has the right to reign.   Truth and life grow as twain trees.   Creed and life are a ring, of which every point is at once a beginning and an end.

The first feature of the Mosaic institutions is a teaching that the God who rules men is the Cause of their existence and of the universe, and is a Person.   This fills the Old Testament, as the chief truth to be expressed and impressed.   It is the doctrine that first distinguishes The Bible from all other books of religion or philosophy.

Teaching about God's person and rights.

The reign of Jehovah is declared to be based, not on his power, or his wisdom, or his goodness, but on his rights as universal Creator. His law is advice and persuasion; but first it is commands. His rule is right because it is his rights. And it is rights of a person, not a necessity, nor an impersonal good end, but a right that has its existence once for all in the personality of the self-existent Cause of all things, and Father of all persons.

The outward forms of the revelation of Jehovah as a person are adapted to make, as they did make, the strongest impression, not only on the ignorant minds that first received it, but on all men. Direct appearances and personal acts of God, if not absolutely necessary for men's instruction, are, at least at the beginning of revelation, so beneficent and useful as to be reasonable and probable. Miraculous performances of God, who is a Creator, and is claiming his rights as First Cause, are such beneficent ministrations as are rationally to be expected, especially when the philosophy and exhausted theology of the whole World were to be revolutionized.

Then the presentation of moral principles, of purity, rightness, holiness, justice, love, goodness, duty, was made, not by urging their theoretical excellence and their utility, but by declaring them to be God's Will. And then, the comprehension and admiration of them came in the experience of living by them, slowly and sometimes painfully. He will fail to apprehend the character of The Old Testament who does not notice its iteration of the personal Will of Jehovah.

The mission of Moses was inaugurated with the formula, "I AM hath sent me to you." The Ten Commandments have the preface, "I am Jehovah thy God."

The law of the Sabbath, the one statute that most plainly rests on God's Will, is enforced with the words, " For The Lord made heaven and earth, The Lord blessed the Sabbath day, and hallowed it." In *Deuteronomy* v, the phrase, " I am Jehovah," is reiterated five times as the basis of four laws.

The name Jehovah is repeated more than five hundred times in the single book of *Deuteronomy*. In *Leviticus* xviii to xx, command after command is given, with the added phrase, "I am Jehovah." Moses epitomizes the law in these words (*Deut.* vi, 4-5), "Jehovah our God! Jehovah one! And thou shalt love Jehovah thy God with all thy heart, and with all thy soul, and with all thy might." In the Old Testament the repetitions of the name Jehovah are many thousands.

After enforcing the principle that Jehovah rules by right of creation, the institutes of Moses proceed to inculcate the idea that the Will of Jehovah is so causative of, and so protective to, all that we call Exalted being, and Harmonies of ends, and Values of personal life, that he is what we call holy, and his personal Will enjoins holiness on us; and this holy Will of God is finally and essentially a principle and operation of supreme love.

Inst uc-
tionнas
to the
holiness
of G d

The World has learned these principles only from the Hebrew Scriptures. No other theology or philosophy contains them. Many others do not conceive their gods to be holy. All conceive holiness as something self-existent, and impersonally excellent, and self-authoritative. If any theology like Buddhism conceives holiness in Deity, it spoils the conception by declaring the God impassive, inactive, and without part or interest in the World or in men.

The holiness which the Old Testament inculcates is the perfection of personal active life of souls, and has its origin and authority in the imperious, but loving, movement of the personal spirit of God towards the highest personal excellence of thought, feeling, and action, in all spirits.

Training in this idea began for Moses at the burning bush with the lesson, " Take off thy shoes, for the place is holy ground"; as any place is holy where the spirit of a man recognizes God. Then came many a lesson and many symbols, which had for their effect a training in habits of self-restraint, of high ideals, and of approach to God.

By commands not to mix materials in garments, nor make shameful alliances, nor bear personal defilement, nor invade consecrated places, the Hebrews were taught that there is something, in the Will of God, that has character above all material worth, and they were trained in that obedient exercise by which ideas become tastes, and habits become ideas.

Wonderful agents for training, not merely for the Hebrews, but for all the World, were the lessons at Sinai, and then the sanctuaries in the tabernacle and temple, from which every pollution, except for confessional sacrifices, was barred, and then the priestly offices of mediation, and the bathing and changing of garments, and in general, everything that inculcates a sense that wrong was personal defilement, because it was unlike the character of The Lord Creator, and made the defiled Person unfit to approach the Person of God.

In the teachings and writings of the Hebrews, God's holiness is the aspect of The Creator's will, as viewed by men, in its relations to the best values of life for spirit beings; and all the books of the Old Testament, with wonderful uniformity and consistency, and with skill and forcefulness of teaching, inculcate the idea that unholiness is personal offense against personal God.

These books do not teach that God, having discovered holiness in the universe has chosen to champion it ; but he made it, in setting his Will into actual life-action. If his Will had been different, holiness and sin would be different from what they now are.

Instruction about sin.

And so, with precept and government, with principles and experiment, with commands and threats and appeals, with charm of words that lead souls by the power of sympathy and fellowship of expression, and with addresses to all the best faculties and sensibilities of souls, the Hebrew training, by these books, taught that The Creator has personal interest in the rightness of men, personal interest in maintaining his plans, personal approving love for the spirits that respond to him, and personal indignation towards spirits that are vile or rebellious.

God is shown moving, with terrible majesty and force, to defend the rightness and justice which are the law of the universe because he is God. And this is the chief objection which Infidels urge against The Old Testament. Of course they would scorn a God who lacked either feeling or action, and they would defy a God whose law was only feeble theory, and advice without authority ; but because God is a personal nature, and his law is his Will, and moves with awful force to defend its rights and its rightness, they hate and scoff.

The manner of the teaching was suited to the circumstances and people, and to its greater and grander work as the inauguration of the moral education of all the World in all time. If the manner was not necessary, it has at least been useful.

Because Man is a free moral being, both the formal theory, and the actual fact of the certainty of punishment for sin against God, had to be exhibited to him. For this, the destruction of wicked communities had immeasurable educational value. For this, imprecations on sin, and the twain blessings and curses from Ebal and Gerezim are priceless lessons. For this, the twenty-eighth chapter of *Deuteronomy*, proclaiming terrible alternative law, which, after all, that intractable people chose to put to the test of experience, is of inestimable worth to the faithful of that people, and to those who come worshipfully to God out of all races.

That the education was useful and necessary, is shown by the fact that, to-day, no philosophers in all the World, except adherents of the Hebrew Scriptures, declare, as principles of moral science, the reign of a personal Creator, authority of moral law in his Will, and certainty of retribution for disobedience and rebellion: but the Hebrews, even at the Christian era, called their system of belief "Our National Philosophy." (See Philo.)

Whatever may be the truth as to the authorship of the Mosaic Institutions, they constituted a marvelously sagacious educational device for training a people in such philosophical principles. Every part is a type, that is to say, a pattern or illustration, of a principle. And these principles, beginning in the personality, holiness, and reign of The Creator, include at last hope and cheer and promise, through repentance and reformation and love in men, and grace and help in the personal ministry of The Lord.

Types.

The sanctuaries lead the system of types, teaching that in character there are separations between God and men, that if a man would come to God he must come with self-examination, with penitence and reformation, turning from sin, and outwardly condemning it, and publicly honoring his Lord. Even so he can best come in God's appointed ways, because these are the best public demonstrations of his sentiments, and in them there are beneficent ministrations. And in these sanctuaries of the tabernacle and temple there was spiritual access to the presence of God. As at the outer line of Eden, so here, cherubs, flaming altars, and shekinah glory, both hindered and protected the way to life in God.

Tabernacle and temple.

Interwoven with the typology of the sanctuaries, all the offices of the Priests were types of principles of the relations of men to the personal God. In these the sinner came with his confession of sin, and his profession of penitence, reformation, and obedience. In the act of his representative, the Priest, the sinner first condemned himself, and then worshiped.

Priests.

In the blood sacrifices, the sinner confessed his guilt, his ill-desert, and his submission. In these he honored the law and its Maker. In them he declared sin awful and deadly. In the ceremonial purifications, the changing and washing of garments, the seclusions, the washings and bathings and sprinklings, he professed his abandonment of sin, and his desire for purity. And these types were agencies to teach him to bring himself in this attitude to God.

Sacrifices. Purifications.

If now we turn to the divine side of these types and their lessons, how graciously they bring, to the erring

man, the assurances of divine love! The God invites.
Divine side of the types. The Divine Person has spoken and called. The Father has opened the way, and bidden the Children to come.

Only one chief truth is kept covered. How God can forgive, how he is satisfied, how justice is met, this is not told. That mystery rested still in God. It never can be fully told. Almost all that can be told, or that philosophy can comprehend, of the reconciliation of God, seems to be the mere fact that, in the personal life of The Father, and the personal relations and influences of Triune Deity, there are possibilities of divine grace, as there are certainties of divine indignations, which are great as the infinity of the personality of God.

All except that one thing the lessons of the Old Testament do. They give the invitations of the person of God. It is the Creator, Jehovah, The Lord, who calls. It is the Maker of Man who helps the returning sinner. It is the Law Maker who forgives. It is the Ruler who pledges grace. And he who came to Jehovah had reached the goal. He whose heart was with his Lord and Father was at home. It was enough that Jehovah knew the facts and principles of atonement; the penitent sinner rested his faith in the person of his Lord.

So the divine side of the types, and the lessons, displayed personal benedictions of reconciled God. These can almost all be embraced in one word, common in the Old Testament; but unknown in all other philosophies and theologies, and meaningless in any moral science that does not rest all its principles on the personal nature of God.

This is the word *Covering*, which we usually translate *atonement.* By direction of Jahoh, the Priests made ceremonial, or typical, coverings of sins of penitent souls; and such souls found assurance that sins, which could not be undone, were truly covered when conscience rested near the heart of the Lord, and the same voice that declared the dreadfulness of sin, said, "It is covered."

There is one matter in the Mosaic institutions which demands a large attention, which it does not get. It is something so great in its pretensions, so far-reaching, and so important, that it must be noticed. Christians, timid, with bated breath, pass it gingerly; and infidels make it the butt of scorn and sarcasm. This is the Oracle of God.

Oracle. Breastplate of judgment. Urim and Thummim.

In *Exodus* xxviii and xxxix, and *Leviticus* viii, there is described an article of the regalia of the High Priest, which we call "The Breastplate of Judgment." In Hebrew it is *hhoshen,* a word of very doubtful, if not unknown, meaning. It has been variously translated bag, covering, and ornament. We have called it breastplate, because it was worn on the High Priest's breast. It was a square plate, or frame, carrying twelve precious stones, and having two pockets, in which were some indescribable emblems, called *urim* (light) and *thummim* (truth).

There is not much said about this; but there is enough to have caused a belief that it was declared to be an instrumentality by which the High Priest communed with God, and obtained revelations from God, or answers to questions. We shall not say much here about this, simply because the Old Testament says so little.

We only say here that its symbolism and use have been misapprehended. If it had, even fraudulently, been used as a means of inducing faith in alleged revelations, it would have been much mentioned, and would have degenerated into a device for trickery and for the advancement of superstition and priestcraft. But its effect was exactly the opposite; and it led in the opposite direction.

Its chief service was in accompanying a High Priest into the sanctuary, when he presented the people's confessions and sacrifices, and asked forgiveness of sins. It was a companion in ceremonies of most solemn advocacy, and especially in those of which the Scriptures imply, and the best Jews declared, the efficacy depended on the spiritual attitude and intent of the worshipers.*

In fact, as we shall show hereafter, this thing and its use were most philosophical and beneficial in their effects. They gave names† and character to the two largest, most philosophical, and most pious, sects of the Jews (the Essenoi and the Pharisaioi); were intimately connected with the logos doctrine, which is so large an element of Jewish philosophy, and of the New Testament; have a close relation to the doctrine about†† The Paraclete (advocate), and seem to have been instrumental in the introduction of the terms *consciousness* and *conscience*, and all that is connected with them, into philosophy.

It must be observed that its name was *hhoshen* of *Mishpat*. *Mishpat* means *judgment*. It is associated a great deal in the Old Testament with *choq* (statute). So far as names give indications, the breastplate was connected with conceptions of moral law and moral decisions. The Greeks condensed its whole name into one word, *logeîon* or *lógion*.

* See Philo, *On The Life of Moses. Books iii, ch. 10.*
† See pages 189, 190.
†† See hereafter. Pages 174, 189, 280.

Later Greeks connected the name *logeion* with the logos doctrine. The name had adaptations to all the significations of *logos*, especially *word*, *truth*, and *law*. *Logos*, from *lego*, *I set*, is equivalent to Latin *lex*, and English *law*; but the Greeks did not choose to use it in that signification.

The name *logeion* seems to have been given with regard to both the meanings of *logos*, viz., *word* and *decision* (or *law*). In inquiring about its use, we must notice that, if it had been used by the Priests to give authority to supposed messages from God, it would have been at variance with the whole tenor and spirit of the Old Testament,

The Jews had Priests and Prophets; but they never had both these offices, nor one of these and government, combined in one man. Such combinations are the beginnings of tyrannies; but Judaism was freedom, and grew freer as it grew older.

It is certain that among later Jews (of the Greek period) the idea of inquiring of the *logeion* for revelations did not prevail; but this oracle was associated with spiritual, pious exercises, and with culture of conscience, and with study of God's natural laws, or his decrees.

§ 3. DIVINE SPIRIT

We have now shown in the personal philosophy in the Old Testament, a wonderful wisdom and great agencies of personal beneficence; but if this were the whole system, it would still be deficient, and unable to rescue or preserve men.

Divine Spirit's help.

Fallen man needs to be saved from himself. His will must remain free, and yet his loves and ideas need radical changes. His corruption is in his spiritual being, at once the noblest and worst, the most enslaved yet freest, the most exhibited yet most concealed, of all the elements of his person.   Philosophy knows no way to save man without changing his will, while leaving him free.   Philosophy and science know no agent, except God's Spirit, that can convert a human spirit, while leaving him free.

No philosophy except the Hebrew has taught that such reformation is possible, and so opened broad avenues of hope for men.   The Hebrew teaching is unique, not only in its basing all its moral principles on creation by personal God, but in its exhibiting that God as a Spirit, and as acting in spiritual methods on the spirits of men.

There is probably no word in the Bible which is more carelessly read than the word *spirit ;* nor any which by negligent reading can lead to more mischievous errors.   Careful study often fails to attain certainty of its meaning in a sentence ; for it has the meanings, *personal being, disposition, courage, moral character,* and *influence.*   But to take out of The Old Testament the word *spirit,* would be like taking out of the World all sunlight and color.

The doctrine of the nature of God as a Spirit began at the very overture of *Genesis* in the saying, "Spirit of Elohim hovered over the face of the waters."   The very ancient book of *Job* says, "Spirit of El made me" (xxxiii 4), and, "By his Spirit he garnished the heavens" (xxvi, 13).   But in general the divine Spirit is most often called Jehovah's Spirit; and when the phrase is "God's spirit" it is usually evident that Jehovah is meant.

Gen. ii, 7, " Jehovah Elohim breathed into his nostrils the breath of life, and Man became a living soul," does not use the Hebrew word for *spirit*, although that word means breath. This verse says that Jehovah gave Man vitality. If it had said that God thus gave spirit, it would have implied that spirit is not personality, but is matter. Philo Judæus, who says a great deal about this verse, actually, while he is trying to honor spirituality, falls into the error of saying that spirit is æther.

The doctrine in The Old Testament about God's Spirit is in several forms. Sometimes The Spirit is the Divine Person. Sometimes it is an influence exerted on men. Sometimes it is the result of that influence in the spirits of men. In this teaching about divine and human spirits, the Hebrew Scriptures bring to men light and hope. In this they show how truth may be illuminated, pure will awakened, moral health quickened, and the Child and the Father brought together. In this they open up endless vistas of infinite possibilities of help, persuasion, and even transformation of wrecked souls into saintliness and worthiness for the Father's home.

In this doctrine the philosophy of the Hebrew Scriptures is rounded into the fulness of a perfect system. In it the truth that God is the Father, and that the Child is in the likeness of God, receives consummation ; for it shows how in free beings the truths, which to intellects are only ideas, can be made forces of best life.

§ 4.   IMMORTALITY

To complete a survey of the philosophy of personality in The Old Testament we ask now, Human What is its doctrine as to immortality of Immorhuman spirits ? We could wish that its reve- tality. lation of this were clearer and fuller ; but men will always wish so ; for nothing but actual experience, or a testimony of sure witnesses, can amount to a demonstration.

It is denied by many that The Old Testament says that souls are immortal; and it may be admitted that The Old Testament is so much more intent on teaching right moral principles, and on declaring God's personal rights, that it does not strongly emphasize the doctrine of human immortality, for a motive to righteousness.

The immateriality and immortality of souls was implied in the declaration that man was made in God's image; and it was so understood by Hebrews, who knew the first chapters of Genesis, and especially by the most intelligent, such as the Platonists and the Pharisees.

The doctrine was obscured to them, as it is to Christians, rather than helped, by what was written about The Tree of Life; for whoever thinks that those words are written about prolongation of vitality, leads himself into all errant paths of skepticism. But no Hebrew believed, or can believe, that the declaration of the likeness of Man to God referred to anything but likeness of soul and spirit, and implied anything but a glorious nature and immortal being.

Intelligent Hebrews also believed that the declaration that "Jehovah breathed into Adam the breath of life," implied an impartation of vitality like Jehovah's, spiritual and eternal. And this conception grew in fulness and breadth and splendor, as their ideas grew of the spirituality of men, and of the moral influence of The Spirit of God.

That men were spirits, was a doctrine that infused a special character into all the Hebrew Scriptures, and into all the Hebrew conception of moral nature and moral law. Belief in immortality is contained in the belief that a man is a spirit.   No person ever believed the one doctrine without believing the other.

No person seems ever to have supposed that it was necessary to prove or to argue that spirits are immortal. The Hebrews not only had, as one of their first principles, the belief that a man is a spirit ; but they also had the philosophical conception that spirit, and only spirit, can act on spirit, and that the spiritual influence and ministry of God is effective in beneficence, and, in exalting power, because the spirit of a human person is akin to God's.

The belief in spirit-immortality became degraded among the Hebrews ; but this degradation became an evidence of the belief.   It became a dark and cheerless belief ; but it has been that to almost all peoples except Christians.   This degradation took the forms of belief in Sheol (Hades) and in necromancy.   Both of them were forms of ghostism.

The first was a conception that the spirits of the departed remained associated somehow with their bodies and with the place of burial.   The name of the grave, Sheol, became a name for a pit, an under-world, an unexplored region, a Hades, in which the spirits lived, but in a kind of life unknown to men on Earth, a life of such a sort that a resurrection to an earthly life would be a joy.

The other conception, necromancy, seems to have been exactly the ghostism which now takes the name of spiritualism.   Moses gives severe laws for its punishment ; and so shows its very ancient prevalence.*   The story of

*See Lev. xvix, 31 ; xx, 6; 27 ; Deut. xviii, 11 ; I Sam. xxviii, 3, 7, 8, 9 ; II Kings, xxi, 6, xxiii, 24 ; I Chron. x, 13 ; Isaiah, viii, 19 ; xvix, 3 ; xxvix, 4.

Saul and the Medium of Endor (I *Sam'l* xxviii) is a counterpart of the modern deceptions ; *but it illustrates the belief in the immortality of the departed.

The silences of The Scriptures are not less eloquent sometimes than words. They pass over without a word the religious theories of the pagans. We are obliged to believe that a wise policy left those temporary errors to die undescribed, because commemoration might have perpetuated them.

The Hebrews came out of long association with the Egyptians, a people whose theology and religion were practically of the grossest kind, but who had, as their most ancient literature, hymns respecting an after life, a judgment of souls, and a sort of immortality. The Hebrews show that they had received and retained the belief in a perpetual life of spirits; but they would not record it as an Egyptian doctrine, because for themselves it rested on the conviction that man is a child of God, and is in the Father's likeness.

The affirmation of human immortality is positive and definite in *Daniel xii, 1 to 4* (See our page 227). This is explained by Saint John in *The Apocalypse*, chs. XIV and XX, in the tableaux of the millennium and the judgment, as we show on pp. 253, 256.

§ 5. SALVATION

After such a view of the philosophy in The Old Testament, we can take up the subject of the salvation of
Salvation.
human beings; and although it is the most momentous problem, and the profoundest mystery, in all the sphere of study, we can, in a few words,

* It is plain that there was no appearance of Samuel except in the pretenses of the medium, who knew Saul.

outline the principles of the Old Testament's doctrine of salvation.

It exhibits The Lord, Jehovah, as Moral Ruler. He is nearest to the offense. He is the wronged One, and the grieved One, and the One in whom all Deity is wronged and grieved. Hence He is the One who is to forgive, help, and restore. That is true philosophy. Grace can begin only where the offense was. And there it did begin.

The offense and wrong in sin are personal to God. It is the clash of two personalities. Hence its enormity; but hence also is the possibility of its forgiveness and remedy. So every hope rests on the person of God. Philosophy can know no covenant of works. The Old Testament, with true philosophy, concentrates all theology in God's Person. To know Him is to know all truth. Salvation is a personal relation to God, because sin is a relation to Him. Hence the Old Testament does not require, nor permit, men to know all the depths of the problem of the ways of God, even in salvation. It only exhibits Jehovah as Judge and Savior, and only requires a sinner to become righted towards the Person of his Lord.

It requires the sinner to come to Jehovah, loving, obeying, confessing, worshiping, and then trusting and honoring him. When he has done that, he has reached home, and rests in God. When the earthly Self is in the embrace of the Divine Father, the eternal peace and bliss have begun.

We have in the first part of this book shown principles of philosophy promising spiritual help for human souls. And this, too, the Old Testament promises so fully that to many Jews the Spirit's help. belief in a spiritual ministry of God to human spirits had become not only a profound conviction, but a rich and precious experience.

If we further ask if there is in the Old Testament an announcement of a Mediator, or of a redemption by sacrifice, we find that before Jesus came, the old Scripture had not only educated the Hebrews in recognizing the value and necessity of the principles of mediation and of sacrifice, but had induced the expectation of the coming of a self-sacrificing Mediator. We are not, perhaps, able to say where John the Baptist learned the name "The Lamb of God, who takes away the World's sin"; but as we see where he was taught the other names of Jesus, we come very close to the origin of the name "The Lamb slain from the foundation of the World."

Mediator Sacrifice.

From our survey of the outlines of philosophy in the Old Testament, we perceive, not merely that it is in harmony with the facts of science and the deductions of Reason, but that it presents to the World such a complete and rational system of philosophy, theology, humanity, and morality, as has nowhere else in the World been suggested.

We may even maintain that all that is recognized as wisest in philosophy, and even the words and formulas of the truest modern philosophy, apparently would not have existed if they had not been initiated and cultivated in the Hebrew literature.

And in that literature the best principles were not the later evolutions, beautiful and precious as they are; but the oldest, the constructive, basic ideas, are the formulative ones, which control and give character to the whole structure, making it at once coherent, symmetrical, harmonious, and true to Reason and to Consciences.

CHAPTER VIII

THE EXPOSITION OF THE BIBLE BY PHILO, THE ALEXANDRIAN JEW

§ I. PHILO JUDÆUS INTRODUCED

In the middle of the reign of Caius Cæsar, called Caligula, about A. D. 39, there stood one day before the Emperor, in his gardens near Rome, a commission of three persons. They had been sent by the Jews of Alexandria to plead with the tyrant for relief from the persecutions which threatened the ruin of their race. Caius was furious because the Jews alone refused to honor him as a God.   He was bent on setting up his statue in the temple of Jehovah in Jerusalem, and had given favor to the enemies of the Jews.

In Alexandria murderous assaults by mobs had been encouraged, and the governor and officers had made public exhibitions of torture, robbery, and killing, almost equal to those which, a little later, under Nero, attended the desolation of the Christians.   The leader of this commission was Philo, of Alexandria.   He was an old man, of high repute for his piety and his learning.   His social standing also was of the best; for his son married a daughter of Agrippa, King of Judæa, and his brother was Governor of the Jews in Alexandria.

Philo, probably between A. D. 10 and 50, wrote many books on the meaning and philosophy of the Hebrew

Scriptures, and on the customs and spirit of the Jews. He wrote as an ardent Jew, believing that the Old Testament was written by men directly inspired by God. He was not a representative of the best Jewish beliefs or hopes; but he does represent admirably their best spiritual temper. From his pen came no word that was not pure and sweet, and redolent of love for God and men. He was a loyal worshiper of God, an enthusiast for virtue, a high toned, spiritually minded man.

In philosophy Philo was a Platonist, believing that the leading tenets of The Bible and of Platonism were in perfect harmony, and explained each other. He, however, held that the Scriptures were in many parts allegorical, and taught principles rather than history. His discussions, and his numerous quotations from The Bible, are almost confined to the first few chapters of *Genesis*, and his Platonism is restricted to the lines of Plato's *Timæus*. He is a man with a mission to discuss the principles of Creation and The Creator, and of the philosophy of Divine and human personality.

Platonism and Hebraism are the only systems of philosophy which commence their studies in the upper ranges, with principles of creatorship, personality, and moral science. They alone had recognized that in these principles all philosophy is involved. Philo was a product of the Hebrew cult, a man in whom the chief features of a coherent and supreme philosophy had become established by his education, and by their natural systematization. His mission was to hold his people to first principles and to extol their oldest scriptures. The poetry of *Job*, the *Psalms*, and the Prophets passed him unheeded, and he gives no sign of any of those hopes that animated the piety of the saintly souls who delighted in Isaiah and Daniel, and who looked for a Messiah, and welcomed Jesus.

The writings of Philo have a permanent and great value as illustrating the habits, theories, biblical interpretations and phrases, of one of the best classes of the most intelligent and pious Jews, in those years in which Jesus lived and the Apostles wrote. Some of this value we will exhibit.

§ 2. PHILO'S DOCTRINE OF DEITY

We begin the survey of Philo's philosophy by noting his doctrine respecting God and his works.

Philo saw clearly the place that an intelligent apprehension of the facts and principles of causation holds in philosophy. He went far beyond any known earlier writer in apprehending the importance Causation. of seeking the firstness of causation, and of Nature, and of personality.

He saw, even more clearly than Plato, the necessity and the principles of a science of psychology, as the science of the being of God and men, and of the relations of the two. He found these principles in his Bible, and in its oldest parts; and yet he speaks of them in terms of which many are now so common and approved that they do not seem like words of a man who lived nineteen hundred years ago. But he must be read in his wholeness, and not in disconnected sentences, or he will not be understood.

Philo's books are treatises on causation and the activities of personal beings. He starts from The Cause of all things, the absolutely first. His philosophy is drawn like a line from a skein, and the beginning, the germ and

epitome of all, is the first verse of Genesis.   There, he
says,* "In the beginning, means *first*" (*próton*).

Like Aristotle and others, he wrestles with the descriptions and explanations of *being, nature,* and *energy;* but
he rises to a higher thought, and declares that the Author
of all these, and of heaven, matter, spirit, law, truth,
time, and goodness, is the One First Being, The God.
Him he calls The Cause (*aítion*), The Maker (*poietes*),
The Artisan (*technites*), and finally† says, "He is not
merely The Fabricator (*demiourgós*), but The Creator
(*ktistes*)."   And to complete the description, he calls
him The Generator (*ho gennēsas*), and "The God and
Father of The All" (*Theos kai Pater tōn hólōn*).‡

The philosophy of causation, which Philo found in
his Hebrew Bible, is not a side thought.‖   It is the sum
and substance, the warp and woof, the clew of the whole.
It shapes the beginning, the middle, and the end of
every discussion.   Even the supreme principle of moral
science, the founding of God's moral law on his causality,
Philo found in his Bible, and affirmed.   He says:§ "The
World and all things in it are the property of Their
Generator.   All things are confessed to be the posses-

---

*On The Creation of the Kosmos, ch. 7.

†On Dreams, Book I, ch. 13, end.

‡This name occurs all through Philo's books.   See On
Joseph, ch. 43; On God's Unchangeableness, ch. 6.

‖He carefully distinguishes the various kinds of causes. by
(*hupó*), through (*di'hou*) and on account of which (*di' ho*) anything is done, and says, "God is The Cause by whom (*huph'
hou*) the World came to exist."   *On Cain and His Birth, chs.
33 and 35.*

§Same references as ‖.   Also see *On The Heir of Divine
Things, ch. 24.*   He says, "Moses was the first man who had
an accurate and positive notion of God, believing that there is
one supreme cause."   *On the Kosmos, ch. 1.*

sions of God, and proved to be so by true arguments and testimonies; for the witnesses are the sacred oracles which Moses recorded."

If some of Philo's sentences* were taken by themselves he might seem to have believed, like the Greeks, that matter had existed from eternity, an unformed basic material, which God took in hand, and endowed with form and qualities. Origin of matter.

But in other passages,† and in no uncertain terms, he affirms that God is Author of Nature and all material things, and these are not even the productions that were first and nearest to him, but are creations of The Divine Word, which is the likeness of The Image of God.

When Philo sets himself to the task of describing The First Cause of All Things, it is his Bible which gives to him his doctrine; but his Greek philosophy modifies his phrases and words. Like all his people, he has learned to regard the name of Jahoh as too holy and awful to be spoken. Supreme Being not knowable by men.

He would speak of God by titles, and by words

---

*The World-former (*kosmoplastes*) leading the unarranged essence into order and regularity, began The Kosmos." *On The Kosmos, ch. 1.* "Essence (*ousia*) had of itself nothing good, but might become anything. It was of itself destitute of arrangement, quality, animation, or distinctive character." *On The Creation of The World, ch. 5.* See also *On Noah's Plantation, Book II, ch. 1; On The Decalogue, ch. 8; On The Incorruptibility of The Kosmos, ch. 2; On Those Who Offer Sacrifices, ch. 13; On Cain and His Birth, ch. 35.*

†*On The Creation of The World, chs. 1 to 7; On The Incorruptibility of The Kosmos, chs. 1 to 12; On The Kosmos, chs. 1 and 2.*

"He produced this most perfect work, The Kosmos, out of non-existence (*tou me outos*) into being (*eis to cinai*)." *On The Life of Moses, Book III, ch. 36.*

descriptive of his acts; but never by a name,* nor by a word descriptive of his being.   Like all the Jews, he held God's words in *Exod.* iii, 14, and xxxiii, 13, 23, to mean that God should be called "He Who Is," and that every descriptive name should be prohibited, and that knowledge of his essence is impossible.

This conception of Deity produced in Philo the logical effect that he speaks of Supreme Deity as

Supreme God as of neuter gender. of neuter gender, or of no gender.†   He calls him *To On* (That Which Is), and *To Hen* (Unity, or The One), and *To Theion* (Deity, or The Divine), and *To Aítion* (The Cause).

This, however, is not, in Philo's conceptions, an implication that God is impersonal.   Philo pro-

Supreme God a person. claims a personal God.   His God is the ideal of personality.   He says that a man cannot know his own Self ; but the best that he knows of his Self is, that what is best in him is a likeness of the image of God.

On The Life of Moses, Book III, ch. 26; On God's Unchangeableness, chs. 11, 12, 13 ; On Cain's Posterity, ch. 5 ; On Dreams, Book I, ch. 11 ; On Rewards and Punishments, chs. 6-9 ; On Change of Scripture Names, chs. 2-4 ; On Monarchy, Book I, ch. 6 ; On Immortality of God, ch. 13.
He says: "I am The Lord is equivalent to I am the perfect, incorruptible, and true good" (*to teleion agathon*). *On The Giants, ch. 11.*
"*To On*" is not of a nature to be described; but only to be. *On Dreams, Book I, ch. 39.*
"God is in nature according to the unit and the monad." *On Allegories, Book I, ch. 1.*
†*On Nobility, ch. 5 ; On The Kosmos, ch. 1 ; On The Worse Plotting Against The Better, ch. 42 ; On God's Unchangeableness, chs. 3-11 ; On Giants; ch. 11 ; On Rewards and Penalties, ch. 9 ; On The Freedom of the Virtuous, ch. 7 ; On The Change of Scripture Names, chs. 2, 3, 4 ; On Abraham, chs. 24-25 ; On The Allegories of The Sacred Laws, Book I, ch. 29 ; On The Creation of The Kosmos, ch. 61 ; On Noah's Plantation, chs. 6, 14, 15 ; On Dreams, Book I, ch. 39.*

By many lines of representation, Philo builds up a description of a man, his mind (*dianoia, logismos, nous, logistikon*), his character, his will, his spirit, his intelligence and wisdom, his consciousness (*suneidesis*), and his conscience (*to suneidos*), and then he declares that man's best is like what God is, and God is the model and pattern, and man is an image of God.

To make the representation of God's personality complete, Philo gives to him, as his chief title, the name Father. This representation and this title distinguish Philo's philosophy from* all other philosophies and religions. This is the characteristic of his pages. No matter what other form his representations may take, he never dims the light that shines on the name of God as " Our Father." <small>God our Father.</small>

When Philo desires to exhibit The Unknowable God as a Creator and a Moral Lord, he takes the first two chapters of *Genesis* for his guide. He says that the known Creator is *Elohim* (*Theós, God*), and *Jehovah Elohim* ("Lord and God," *Kurios kai Theos*). These are not lesser Gods, nor Second and Third Gods, but powers or faculties (*dunameis*) of The One God. <small>Creator and Lord.</small>

He says God† has many powers, chief of which are his beneficent faculty,‡ which made him a Creator, and

---

*Plato, indeed, in one passage (*Timaios, 37, c.*) calls God "Father," but this is the passage which is most like Genesis I and II and which makes it hard to believe that Plato did not borrow from the Jews.

See *On The Kosmos, chs. 5, 6, 7.*

†*On Change of Scripture Names, chs. 2, 3 ; On Abraham, ch. 24 ; On Those Who Offer Sacrifices, ch. 9 ; On Fugitives, ch. 18.*

‡*On God's Unchangeableness, chs. 23, 24.* "If any one were to ask me what was the cause of the creation of the universe, I,

his ruling faculty, by which he is Lord.   Through these he acts, and in his doings he is revealed to men.*

This is Philo's way of saying the philosophical truth, that The Creator, who cannot be known in his being, comes into human view in his doings, and, in this view, is chiefly known as loving and willing.   This is to say that The Creator acts first in love, and then in holiness; or to say that by love he becomes a Creator of beings designedly lovable, and instantly stands in moral relations to them as Holy Ruler.

The first part of this doctrine seems like an echo of Plato, who has said† that the Creator's goodness was the cause of creation; but Philo‡ connects the doctrine with those verses of the first chapter of Genesis which say that God saw the goodness of his work.

Philo does what had been done by no heathen religion, in saying that the foundations of moral law are laid in the character and will of The Creator, revealed in his first relations to the beings whom he made.

Here he sets a broad gulf between his doctrine and Plato's; and he founds his on the second chapter of *Genesis*.   Plato describes goodness as being homogeneity, or a oneness, sameness, and simplicity of being, in which there is nothing that can produce change.   Philo sees goodness as the law and will of The Creator.

Plato describes virtue as utility gauged by the Right Reason of Nature.   Philo gauges it by the will of The having learned from Moses, should answer: It is the goodness of The Living One, which is in itself the oldest of graces." See also *On Fugitives, ch. 19.*

On The Life of Moses, Book III, 9; Questions and Answers, Book II, 16.

†*Timaios, 29 E, 30 A.*

‡*On Abraham's Migration, ch. 24; On The Heir of Divine Things, ch. 32.*

Lord God. Plato's conceptions of goodness and virtue are, in one aspect, similar to those defined on page 43 of this book; but they lack the vital and the sentimental elements of the will of the personal Lord Creator. Philo's conception, drawn from his Bible, recognizes God as at once Creator good and loving, and Lord holy and authoritative.

To bring into description as a doer this God whose being is not conceivable, Philo develops what he understands to be the doctrine of the first chapter of *Genesis*. He lays hold on the phrases, "God said, Let there be," and "God said, Let us make." His theory is as follows :

God's speaking these phrases made his word a living being, a conceptional or ideal image of himself, an expression and agent of his activity. Of the speaking, Philo says little, except this,* "Speaking, he at the same time made. The Word is his work." Philo conceives the first Word of God rather as an objective result than as a causal act of God. But this Word, when he has become a Being, is the revealer of God, and is the active power of God, and† "The Cause of All Things." Philo calls him "The Second God."‡

God's Word.
The Logos.

Of course Philo cannot make any definition of the being and powers of this Word of God at the point of

On The Sacrifices of Cain and Abel, ch. 18.

†*On Noah's Plantation, ch. 5.* On the Creation of the Kosmos, ch. 6.*

‡*On Allegories of The Sacred Laws, Book III, ch. 73 ;* The Fragments, 1. On Dreams, Book I, ch. 39; On the Heir of Divine Things, ch. 48 ; Questions and Answers, II, 62.*
He says, "The Word is, as it were, the charioteer of the Powers; and he who utters it is the rider who directs the charioteer, with a view to the proper guidance of the universe." *On Fugitives, ch. 19.*

his initial appearance; but he tries to. He makes him a power in God, joining his other two chief powers which are not distinct Deities, or persons, and bringing them jointly into activity as Nature's God. He says,* "In regard to the one living God (*ho ontōs ōn Theos*), the supreme and primal powers are two, goodness and authority; and a third thing, between the two and joining them together, is Word (or a word); for it is owing to a word (or speech) that God was a ruler and good."

This Word of God in his first aspect is a person.† He is the image of God, and also the image of that image, and the archetype of Adam, who was the third image of God‡ He is "The First-begotten (*protogonos*) Son of God, and "The Eldest of his Angels, The Great Archangel of Many Names, The Beginning, The Name of God, *The* Word."‖ He is "first and eldest of all things that had a beginning," and§ "The Eldest and First-begotten Son."

But in all these aspects this First Word of God is only conceptional (*noetós*), intellectual, an idea.** Philo says,†† "Man according to God's image was an idea, or a genus, or a seal, or a conception, incorporeal, sexless, imperishable."‡‡ As to his personality he is the ideal

---

On The Cherubim, ch. 9; On Fugitives, ch. 19.

†*On The Creation of The Kosmos, chs. 4 to 8, 23, 24, 46; On Monarchy, Book II, ch. 5. On Noah's Plantation, ch. 5; On Dreams, Book I, ch. 11; On Abraham's Migration, ch. 1; On The Confusion of Tongues, ch. 28.*

‡*On Noah's Plantation, ch. 12; On Dreams, Book I, ch. 37.*

‖*On The Allegories of The Sacred Laws, Book III, ch. 61.*

§*On The Confusion of Tongues, chs. 14 and 28.*

**On Dreams, Book I, ch. 11.*

††*On The Creation of the World, ch. 46.*

‡‡*On The Creation of the World, chs. 47 to 50; On The Allegories of The Sacred Laws, Book III, ch. 31.*

image of God's mind and faculties. As to his projected being he is* the idea of the universe, and so the ideal universe (*kosmos noetós*) with its things and forces, the antitype of all actual things.

When God made the first earthly man, after the likeness of the conceptional model man (The Divine Word), he said "Let *us* make Man in *our* image."† He was speaking to his own powers, to whom he had given a lesser work than his own work of making the ideal man.

To this "Word of God," when considered as an objective persistent result of God's speaking, Philo usually gives the name "Divine Word" (*Theios Logos*). And he has a great deal to say about Him, or perhaps we ought to say *It;* for Philo The Divine Word. has the same impersonal notions of the "Divine Word" that he has of Supreme Deity, *to on.* He says‡ "It is impious to attempt to describe or even imagine it" ; and‖ "The word that God speaks is incorporeal and bare, not differing from an unit (*monas*). God utters unmixed units (*monades*)."

Out of the multitude of things which Philo says about The Divine Word we select a few sentences as general examples:

On The Allegories of The Sacred Laws, Book II, ch. 2.

On The Creation of The World, chs. 5 to 10; On Dreams, Book I, ch. 13.

On Special Laws, Book III, ch. 36.

†*On Fugitives, ch. 13.*

‡*On The Creation of the World, ch. 4.*

‖*On God's Unchangeableness, ch. 18.* He says also, "Unity is the image of the only complete God. The Divine Word is a glue and chain, filling all things with its being. It is full of itself, having no need of anything beyond." *On The Heir of Divine Things, ch. 38.* Does Philo here have in his thought the Latin verb *ligo, to bind,* or does he have in view the fact that one of the meanings of *lego* is *to collect together?*

"The Divine Word is very sharp-sighted. By participation in it, all other things can repel mists and darkness."*

"The instrument of creation is the Divine Word."†

"The Divine Word can at all times divide everything." On this idea Philo several times says much. Sometimes his phrases closely resemble those of The New Testament in *Heb. iv, 12.* "The Word of God is living and powerful, sharper than any two-edged sword, and piercing to the dividing asunder of soul and spirit."‡

"The Divine Word is the helmsman and governor of the universe."‖

"The Divine Word, like a river, flows forth from wisdom."§

"The Divine Word is the best city of refuge   *   *   * and a fountain of wisdom   *   *   *. It is an image of God, the most ancient of intellectual objects, and that which is nearest to God, no distance being interposed."**

"From The Divine Word flow all kinds of wisdoms."††

"Place is The Divine Word, which God has filled wholly with incorporeal powers   *   *   *. He who is

---

*On *The Allegories of The Sacred Laws, Book III, ch. 59.*

†*On Cain and His Birth, ch. 35.*

‡*On Cain's Posterity, ch. 46.* On *lego* as meaning *to divide,* see page 19 of this book. Philo says also, "The Divine Word divided and distributed everything in Nature." *On The Heir of Divine Things, ch. 48.*

‖*On The Cherubim, ch. 11.*

§He says, "It flows to irrigate the heavenly shoots and plants of souls that love virtue.   *   *   * It is full of the streams of wisdom.   *   *   * Being borne on rapidly and regularly it is diffused universally, giving joy to all." *On Dreams Book II, 37, 38.*

**On *Fugitives, chs. 18 and 19.*

††*On Fugitives, ch. 25.*

conducted by wisdom comes to The Divine Word, * * * being fixed in this, he does not penetrate to the being of God * * * but discerns that any comprehension of Him is far from all human intellect."*

"The word of The Maker is the stamp (or seal) by which each of existing things receives form * * *. Quality (distinctive character) is stamped in it by The Divine Word which is permanent and unchangeable."†

"The Divine Word is The Royal Shepherd."‡

"The Divine Word, like a river nourishes souls that love God." ‖

"The Divine Word brings around its operations in a cycle, which most men call Fortune (or chance, tuché)."§

"The Divine Word is an Angel guiding our feet."**

"Every man, in respect to his intellect, is connected with the Divine Word, being a fragment or ray of that blessed nature."††

Besides regarding God's Word as his first act and his first-product and Son, Philo recognizes him as a persistent living and‖‖ acting God, speaking more words for the instruction and elevation of men.§§ Philo makes a great deal of the words in *Deut. viii*, 3, "By every word that proceedeth out of

The Word ever acting.

On Dreams, ch. 11.

†*On Fugitives, ch. 2.*

‡*On The Change of Scripture Names, chs. 19 and 20.*

‖*On Cain's Posterity, chs. 35 and 37.*

§*On God's Unchangeableness, ch. 36.*

**On God's Unchangeableness, ch. 37.* See also, *On Fugitives, ch. 1.* *On Dreams, Book I, ch. 19.*

††*On The Creation of The World, ch. 51.*

‖‖He says, "God is constantly creating.' '*On The Allegories of The Sacred Laws, Book I, chs. 3 and 7. On Cain's Posterity, chs. 25 and 27. Fugitives, ch. 25.*

§§*On the Allegories of the Sacred Laws, Book III, ch. 61.*

the mouth of God shall men live." He holds this work
of The Word and the inspiration of The Divine Spirit
to be the two greatest blessings bestowed by God.

But he confuses this doctrine by declaring* that
many words of God are personal ministering beings, the
chief of them being Gods, and the others Angels and
daimones, some with bodies, and some without.

We have now observed the chief features of Philo's
doctrine of the Word of God. We see it filling almost the
whole horizon of his mind. It is to him a
wonderful revelation of God as living, wise,
and omnipotent. This doctrine we cannot
ascribe to Philo alone. It bears all the marks of an old,
slowly developed, and widely disseminated theory, not
growing out of Platonism, and not altogether agreeing
with it, but going far beyond it in important features.

Philo's logos
doctrine is
Jewish.

We must suppose that in this doctrine Philo is but
one of a class of Jews, who found in their Bible a full
system of philosophy, and had developed that system
into formulas and phrases, which, as we shall see, appear
in The New Testament in new lights, perfected and symmetrical, divested of their crude and irrational features.

But we come to a place where Philo's Hebrew philosophy and phrases meet and lap upon those of the common Greek modes of thought and expression. His
" Divine Word " passes over into that *logos* of an uncertain nature, which the Greeks conceived as neither a personality of God nor a faculty of Man, but yet a wisdom,
or truth, or law of thinking, which holds sovereignty

*On Creation of The World, ch. 50. On Fugitives, ch. 14.
On The Confusion of Tongues, chs. 33 and 34. On The Heir of
Divine Things, chs. 34 and 35. On Dreams, Book I, ch. 19.
On The Giants, ch. 2. On Cain's Posterity, ch. 25.

over human minds, and contains all reasonableness. (See page 19 of this book.)

This *logos* Philo, like all other Greek writers, calls "The Right Reason of Nature" (*ho orthós lógos tes phúseōs*), or simply "The Right Reason." Of this, Philo says a great deal.* He extols and exalts it so much that if he had not written that theology which we have detailed, he might appear as an extreme rationalist. But he is not this; for he so declares definitions and principles that he lifts himself far above mere rationalism. He does this in part by defining each of the words *right, reason*, and *nature*.

He explains *right* by using as equivalent such other words as *pure, sound, healthy, wise, perfect, highest, most sacred, sublime,* and *heavenly*.

He says† a great deal about Nature, but always as having been created by God, either in or through "The Divine Word."

Orthos logos, he says,‡ is Law. As if he foresaw the use of the word *law* as a catchword of Deists in our day, and recognized what there is as a philosophical basis in God's Will for the use of that word in that connection,

On the Allegories of The Sacred Laws, Book III, ch. 25 :52 to 58 :90. On The Cherubim, chs. 9 to 11. On The Sacrifices of Abel and Cain, ch. 12. On God's Unchangeableness, ch. 26 and 27. On Cain's Posterity, chs. 35 to 37. On The Worse Plotting Against The Better, ch. 40. On The Change of Scripture Names, chs. 19 and 25. On Joseph, ch. 46. On The Freedom of The Virtuous, ch. 7. On Humanity, ch. 17.
He says, "The right reason of Nature is, in fact, alone the beginning and fountain of virtues."—*Life of Moses, I, 9.*

†*On Dreams, I, 37, 41 ; On Fugitives, ch. 31 ; On Rewards and Penalties, ch. 4.*

‡*On The Creation of The Kosmos, ch. 50. On Drunkenness, ch. 35.*

he says,* "The infinite (*aïdios*) law of eternal (*aïonios*) God is the fixed and sure support of all things."

He says,† "This law (for free souls) is Right Reason; not a soulless law, for the soulless; but imperishable, stamped by imperishable Nature in an immortal intellect" (*diánoia*).

He says,‡ "The Right Reason is man living according to the law."

The complete doctrine of Philo, in this matter, is this: "The Word of God" became two words.‖ One
Two Words. is "The Divine Word" (*Ho Theios Logos*),
Two Sons of containing and constituting the intellectual
God.   ideal World of incorporeal ideas.   It is the likeness of "The Image of God" (which is The Word that Philo§ calls "The Second God"). This he** says is "The First-begotten (*protogonos*) Son of God." The other is "The Right Reason," that is the laws of Nature and of Intellect (*dianoia*).   And this also, he†† says, is "The First-begotten Son of God."

We hardly know whether here we must credit Philo with special philosophical acumen, or must consider
           him as representative of common Jewish
Logos   ideas, and especially of those connected with
is law.   the *logeion* as emblematic of divine law.   In connection with that, we have said, that one meaning of

**On The Kosmos, ch. 2.*
†*On The Freedom of The Virtuous, chs. 7, 10.*
‡*On The Allegories of The Sacred Laws, Book III, ch. 51.*
‖*Questions and Answers, Book III, 3; On The Heir of Divine Things, ch. 48; On The Life of Moses, Book III, ch. 13.*
§*Fragments from Eusebius.   Also Questions and Answers, Book II, 62.*
***On Dreams, Book I, ch. 37; On The Confusion of Tongues, chs. 14, 28.*
††*On Agriculture, ch. 12.*

logos is lex (law), and that this was probably recognized in the name *logeîon.**

There are other doctrines of Philo respecting the Word of God, which are worthy of the study of biblical scholars; but for many reasons their exhibition here would be premature, and they are therefore treated later.

Having surveyed one part of the doctrine about God, which Philo and his class drew, or thought that they drew, from the Hebrew Scriptures, we turn now to the other part, which equals and perhaps exceeds it in importance. This is the doctrine of God as Spirit. Spirit of God.

Philo is sensible of the important place which a true doctrine of divine and human spirit holds in a system of philosophy. He sees it in its bearings on doctrines of God's Fatherhood, and of divine operation and influence in men, and of moral science, and of human immortality.

As to all of these he produces doctrines positive and strong; but in regard to everything in which a conception of the fundamental nature of spirit is an element, he is vague and confused. This is not merely because The Bible is not clear, but because Philo, with all his efforts to be an idealist and a rationalist, is somewhat involved in a haze of materialistic conceptions.

In his theory of God's Spirit Philo makes his start from *Gen. i, 2,* "Spirit of God soared (or brooded, or hovered) over the face of the waters." But he says little about this text. He is far more influenced by *Gen. ii, 7.* "God breathed, etc." He is eager to magnify everything that is personal in God; and hence extols the breath of God rather than the wind of Nature.

* See in this book, page 135.

Philo does not regard God as a spirit, nor spirit as
a part of The Creator. He holds God's Spir-
Divine
Spirit was
created. it, or rather " The Divine Spirit," to be a created result of God's speaking. It is part* of
the ideal conceptional, incorporeal world. He calls it
"A fifth substance (*ousia*), more ethereal than the four
elements, earth, air, water, and fire." †

Philo conceived that even the four gross elements
were first ideal in God's Word; but he seems to have regarded spirit as having retained more of the incorporeal
nature, remaining nearer to God, and in closer union
with The Second God.‡ He says, " The four elements
are mixtures rather than elements, * * * but the
fifth essence is the pure and unmixed one, * * *
for the indivisible nature is of a fifth essence, more re-
sembling unity."

There inhered in it a living and divine power. When
The Word gave men truth, The Spirit gave them higher
truth. When the Word gave them intelligence, The
Spirit gave them character and disposition. When the
Word gave them life, that life was spirit.‖ It imparts
the purest life, the best moral power, the perfection of
personality.§

*"After the conceived model world The Maker made a bodi-
less essence of water and spirit . . . and he called it God's
Spirit because God is the cause of life, and the spirit is most
life-giving." *On Creation, chs. 7, 8.*

†" The fifth essence is superior to the other four, and from it
the stars and whole heavens appear to have been generated." *On
The Heir of Divine Things, ch. 57.* See also *On Coveting,
ch. 11.*

‡*Questions and Answers, III, 9.*

‖"The Creator breathed into man from above (*anothen*) something of his own Divine Nature." *On The Worse Plotting
Against the Better, ch. 24.*

§"That power of a man is spirit, not moving air, but a repre-

Philo seeks earnestly to eliminate materialism from his notion of God's spirit. He makes a distinction between two spirits of God. One is air. The other is breath. One is of Nature. The other is Divine. He says,* "Spirit of God is spoken of (in Gen. i, 2) as being air flowing upon the earth. * * * In another manner Moses shows us, saying 'God called Bezaleel, and filled him with Divine Spirit, with wisdom, understanding, and knowledge.' So, what Divine Spirit is, is definitely described in these words."

Philo therefore does not say "God's Spirit," nor "Holy Spirit"; but he says, "Divine Spirit." (*Theion Pneuma.*) If this spirit is not God, and is in any sense substantial, it is yet, of all things, nearest to the incorporeal ideas of God. It is† the common element of "The Divine Word" and of the corporeal essence of the human soul. And it is holy, and the source of goodness in men.

sentation and stamp of the Divine Power, which Moses calls by its proper name, an image." *On The Worse Plotting Against the Better, ch. 23.* See also *On The Creation of The World, ch. 50. On Special Laws, Book IV, ch. 8.*

*He adds, "The spirit that was on Moses (Num. xi. 17) is the wise, the divine, the indivisible, the undistributable, the good spirit, the spirit which is everywhere diffused, so as to fill the universe." *On Giants, ch. 6.*

"Spirit is to be thought of with reference to strength, intensity and power." *On Allegories of The Sacred Laws, chs. 8, 49 51.*

"The Divine Spirit is able to do everything, and to subdue all things below." *On Noah's Plantation, ch. 6.*

†*On The Creation of The World, ch. 8. On The Worse Plotting Against The Better, ch. 23.*

§ 3.   PHILO'S MAN

Philo's ideas of a man are the logical complement of his conceptions of the personality and nature of The Creator and Father. He thinks also that they are the truths taught in The Bible. The man is* a Child of God, in the likeness of the likeness of the image of God, having a soul, because God breathed spirit into his face, and gave him a mind from above.

When Philo attempts to describe this Son of God, he becomes incoherent and inconsistent. This is partly because the word *being* (*ousia*) is a clog to him, and partly because his conception of spirit is materialistic, and partly because his ideas are grouped around phrases of The Bible.

Out of the mass of Philo's phrases, the elements of his theory emerge as follows:

In the human body water is the chief element. This doctrine is from the second verse of *Genesis*. He speaks Human of men as composed of dust and water; but bodies are this he does in commenting on the use of of water. water in religious ceremonies; and he makes these serve as occasions for saying that water is the emblem of natural birth.

He says: †"By men who are learned in natural science, water is said to be the corporeal essence of children. * * * It is not the nature of anything on earth to exist without a moist essence." ‡"Our bodily substance is earth and water."

*Page 152.
†*On The Creation of The World, chs. 44, 45.*
‡*On Those Who Offer Sacrifice, ch. 2. On Dreams, I, 36.*

Out of *Gen. i, 2*, there came to Philo (and he writes as of something familiar to his readers), an association of the words *water* and *spirit* in symbols and ~~Water and~~ in metaphors. The water is an emblem of ~~spirit as~~ physical life, the life of the senses and the ~~emblems.~~ body; but Philo sees this life as psychical, blending with the life of the spirit. Hence he quotes many texts of the Bible that mention water; and he connects water, soul, and spirit, in his phrases, in ways that are very suggestive as to the meaning of many passages in the New Testament.

When we turn the pages of Philo, we seem almost to read: *"Born of water,"—†"He that drinketh of God shall never thirst,"—‡"Out of his body shall flow rivers of living water,"—‖"The river of the water of life."

Having recognized water as the physical germinal element of men, Philo next recognizes blood as the element in which is the force of the soul-life. This doctrine comes to him out of many texts ~~Blood in~~ ~~men.~~ of Scripture, but specially from *Leviticus xvii, 14.* "The soul of all flesh is its blood" (as the Greek version reads), and *Deuteronomy xii, 23.* "Its blood is soul."

He sees § in blood, however, two souls. One is the

*Compare *John iii, 5*, with *On The Creation of the World*, ch. 45.

†Compare *John iv, 14*, with *On Fugitives, ch. 36; On Cain's Posterity, ch. 41.*

‡Compare *John vii, 38*, with *On Fugitives, ch. 32. On Cain's Posterity, ch. 37. See On The Allegories, Book I, ch. 11.*

‖Compare *Rev. xxii, 1*, with *On The Allegories of The Sacred Laws, I, 19.*

§*On The Worse Plotting Against the Better*, chs. *22, 23, 25.* He says, "It seemed good to the Law Giver that the essence of the soul should be twofold; blood being the essence of the life force of the animal.   The other is the best psychical life; the blood being but the vehicle, or the medium element, by which mind, spirit, soul, and body, join into the vigor of one combined life.   On the pages of Philo, we almost read: There are three, the spirit, the water, and the blood, and the three join in the one.

The chief and best part of a man is a soul (*psuché*, or in Latin *psyche*).   Two texts of The Bible furnish the chief elements of Philo's conception of a soul.

Soul.

One is *Gen. ii, 7*, "God breathed into his nostrils the breath of life, and the man became a living soul."   The other is *Lev. xvii., 11*, "The blood is the soul."

Philo, in fact, finds in a man two souls, or two phases which are nearly as distinct as two souls.   One is in the physical instincts.   The other has spirit, mind, intellect, and reason.   Soul is the generic name for the living being that has the vital force.   It is a word that occurs everywhere in Philo's pages.

When Philo attempts details of the definition of a soul, he becomes incoherent.   When he writes of the powers and doings of a soul, he is wise and philosophical.   When he tries to describe its being, he is confused, weak, and materialistic.   He never escapes from the idea that a soul is a breath, and this idea taints all his descriptions of the soul's nature.   He tries, however, to escape the taint, and to make his ideal of the soul the next in glory to the idea of God.

whole soul, and the Divine spirit being the essence of the dominant part." *On Who is The Heir of Divine Things,* chs. *11, 12*.

He changes his translation of Moses to "Blood is the spirit of all flesh," and says, "Spirit has not a place apart from the blood in the body, but is mixed with the blood." *Questions and Answers, 59*.

First in his analysis of a soul, as also first in the order
of his Scripture texts in this matter, he puts the declaration that a soul is a spirit, or has a spirit. Spirit.
We have seen* that his notion of spirit is
materialistic. True, this spirit is matter ethereal, the
divinest substance nearest to the ideal and incorporeal
being of God and The Word, and is part of the image of
God;† but it is material in man, if not so in its origin.

But this creative Spirit is not God. It is Divine, but
not a person. "The Word" is a person, and so is "The
Divine Word," but The Spirit is not a person, although
in that secondary divine person. "Divine Spirit" is a
substance, of which Philo‡ says "A great deal flowed
into Adam." It has quantity.

Philo says:|| " A human soul is a fragment (*apóspasma*)
of the fifth essence, from which the stars and heavens
originated." " Divine Spirit is the essence of the dominant part of souls."§

Divine Spirit comes to men from the Spirit is
upper ranges of the universe. It is breathed from above.
down into men; but it does not and cannot *Anothen.*
stay.** Its own nature will not let it stay. The men

*See pages 160, etc.

†*On The Worse Plotting Against The Better*, ch. *23*.

‡*On The Creation of The World*, ch. *50*: " Breath (*spirit*)
is the essence (*ousia*) of the soul; but it resembles and is combined with blood." *Fragments*.

||*On Who Is The Heir of Divine Things*, ch. *57*; *On The
Allegories*, *Book III*, ch. *55*.

§*On Who Is The Heir of Divine Things*, ch. *11*. See also
Fragments and *Questions and Solutions*, *Book II*, ch. *59*; *On
The Allegories of The Sacred Laws*, *Book III*, ch. *55*; *On The
Creation of The Kosmos*, ch. *46*; *On Special Laws*, *ii, 11*; *On
The Worse Plotting Against The Better*, chs. *23, 24*; *On
Dreams*, *Book I*, ch. *6*.

**On The Giants*, chs. *5, 7*. Here he is discussing *Gen. vi, 3*.
" My spirit shall not always remain with men." See also *On
The Heir of Divine Things*, chs. *55, 57*.

must die, and the spirit must return to its place and its like.* It comes from above (*anothen*) to men. This declaration is frequent.†

However materialistic Philo's doctrine of spirit may be, he thought it an assurance of nearness to God, of nobility, of pure influences, and of vital help. And it was only a secondary doctrine, an adjunct and explanation of the primal doctrine that The Word of God is the source of all kosmical life.

Philo holds mind to be superior to spirit. To a mind the spirit is a vehicle, a quickening force, and an influ-

Mind. ence. Spirit is almost pure form and char-acter vitalized; but mind is a child of the Omniscient Supreme Being. Philo glorifies a man's spirit only because it is a *rational* (*logikón*) spirit. It is only of "Our rational spirit" that he says, "This is the dominant part in us," and this "was fashioned after the archetypal pattern of The Divine Image."‡

Philo glorifies a human mind as the noblest part of the soul; and the word *nous* occurs probably thousands of times on his pages. He says,‖ "It is holy, being a sort of a divine fragment, according to the statement of Moses. * * * It is not a body, but must be called bodiless (*asomatos*)." "It§ came down from above

---

On Who Is The Heir of Divine Things, ch. 57; On The Allegories, Book III, ch. 55.

†*The Worse Plotting Against The Better, ch. 24; On Fugitives, chs. 30, 34; On Abraham's Migration, ch. 7; On The Heir of Divine Things, chs. 11, 13, 38, 55; On Nobility, ch. 5; On The Life of Moses, Book III, ch. 2.*

‡*On Animals Fit For Sacrifice, chs. 2, 3.* See also *On The Allegories of The Sacred Laws, Book I, ch. 13; On The Change of Scripture Names, ch. 21; On The Heir of Divine Things, chs. 11, 13.*

‖*On Dreams, Book I, ch. 6.*

§*On The Heir of Divine Things, chs. 55, 56; On The Sacrifices of Abel and Cain, ch. 3.*

(*anothen*). ∗ ∗ ∗ It cannot die, but only departs, as migrating from Earth to Heaven." "It has been taught to think of divine things in a divine manner."∗

But Philo views mind from two points, and hence calls it by two other names. It is *diánoia* (intellect) when considered as intuitively intelligent; and it is *logismós* when considered as knowing by reasoning. These words were common in philosophical Greek, but they came to Philo biblically,—*diánoia* in *Deut. vi, 5,* "Thou shalt love the Lord thy God with all thy intellect,"—and *logismós* was part of the phraseology of the logos doctrine.

Philo glorifies† Intellect, but reverently and philosophically ascribes its powers and excellence to God and his grace. He says:‡ "It is the most excellent part of a man." ‖"Every man, as to his intellect, is an impression, fragment, or ray (*ekmageion, apospasma,* or *apaugasma*) of The Divine Word." §"Man is immortal as to his intellect." ¶"The intellect alone, of all the powers in us, appears to be imperishable." *(margin: Intellect. Diánoia.)*

Philo glorifies ∗∗Reason, but not quite as he does Intellect; for the faculty that knows directly is superior to the one that uses reasoning. He recognizes its liability to err in its processes. He recognizes its perversions, and warns against its misuse. *(margin: Reason. Logismós.)*

∗*On The Change of Scripture Names, ch. 37.*
†He uses the word *diánoia* hundreds of times.
‡*On The Change of Scripture Names, ch. 43; On Fugitives, ch. 26.*
‖*On The Creation of The World, ch. 51.*
§*On The Creation of The World, ch. 46.*
¶*On The Kosmos, ch. 5; On God's Unchangeableness, ch. 10.*
∗∗He uses the word *logismós* scores of times.

He says:* " Logismós is a short word, but a most perfect and admirable thing, a fragment of the soul of the universe, or, as it is more pious to say, for those who study philosophy according to Moses, a very faithful copy of the Divine Image."†

Logismós‡ is the faculty which has to do with virtue, or has virtue; because virtue must be considerate and deliberate. It is "An incorruptible Judge, to be guided by the considerations of ' Right Reason ' (*orthós logos*)." ‖ " It is the better part of the soul."§

We have reached the place where Philo's analysis of a human mind passes out from biblical philosophy, and as that alone is what we wish to delineate here, we must make but scant mention of a matter intimately connected with the philosophy of Reason, as Philo and other Greek writers saw it. This is the doctrine about the human logos.

Speech. *Logos.*

When Philo uses the word *logos* alone, he means usually that wise faculty by which a man defines truth.** This is speech, or *logos.* It is not part of a man, as soul, mind, or reason. But it is a faculty, or exercise of all of these, and it is also that which a man attains by the exercise of all of these, if he attains " The Right Reason of Nature."

Logos was to Philo very nearly what "The Dialectic

On The Change of Scripture Names, ch. 40.

†See also *On The Worse Plotting Against The Better*, *ch. 23.*

‡Probably in half his instances in the use of this word Philo connects it with philosophy of virtue.

‖ *On God's Unchangeableness, ch. 10.*

§ " Every person who is deprived of it is changed into the nature of a beast." *On SpecialL aws, i, 18.*

** " The test (*basanos, chrusial test, touchstone of gold*) is the beliefs that are with *logos.*" *On The Creation of Magistrates, ch. 1.*

Art" (*hē dialectikē*) was to Plato. Philo* describes a human being's *logos* as of two kinds: One is his speech that dwells in him. It is in fact his wisdom, or what he would say if he spoke wisely. This is "Inherent Speech" (*logos endiathetos*). The other is what he does say. This is "Uttered Speech" (*logos prophorikós,* or *katà prophorán*).

Having described the being and personality of a man, as we have detailed, Philo has a great deal to say of his faculties and endowments. Even in this his Bible is his guide, inasmuch as his conceptions of the nature and powers of a man, as also his notions of truth and knowledge, are logical sequences of his doctrines of The Cause, God, and Man as God's Child.

Philo's Psychology. Endowments of a man.

†He nowhere has a methodical (according to modern methods) treatise on psychology; because he makes it so subordinate to his theology and moral science, and follows the biblical order of the doctrines. And yet it would not be a strange thing if the twentieth century should return to the biblical and Philonic method, and, instead of placing human *being* first in the list of categories, as an inference from man's activities, or a postulate, should initiate its list with God's unity, God's *being*, God's causation, and man's *being* as a corollary of God's.

Life of Moses, Book III, ch. 13 ; On Abraham's Migration chs. 1, 2 ; On Fugitives, ch. 17 ; On Abraham, chs. 5, 18. He never connects these two adjectives with the *logos* of God.

He says, "Speech is an interpreter of the things which the intellect has decided upon in its tribunal." *The Worse Plotting Against The Better, chs. 12, 35.*

†Yet his treatises on *The Cherubim, On Cain and His Birth,* and *On Noah's Plantation,* and *On Drunkenness,* deserve a high place among even modern treatises on psychology.

If, having in our minds a philosophical schedule of the characteristics and powers of a human person,* we look for the same elements in Philo, we may be surprised by what we find.   He builds philosophy on the doings of persons, and almost makes three lists, psychical, rational and moral.†

He describes men in the two philosophical ways, i. e. as Children of God having divine endowments and as active persons in relations with God and His works. And the World must accord to Philo this honor, viz., that, in the infancy of psychology and moral science, he saw and declared the place and functions of freewill and consciousness and conscience.

That puzzle of all thinking minds, and riddle of the unthinking, the freedom of will, which is the cause of all wickedness, was, for Philo, solved as it must be for all right-minded philosophers. He saw it as the condition on which moral law, moral life, true human nobility, and human happiness were possible.   He declares,‡ " It was necessary that freewill (*to hekousion*) should be displayed as a counterpoise to involuntariness (*to akousion*), for the perfection (*sumplerosis*) of the universe."

Free-will.

*See pages 72, 73.

†He names Aristotle's categories, and impugns the senses like a modern Professor. His lists of faculties and performances if mixed, are sagacious. He divides philosophy into physical, rational and moral.   One list mentions perception (*nóesis,*) comprehension (*katalepsis*), study (*meléte*), acuteness (*eustochia*), memories (*mnemai*), arts (*technai*), habits (*hexeis*), disposition (*diáthesis*).   *On Noah's Plantation ch. 7.*

Another is conceptions, sciences, arts, reasonings, senses, energies. *On Cain and His Birth, ch. 22.*

Another is, piety, holiness, nature study, moral science, sociology, business, ruling, legislation. *On Drunkenness, ch. 22. See also ch. 48.*

‡*On The Confusion of Tongues, ch. 35.*

He sees it as part of the likeness of God, and says,* "Intellect is the only kind in us which The Father thought worthy of freedom. Loosing the bonds of necessity, he let it go unrestrained, bestowing on it that most admirable gift, and the one most connected with himself, the gift of freewill (*to hekousion*) * * * The soul of man, being the only soul which has received from God free movement (*hekousian kinesin*), and which in this respect, has been made like God, may rightly be reproached if it does not pay due honor to the Being who emancipated it. * * * God made man free from all bondage and restraint, able to exert his energies in accordance with his own will and deliberate purpose, to this end, that comprehending what is just and what is unjust, and what things flow from virtue, and what from wickedness, he might make a choice of the better objects. And this is the meaning of the oracle, recorded in Deuteronomy. 'Behold, I have put before thy face life and death; good and evil. Do thou choose life.'"

Philo has left a treatise of some fifty good pages entitled, "Proof that Every Virtuous Man is Free." It is full of pure thoughts and noble sentiments and wise philosophy. A few sentences will show its doctrine. †"That man alone is free who has God for his ruler." ‡"The man who is possessed with love of God, and who serves only 'The Living One,' is like a God." "The unerring law is 'The Right Word,' an imperishable law, stamped by immortal Nature on the immortal mind."

We have said that Philo saw and declared the func-

---

*On God's Unchangeableness, ch. 10. On The Kosmos, ch. 5.
†Chap. 3.
‡Chap. 7.

He does it . . . the likeness of God and sees . . .
. . . . in the only God in us . . . . . . The united
. . . will work . . . between . . . . . . to the fate . . . . .

hat
nd
nt-
not

six
up
of
ure
ns,
in
oc-

hn
the

the
ms

ci-
d's

tions of consciousness, and its place in philosophy.

Consciousness and Conscience. When the history of the literature of philosophy shall be correctly written, high honor will be accorded to Philo for having done this so many centuries before modern psychology began to make consciousness its initial fact and principle.

Before Philo, the word *suneidesis* was used a little in common speech, to signify *consciousness;* but it was not a term of philosophy. Even Philo uses it only a few times.* He uses, in preference, *to suneidôs;* and the preference is significant; for *suneidesis* means sure knowledge, and to *suneidôs* means that which is self-sure or self-knowing. In fact, *suneidesis* and *conscientia* have both served to fix the attention of philosophers on the fact of knowing, to the exclusion of proper regard for what it is in man that knows.

The way in which Philo came to the use of the term consciousness (or conscience) furnishes a curious and profitable study ; for it is a part of his moral science, and comes from his Judaism.

His philosophy, beginning with recognition of universal causation, God as Cause, and God as a Person, passes, as we have seen, immediately into doctrines of Man as a person, and of man's knowledge, and of the causation of a man's intelligence. But in all this, the moral philosophy is foremost. Philo's Hebraic philosophy takes shape in the logos doctrine. This puts the principle of causation in the advance, and the *orthos logos* which to other Greeks was only reasonableness, is to Philo truth created by the Word of God.

How this truth is known to human minds, has always

On The Worse Plotting Against The Better, ch. 40 ; Fragments, from John of Damascus, page 782.

been the great study of human intellects. It is the crucial question in philosophy. The most Greeks simply assumed that the intuitions of mind (*nous*) must be truthful. Plato attempted the confirmation of rational beliefs by a doctrine that human minds saw the truths while living in some other state, before their birth in the World. This was an attempt to construct a psychology; but it was so defective that it left the Hebrews, represented in Philo, the first philosophers to base knowledge on real psychology.

Philo's theory is as follows: Truth is God's Word, which God by his own acts and by spirit impresses in human minds. This is known to human minds, partly by the likeness of intellects to God, and partly by the ability of Reason (*logismós*) to apprehend God's *logos*, especially in respect to virtue and the relations of God and men.

This apprehension Philo calls conviction (*élenchos*), and that which apprehends is conscience (*to suneidós*). Philo uses each of these words about twenty times, and in nearly as many treatises; and almost always uses the two words together. The words are a pair. They are the two sides of one doctrine, and are mutually explanatory. Each is the man's self-knowledge.

Of conviction he says: *"The conviction which dwells in, and never leaves, the soul, * * * preserves its own nature always such as to hate evil and love virtue." †"The real man, conviction, that dwells in the soul, says this." ‡"The healthy and living color in the soul, in very truth rising there, is conviction."

On the Decalog, chs. 17, 18.
†*On Fugitives, ch. 33.*
‡*On God's Unchangeableness, ch. 26.*

Of conscience he says, *"Conscience is an incorruptible conviction, and the most unerring of all judges."
† "Conscience, a conviction most incorruptible and
truthful."   ‡ "Conscience has derived from nature this
most special honor, that no error of thought can find
place in it."||

Out of Philo's phrases about conviction and the conscience, there comes a matter, curious and of great interest for two reasons. It has a bearing on the
meaning of Christ's words about " The Advocate" (commonly translated Comforter) in
John xiv, 16 to 26 ; xv, 26; xvi, 7 to 14; and by the way
which Philo presents it, it appears to indicate that
Philo's doctrine, that consciences were convicted (or
convinced) by The Word of God, was a common idea
among the Hebrews.

The Para-
klete or
Advocate,

To exhibit this matter we must introduce two facts;
one of which is a pair of verbs, and the other is "The
breastplate of judgment."

The Hebrew verb which means *to convict* is *iakach.*
Its first meaning is *to be right.* It has secondary meanings, §*to arbitrate*, and *to judge*, and *to convict.* In Greek

Fragments, 349, A.
†*On Cain's Posterity, ch. 17.*
‡*On Fugitives, ch. 21.*
||For the word *suneidós*, see *On the Worse Plotting Against
the Better, ch. 8; On the Creation of the World, ch. 43;
On God's Unchangeableness, chs. 26 to 28; On the Confusion
of Tongues, ch. 24; On Animals fit for Sacrifice, ch. 11;
Against Flaccus, ch. 17; On Dreams, Book I, ch. 15; On
Abraham, ch. 26; On Special Laws, Book IV, ch. 10; On
Fugitives, chs. 37, 38; On Joseph, chs. 9, 14.*
§See *Gen. xxxi, 37.* "That they may judge (or arbitrate)
between me and thee." This is the word used in *Job ix, 33.*
"Neither is there any arbitrater between us,"—where the Greek
version says, "O that he were the mediator of us, and a con-
victor (*elenchon*) and a hearer between both." See also *Isaiah
xi, 3, 4.*

there is the verb *parakaléo, to call to one's side,* either for a companion, or an advocate, or for any other purpose. Out of this verb is made *parákletos,* meaning usually *an advocate,* or *a mediator.* Philo uses it in this sense several times, as a common word;* and he connects its use with that of the Hebrew verb *iakach.*

There was among the institutes of Moses the priest-hood,† in which the Priests were advocates for the penitent worshipers. The High Priest had, as part of his official regalia, the "Breastplate of Judgment." Philo has written a great deal about this, calling it *the logeîon.* In the Greek Bible it is called *lógion* or word-thing, or oracle.‡ We have expressed the belief that it was associated with the most pious exercises of conscience and of the spirit of worship.

This belief Philo confirms. He associates the *logeîon* with the inmost spiritual exercises, the secret voice of conscience, the holy laws of God, the purest worship. He gives reason to believe that the name *hhôshen* had passed into the name *Parákletos.* Or if this was not so, the High Priest seems to have been called *A Parákletos,* and the breastplate was the Paraklete of the Priest, the meaning of the word being *Advocate.*

He associates many of the meanings of *logos* with the name *logeîon,* and finally shows that the Paraklete Logeîon was understood to represent The Logos, Son of God.

Against Flaccus, chs. 4 and 18.

†Philo says, "The Priest is, if one must say the plain truth, on the borders between the two natures (divine and human), in order that men may propitiate God by some middle (*mesos*)." *On Monarchy, ch. 12.*

‡See in this book, page 134.

*He says, "The Priest's dress is a representation of the World. * * * The breastplate also is divided according to that unchangeable, lasting, really Divine Logos; wherefore they attached it to that which is with great propriety called "The Logion." * * * And this *logion* is described as double with great correctness; for speech (*logos*) is double, both in the universe and in human nature. * * * The speech of Nature is true, and calculated to make manifest. * * * The High Priest equipped in this way is properly prepared for the performance of the sacred ceremonies, that, when he enters the sanctuary to offer the prayers and sacrifices, all the World may likewise enter with him * * the twelve stones, *the lógion*, being an emblem of that logos which holds together and regulates the universe. It was indispensable that the man consecrated to The Father of the World should have as a *parákletos* his (God's) Son, to procure forgiveness of sins and unlimited blessings."†

This whole conception (of The Paraklete) Philo finishes out for us by two or three peculiar paragraphs, by which he connects together the lógion, the Priest, the Word of God, conviction, and conscience.

‡"The most undefiled High Priest, conscience (*to suneidós*) has derived from Nature this most especial honor, that no error of thought can find place in it. Wherefore, it is well to pray that the High Priest, who is

---

*On *The Life of Moses*, *Book III*, chs. *12, 13, 14*. He says also, "It is very becoming that the man who is consecrated to the service of the Father of the World should also bring his Son to the service of that generating Father." *On Monarchy*, Book II, 6.

†See also *On The Allegories of The Sacred Laws, Book III*, chs. *39, 41; On Who Is The Heir of Divine Things*, ch. *42*.

‡*On Fugitives*, ch. *11*.

both a judge and a conviction (*elenchos*), may live in the soul." This is said after saying "The High Priest is not a man, but is God's Word. * * * As long as this most sacred Word lives in the soul, it is impossible for any voluntary error to enter into it."

Referring to *Leviticus vi, 1 to 6*, where a statute is made for men self-convicted of undetected sins, he says,[*] "When he appears to have escaped all conviction by accusers, but himself becomes his own accuser, being convicted by his conscience residing within, * * * the law proceeds to say, After this let him go into the sanctuary, to implore remission of the sins which he has committed, taking with him an irreproachable paraklete, that conviction of the soul, which has delivered him from his incurable calamity."

In fact, neither in Greek, nor in Hebrew, does the Bible say what Philo does; but it says, "When he is convicted, he shall bring his offering to the Lord, and the Priest shall offer it." It is presumable that Philo quotes from some well-known paraphrase or commentary, and expects his statement to pass, as already familiar to his readers. And it is reasonable to believe, that the Bible had taught the Jews a common doctrine, that a man's conscience, apprehending the Word of God, takes that Word as a mediator to the sanctuary, the conscience and the Word being, each in its own way, a paraklete.

In another place[†] Philo says: "Let us, who are self-convicted by consciousness (*suneidesis*), implore God. * * * He will rectify the sins, sending into our intellects (*dianoiai*) that most proper conviction, his own Word."

We have now surveyed the psychology which Philo

---

[*]*On Animals Fit for Sacrifice, ch. 11.*
[†]*On The Worse Plotting against The Better, ch. 40.*

drew from his Bible. Whatever may be its errors and
faults, it was a great intellectual achievement.
Philo's Psy-
chology as
a whole. In its scope it had no counterpart; for it first
broke through the bondage of the logic that
enslaved philosophy to the verb *to be*. It
honors a philosophy of personality, and of Divine
Fatherhood, and of consciousness and conscience.

It confesses a personal equation, but finds good and
glory in it. It is a philosophy of activity, and of causation, a philosophy that, rising above the tricks of verbiage,
and piercing through many of the enigmas of the relations of infinite and finite being, finds assurance of truth
in the likeness and the association of the earthborn children and the good, wise, and mighty "FATHER OF ALL."

We turn now to a study of Philo's doctrines of hope
and promise of the eventual glory and bliss of those
beings who are a "likeness of the likeness of the IMAGE
OF GOD."

§ 4.   PHILO ON SALVATION

Philo's philosophy is cheerful and hopeful. * It
begins in a conviction that The Father has become a
Creator, only because he is good, and that divine goodness pervades all Nature and all life. Then Philo sees
hope springing up immediately after sin. † He rejoices
in the crushing of the tempter, and in the safeguards
symbolized by the cherubim. He knows there is salvation in the ministry of The Divine Word. He delights
in that verse ‡ which, as he read it, says, "To Seth there

---

* *On God's Unchangeableness, ch. 23.   On the Creation of
The World, ch. 5.   On Cain and His Birth, ch. 25.   On The
Allegories, Book III, ch. 24.*

† *On The Cherubim.*

‡ *Gen. iv, 26.   See On the Worse Plotting Against the Better, ch. 38.   On Abraham, ch. 2.*

was born a Son, and he called his name Man (Enos). At once Enos hoped to call on the name of The Lord (Jehovah)."

It might be supposed from what we have shown of Philo's philosophy that he is a cold theorizer, lost in contemplation of intellectual puzzles. On the contrary, he is a warm-hearted philanthropist, glowing with sympathies for the experiences, the needs, and the capacities of his fellow-men. That which we have detailed, as his philosophy, is but a statement of his principles, which are scattered through his essays, the great bulk of which deals with practical morality and principles of salvation and eternal life.

There is an unfilled place in religious literature which calls for a book, or books, exhibiting the religion and the gospel, based on eternal principles, which Philo drew from his Bible. One short text of Philo, for instance, might invite and tax the best efforts of the ablest and most eloquent pen.

He says: * "The lawgiver, being a most admirable physician of the sufferings and diseases of the soul, has proposed to himself to eradicate the diseases of the mind. * * * Therefore, it appears to me that with the two principal assertions, that God is as a man, and that God is not as a man, are connected two other principles consequent upon and connected with them, namely, that of fear and that of love."

We can here allow ourselves only a meager outline of the principles of salvation, as Philo saw them.

God's rule is for love; but it involves Salvation. indignations, and hostility to sin. Time is filled with ministries of God to men, by his living Word, his Spirit,

* *On God's Unchangeableness, ch. 14.*

his providence, and his angels.   His ancient revelation and institutes were helps towards salvation.   An ever-to-be-remembered name of God is "The Saviour."   Salvation is the health of a philosophical soul (or mind, *diánoia*) quickened by "Divine Spirit," and instructed and nourished by "God's Word."   Wise and pure souls are born from above.   Wicked souls are morally dead; but for sinners there is salvation.   It begins in conviction of conscience, and ends in repentance and reformation, which bring the soul into communion with the Spirit and the Word of God.   And all of this is by the "Grace of God," which brings souls to faith, obedience, love and hope.*

If we do not do an injustice to Philo, unintentionally, his theory of salvation lacks a doctrine as to the way in which the justice of God is satisfied; but it has some of the essential elements of a rational and logical doctrine; viz., The Divine and the human persons must move toward each other,—The Person in God, to whom the sinner must appeal, is the same one who is Creator, the same who is Author of moral law and of human life, the same who is wronged and offended by sin.

With a recommendation to our readers to read Philo's treatise *On Fugitives*, we make a few somewhat disconnected, but sequent, extracts.   †"The oldest, strongest, best metropolis (of the cities of refuge) is The Divine Word. * * * The other five * * * are the powers of Him who utters The Word, the chief of which is his creative power, according to which the Creator made the World with a word; the second is his royal power, accord-

* See *On Dreams, Book I, ch. 15. On Animals Fit For Sacrifice, chs. 12, 14.*   Citations might be made by hundreds.

† *On Fugitives, ch. 18.*

ing to which he who has created rules over what he has created; the third is his merciful power, in respect of which The Creator pities and shows mercy towards his work; the fourth is his legislative power, by which he forbids what may not be done. * * * Therefore he exhorts to run * * * to the highest Divine Word, which is the fountain of wisdom, in order that by drinking of that stream he may find everlasting life."

*"This is the heavenly nourishment which the Holy Scripture indicates, saying, in the name of 'The Cause,' 'Behold I rain upon your head from heaven; for in truth it is God who showers heavenly wisdom from above (*anothen*) upon the intellects which are disposed for its reception. * * * The search for the nature of God delights those who pursue it, * * * and He, out of his own merciful nature, comes forward to meet it.' * * * And this also is written, 'Ye shall turn unto the Lord, your God, and shall find him, when ye seek him with all your heart and with all your soul.'"

†"The intellect which was eager to purchase the most excellent possession, piety toward God, offers three pledges or symbols, * * * a ring signifying confidence and faith, an armlet signifying the connection and union of speech (*logos*) with life and of life (*bios*) with speech, and a staff signifying upright and reliable instruction."

‡"When one falls into error, his conscience will not permit him to be nourished by repentance, * * * § But now that he is about to undertake a labor which

*On Fugitives, ch. 25.
†On Fugitives, ch. 27.
‡On Fugitives, ch. 28.
§On Fugitives, ch. 29.

will have no success and no end, he is relieved by the mercy and providence of God, the Savior of all men, * * * God says 'The place on which thou standest is holy.' What kind of a place is that? Is it not plain that it is the one that understands causation (*ho aitiologikos*), which place he has adjusted only to Divine Natures. * * * But he who, out of his desire for learning, has raised his head above the whole World, begins to inquire concerning the Worldmaker (*kosmopoios*) * * * then he prays to be allowed to learn from God himself who God is."

*"What is the beginning of learning the nature of things? It is plain that it is a nature in the person who is taught. * * * Again, what is the beginning of being made perfect again? Nature! Therefore a teacher is able to effect advancements, but the progress towards supreme perfection, only God, The Noblest Nature, can effect."

†"It is worth while to pray that the High Priest, Conscience, may live in the soul, as at once a Judge and a conviction, who has jurisdiction over our intellect."

‡"I admire those persons who ask 'Where is the lamb for the burnt offering?' and also him who answers, 'My son, God will provide himself a lamb for a burnt offering,' and who afterwards finds what is given as a ransom. * * * And a ram is found caught by the horns; that is to say, The Word is found silent; for silence is the best of offerings, * * * Therefore this is all that ought to be said, GOD WILL PROVIDE FOR HIMSELF; He to whom all things are known, He who illuminates the universe by the most brilliant of lights, Himself."

*On Fugitives, ch.31.   † Same, ch. 22.   ‡Same, ch. 24.

NOTE: There are in the Bible several lines of peculiar phraseology, used by many persons, which resemble Philo's words here in several features, and show a similar interweaving of similar ideas. These, when collated, seem to indicate that a belief had become general that a Messiah had been as a lamb before the creation of the world, and was silent, sacrificed, and connected with lights.

The student of these phrases will discover that the mention of lights is a part of certain symbolisms, having reference to *Genesis i*, and the creation of light by the Word of God. It is a part of the same idea that is expressed in the words, " Before the foundation of the world."

He will find these phrases interweaving the ideas of "The Word silent," and " The lamb silent," and he will find these to be parts of a representation of a Messiah, who is "Son of Gŏd," " Son of Man," " Word of God," and " Lamb," offering himself, or submitting to be offered as a sacrifice.

Among such phrases we may notice the following: *Psalm xix*, which seems to refer to *Genesis i*, and to the creation by God's Word, says, "No language nor speech."

Isaiah liii, 7, which is commonly regarded as introducing the name "Lamb," says, "As a lamb led to slaughter is dumb, he opened not his mouth." (*See Acts viii, 32*).

Christ and the Apostles, in many sentences, express the idea that utterance is often a sin, and silence is often a duty; and Christ's silent submission has been emphasized in history. (See Matt. xxvii, 14; Mark xv, 5; Luke xxiii, 9; I Peter ii, 23.\ Philo, who extols speech as almost the divinest thing in men, speaks of silence as a faculty and an excellence.

It is at least a curious fact that, in Aramaic speech, the names *word* and *lamb* are both written *amr*, although they are not pronounced alike. The name *lamb*, in Hebrew, is probably derived from its bleating. There seems to have been a Hebrew conception that the blood of a victim, although silent, spoke as a voice to God.

For a continuation of this study see our pages 202, 235, 236, 252.

CHAPTER IX

SYRIA AT THE CHRISTIAN ERA

Palestine is a little country, scarcely a hundred miles by fifty; but nature and Providence have given to it an immeasurable place in the history of civilization; because it was the spot where the races of North, South, East and West met and taught, fought and traded.

Along its northern edge ran the highway of commerce and war between the West and the East. Through its center ran the roads of the World from North to South, and of Africa to Europe and Asia. The arts, the trades, the forces and the ideas of the nations of the World could only meet on the soil of Palestine, or by passing over its highways.

Hemmed in by broad stretches of sea, desert and mountains, it was the door of the World. Providence decreed that it should be an open door, into which wisdom, science and art of every sort should enter, and from which wealth, ideas and impulses should go out to the furthest bounds of civilization.

Here have met and fought the armies of probably ten times as many nations as have come together in any other land of the Earth. Here luxury and necessity, affluence and industry, rudeness and elegance, trafficked, or consorted, or contended. Here the letters of Egypt took the forms, and evolved the vitality, that carried the first writing, and the possibilities of literature, over almost all the World. Here the science of Astronomy, which Babylon had made rich by its observations, transmitted its lessons to Egypt and Europe.*

The Palestine of the reign of Tiberius Cæsar, and of Herod The Great, was the resultant of the elements and forces that had been exerted in twenty centuries in this territory. A remnant of one immigrant people, after fifteen hundred years of wars and suffering, counted a national population of a few millions, and held a name and coherence as a nation of Judah. A restricted, tillable or pastoral soil gave sustenance, but not wealth, to a small number. Handicraft, in the many arts, made employment for multitudes. Trade and commerce brought affluence to some and comfort to many, and had scattered the agents and representatives of this keen-witted, this prudent and coherent people, over all civilized countries.

Before this era, Greek civilization had taken possession of the Northern and Eastern borders of the land, and largely occupied its center, where they have strewn the fragments of luxurious houses and magnificent temples in regions now swept or washed bare of all soil. Then Roman sovereignty had come in, with an iron hand, that crushed in its grasp all delicacy and tenderness, except where Roman wealth affiliated with Greek luxury for display and pleasure.

The people of all classes spoke two languages, Greek and Syriac. Greek literature constituted the libraries; and yet, only about two and a half centuries earlier, the Syrian trade had carried the new Syriac letters to Further

* The 49th chapter of Genesis shows that the children of Jacob were called by the names of the constellations of the zodiac under which they were born, as well as by their proper names.

India, and bestowed new alphabets on India, Persia, Mongolia and Manchuria.

To the alphabet of this people the whole World owes its cipher figures and the zero, without which extended performances are impossible in arithmetic. The following are the first ten letters of a Syriac alphabet of about this period, as found on pottery, and are our numerals:

Cæsar Augustus, out of gratitude to Herod for help in war, had constituted the central portion of Palestine into a kingdom, and made Herod (The Great) King, and also greatly favored the Jews, so that they enjoyed a period of great prosperity during the life of Augustus.

With the reign of Herod Archelaus, and of Tiberius Cæsar in Rome, new circumstances and new influences came into control. The Jews were a thrifty people, acquiring wealth everywhere, and arousing the envy and rapacity of the dominant races. More than this, they were the only people who did not worship some one of the three forms of heathen Deities, viz., idols, ideal personages, or powers of Nature.

The pagans could be tolerant to each other; but here was a people who worshiped no visible God, and yet claimed that their unseen God was Creator and Lord of all the Earth. Between Jews and Gentiles there was that line across which men pass only with a passion for killing or for proselyting; and the Jews would not, could not, surrender their faith, which had been taught to them as the infallible truth of both Reason and Revelation, and which they possessed in a literature so unique, so beautiful, so wise, and so elevating.

If we would draw for ourselves a portrait of this people, in respect to the chief element of their intellectual and religious life at that period, we fortunately have materials for the picture. The New Testament, Josephus and Philo give us adequate information of the prevailing ideas and the habits of study.

After the Assyrian captivity, there grew up the synagogue cult, the germ of political and religious republicanism. In little companies, the people organized themselves in parishes, built their halls of assembly, elected for each one a President (or Ruler or Episcopos) of the congregation, and a number of their wisest men for advisers or teachers, under the name of Elders or Presbyters. The name *quahál* which had long been the name of the People of God, and means *called assembly*, and which *by Philo is still used in that signification, was also used, as it is now, to designate the small congregations; being in Greek changed into such equivalent names as *ekklesia* and *sunagogé.*

Drawing together in these congregations, the people had a certain minor organization within the greater political power under which they lived; and here they cherished and studied the ancient literature which shaped their political, social and intellectual character.

Philo says, †"Even to this day the Jews hold philosophical discussions on the seventh day, disputing about their national philosophy; for, as for their houses of prayer in the different cities, what are they but schools of wisdom, courage, temperance, justice, piety, holiness, and every virtue by which human and divine things are appreciated?"

On Cain's Posterity, ch. 43.

†*On The Life of Moses, Book III, ch. 27.* See also *On The Freedom of The Virtuous, ch. 12;* and *On The Creation of The World, ch. 43.*

The result of all this—and was it not the natural one?
—was great freedom of discussion and of opinion. Men
of similar views and feelings drew together, and congregations, or societies, acquired marked characteristics,
while all equally maintained reverence for the same
Sacred Scriptures. Four chief kinds of doctrine drew
some thousands of Jews into distinct classes, known as
Pharisees, Essēnes, Sadducees and Therapeutæ, while the
greater body of the people, with less marked distinctness,
and less organization, studied and loved the books that
cheered their hopes.

*Philo and †Josephus both give us long and enthu-
siastic descriptions of the Essēnes. They were in number about four thousand, scattered among the
Essēnes. villages. They were distinguished by their
faith in God, and their practical piety, and their
communism. Philo says, "Leaving the logical part of
philosophy to the word-catchers, and the study of Nature
(except as to the existence of God, and the creation of
the universe) to others, they devote their attention to
the ethical part of philosophy."

Josephus says that they believed that souls are immortal, and that they come out of most subtle ether, and
that, when released from the bondage of the flesh, they
mount upward.

The origin of the name Essēn, or Essēnós, is nowhere
satisfactorily explained. If we reason from etymologi-
cal facts, there is ground for a belief that it comes from

*See Philo *On The Freedom of The Virtuous, ch. 12;* and
*Fragment from Eusibius' Preparation of The Gospel, Book VII,
ch. 8.*

†See *Josephus, Antiquities, Book XVIII, ch. 1,* and *Book
XIII, ch. 5. Wars of The Jews, Book II, ch. 8.*

the name of the oracle, the *logeion;* for Josephus says,*
that the Hebrew name of this, *hhôshen*, was written in
Greek letters *essēnēs*. They seem to have been a people
who placed the ancient word, the worship of God as
Creator, the communion with God, and the rule of conscience, very high. Josephus also says that they had
special customs of bathing in cold water, while clothed
in white veils. Philo says that they regard much of the
Scriptures as allegorical. In their ethical philosophy,
they used three criteria—love of God, of virtue, and of
mankind.†

Of the Pharisees, Josephus says ‡ that they were
believers in the immortality of souls, the blessedness of
good ones, and the eternal punishment of the
wicked. They loved God and men. They **Pharisees.**
followed the guidance of reason (*logos*). ‖ They declared
the fixity of God's decrees, but also the freedom of
human wills. They were highly esteemed by the Jews,
and exercised great influence. They professed to make
much study of the Scriptures, and to be much in communion with God.

The name of the Pharisees seems to be derived from
the Syriac word *Pharis*, which, in the Syriac version of
the Bible, represents the Hebrew *hhôshen*, and the Greek
logeion. It is made from the Syriac verb *Ph'ras, to divide,*

---

*Antiquites, Book *III*, *7*, *5*.

†Josephus says that they believed that destiny rules all
things; but he evidently means by destiny, God's decrees, as
opposed to the Atheism of the Sadducees. *Antiquities, XIII,
5, 9*.

‡He says there were six thousand who at one time refused
an oath of allegiance to Cæsar and Herod. *Antiquities,
XVII, 2, 4*.

‖What is said of the Essenes and Pharisees respecting the
logos, and divine law, or decrees, confirms our suggestions on
pages 134, 135.

(like the verb *lego*); and *Pharis* is like *logeion*, in the sense in which Philo says so much about the *logos* as dividing, and in which *Heb. iv, 12*, says it is "sharper than a sword," etc.

Both the Pharisees and the Essēnes seem to have derived their names from their being disciples of the Logeion.　They were much alike, except that the Essēnes withdrew more from the world, and favored celibacy.

The Therapeutæ Philo *describes with the same enthusiastic praise, and almost the same terms, that he uses of the Essēnes; but they are found in remoter parts of the World, as Greece and Egypt.　Once in seven weeks they hold their Sabbath assembly all night, at which they partake of a simple meal, as, clothed in white, they sit on rugs, after which they spend the night in studying the Bible, singing hymns, and exhorting one another to virtue and piety.

Therapeutæ.

Of the Sadducees, Josephus says †that they deny an after life and the fixity of divine decrees.　They were the materialists and pleasure lovers, if not the Atheists, of their day.

Sadducees.

If a person in the reign of Herod Archelaus had by turns visited the many synagogues of Jerusalem, he might have found the people in all of them studying and revering their ancient Scriptures, while there was great variety in the cast of thought and sentiment in different congregations.

In one he would have heard read the second chapter of Genesis, or the twentieth of Exodus, and heard this followed by a discourse on Jahoh, The Lord, his rights,

---

*On a Contemplative Life, chs. 3 to 11.
†Antiquities, Book XIII. 5, 9; XVIII, 1, 3.

as Life Giver to men, as Moral Ruler, and as the God whose providence cared for his children.

In another he might have heard a chapter of Daniel read, and followed by a discourse on the promise of a Messiah, an anointed King, a Son of The Most High God, to set up the kingdom of The God of Heaven, of which there shall be no end.

In another he might hear read, "God will provide himself a lamb," followed by the fifty-third chapter of Isaiah, and a discourse on the hope that God would provide some redemption of his children from their sins and afflictions.

In another he might hear the twelfth chapter of Daniel, and a discourse on immortality, or the resurrection.

Probably, in a great many, he would have heard some reading of, or reference to, the first chapter of Genesis, and some reference to "The Word of God" as the revelation of God, and as the active personality God, first creating the World and men, and then instructing and helping men by the ministry of The Word.

Perhaps one speaker would have read from the 33d Psalm "By the Word of The Lord, were the heavens made, and all the host of them by the spirit (or breath) of his mouth." Another might have read, "By every word that proceedeth out of God's mouth shall men live," and might have followed this with a discourse to show how the word of God, uttered by inspired men, had been a growing and advancing truth, till it had become a mass, of which the beauty, the helpfulness, and the convincing power, were a priceless treasure.

Another might have read the nineteenth Psalm, and shown that its first part is declarative of the great principles of the first chapter of Genesis (Causation, God and The Word), and the second part refers to the *logeion* and conscience.

In all this there is great diversity, but nothing clashing. In all there is essential unity in recognition of God as First Cause of all things, and as source of all truth, and all wisdom, and all right living, and as personal Moral Lord.

But, if we could have portrayed to us a view of the characteristics of the Tiberian and Herodian age of Jerusalem, the intelligent elevation of the Jews might, perhaps, not be so noticeable and noteworthy as the ideas and sentiments of the other Syrian and Greek educated and thoughtful classes.

A crisis in the World's history had come. A catastrophe or a revolution was imminent. Students of political history recognize that civilization had come to the parting of the ways, where chaos, moral and social, was at hand, unless new moral principles and forces should intervene. Paganism no longer possessed any moral character or principles. Philosophy had perverted Platonism and Aristotelianism into blank skepticism, and almost into atheism.

But the counter movement had begun; and we must recognize that it had begun through Judaism. Scarcely anything of philosophy survived except rationalism. Plato had exalted Reason, but had discovered no criterion of its reliability. He had magnified the words that mean reason, thought, intellect, and intelligence, till it seems that he was almost ready to say *consciousness* is the touchstone, and Man is God's child, and has the child's understanding of the Father. But Plato had just missed the goal; and Aristotle had turned his back on it.

And yet some force was working as a leaven. **For**

some cause, hearts and minds rose up in protest against the appalling blankness of philosophical unbelief. That cause was nothing else than the training which had produced, in Hebrew schools, the recognition of personal and spiritual God, causation by God, moral government by God, inspiration by the Spirit of God, revelation by the Word of God, conscience as the intuition of relations to God, and consciousness as the criterion of truth.

Already hosts of persons among the Greeks had learned the tendency of the Hebraic doctrines, and had in consequence set up a new word in philosophy, the word *gnosis*. This word is made from *gignosco*, which first meant *I think*, and then *I know by thought*. *Gnosis* is equivalent to Reason, or Common Sense, or Knowledge through one's personal faculties. *Gnosis* just misses being *consciousness;* but having missed it, it is the essence of rationalism.

Multitudes adopted the name of Gnostics, and formulated systems of doctrine about God, causa-

Gnostics.

tion, life, truth, and intelligence; and these were perversions of Jewish doctrines, the most of them involving the first chapters of Genesis. They were, first, theories of creation, of God becoming lesser personalities, *aiôns* good and bad. Secondly, they were theories of right and wrong, of good spirits and bad. Thirdly, they were theories of truth and wisdom, of reason, and of inspiration, and of communion with God.

And already that which later was called "New Platonism" was becoming shaped and quick. And this, too, was beliefs in spiritual communion (almost union) with God, and in divine causation of Nature, and in the trustiness of reason.

Judaism was not becoming platonic; but philosophy

was becoming Jewish; and conceptions, good and bad, out of Jewish philosophy, dominated the world of philosophy, long before the Bible was protected by imperial Rome.

Judaism had brought to the front two chief ideas, and fixed on them the attention of the world. These ideas were personal Creator and human personal intelligence. Judaism has taught that the *logos* of the Greeks lives in the *logos* which is the Word and law of God, and is also the wisdom of men, especially as it is quick in the personal conscience of intellects and spirits.

What a various and incongruous mass we have portrayed! Here are God *agnostòs* (unthinkable), God Creator, Father, Lord, Moral Ruler, Revealing Word, Spirit, Sovereign in decrees and in personal providence. Here is man, God's Image, God's Child, man wicked, perverted, ignorant, dead in sins. Here is man with free will, and intellect and conscience, and with hope and penitence and reformation and faith. Here are hopes of a Messiah (*Christ, anointed*), and of immortality.

Could it be possible that, in this crisis of the world, a doctrine was near, which could take what was chief in all these ideas, and combine them into one philosophy, simple enough for a child, profound enough for the mightiest intellect?

CHAPTER X

JOHN THE BAPTIST

It was in this Syria, in this reign of Tiberius, that there came into public view a character unique, and never to be forgotten; but not such a character as painters have portrayed. Jesus said of him, "There has not arisen a greater than John."

This John was a cousin of Jesus, and his elder by six months. It is presumable that the two had grown up together, connected by family ties and sympathies of spirit. For more than ten years they had been mature men, when John, abandoning the ordinary occupations, communities and resources of men, went into poverty in the wilderness, and began the preaching of a new doctrine, accompanied by a novel rite or symbol.

From all the indications, we must suppose that John was a pupil and herald of Jesus, who had taught him the great principles of the new doctrines, but had not at first made known to him his own claim to Deity. The doctrine of John and of Jesus is in two parts. The first part is an epitome of the oldest Hebrew theology. The second part proclaims Jesus as the completer of the old revelation, and the personality necessary for its becoming perfected.

John a pupil of Jesus.

John's doctrine.

The first part of the doctrine included all the principles of creation, of God the Father, of men as God's

children, of sin as a death, of repentance and reformation, of spiritual help that made men new, as if born
again from the Spirit, from above. It was the essence
of the coherent philosophy that, as a tree from its seed,
evolves from the first verses of *Genesis*, and makes the
beauty and the preciousness of the whole Old Testament.

To souls that received the preaching that came with
a new simplicity and unequaled earnestness,
**Baptism
a symbol
of men's
creation
from water.** it was at once a warning of death and a
proclamation of hope and life. With John
began a new regime of ideas alive, theories
that are forces, and principles that are powers.
It was a doctrine of death out of life, and of new foun-
tains and agencies of vitality.

And with the preaching, John established a symbol,
one unique and simple; but one that, somehow, so
answered to men's convictions of essential truth, that it
remains an ever-persistent power to organize the religion
of half the World; for it concentrates and emphasizes
the germinal truth of truths, while it honors and preserves the words of the old revelation.

As the old book said that the world of living things
arose from the water, by the power of the Word and the
Spirit of God, the new symbol took water as the emblem
of the physical nature of man, and made the idea of
birth the foundation idea of the new gospel.

In this it said, The old doctrine is the true doctrine,
and the old form of revelation is wise and true, and the
old Scriptures have done well to place, at the beginning
of all theology, the recognition of the Creator and
Father, and of his rights, and of our relations to him as
his children.

The new preaching, and the new emblematic rite, thus preserved, utilized and honored the ancient Scriptures, and all the education of the Hebrew people that had come from those Scriptures. The preaching and the symbol went along together; and the preaching of John, although not preserved in long discourses, is the full essence and epitome of the old theology. The chief theme is repentance and new life.

The burden of John's preaching said, Men are dead in sins. They must revive as to a new life, and that life, in respect to its forcefulness and its sources, must, like the natural life, be like a birth from God's Spirit, from above. And the true religion must make its profession in a symbol which recognizes God as Author of life.

But the new preaching advanced beyond the old. The old had been perverted, so that men had veiled the person of God from their eyes, and dared not speak the name of Jahoh. The old religion seemed likely to degenerate into a denial of God's personality, or else into such a conception of it that God would no longer seem a Father, and a near and present Savior.

The second part of John's preaching was a response to the prayers of the best souls trained by the Old Testament, who had, perhaps, mystical and incorrect ideas of the oracle of God, and of communion with him, and of inspiration, but had come to believe in conscience and conviction as being a better Paraklete than the Priest, and as bringing a penitent soul very near to his Lord. For these souls, like Philo, could not conceive how the holiness of God could be satisfied, nor how their own conscience could bring to God an adequate sacrifice, a sufficient lamb.

To these souls the second part of John's preaching said, "There cometh one who shall baptize you with the Holy Spirit and with fire." One who will re-create all things.

Apparently there had been given him the doctrine that the Word, whom so many Jews called God, and "The Firstborn Son of God," might be expected to reveal himself The Only true Son of God, the Person of God who should give men power to become reinstalled as Sons or Children of God.

There came a time when Jesus was ready to begin his own preaching. He came to John for baptism, and said, "So it is proper for us to fulfill all righteousness." On this saying we must linger a little. It is hard to believe that Jesus merely meant to say, This is a part of righteousness, and even I must honor it. He more probably means, "In this way we teach the principles of righteousness." The Greek verb *plero* (fulfill) never means to perform. It usually means *to illustrate the principle of a thing*, and often means to do something like some type or principle or prophecy.

John baptizes Jesus.

Such is its meaning in most of those passages of the New Testament where we read, "That it might be fulfilled," etc. Greek writers even speak of fulfilling in this way a remark made long afterward. Possibly Jesus meant, By my baptism the idea of creation and the spiritual birth will be perfectly presented; for the Jews have believed that The Word, The Creator, is The Firstborn Son of God. They are to be taught that I am The Only True Son of God, the Visible Revelation of his Person in human life.

Then follows the baptism of Jesus by John; and John

describes his recognition of Jesus by a form of expression analogous to the first verses of Genesis. Hebrew scholars know that the phrase in our Bible, "The Spirit of God moved upon the face of the waters" is in Hebrew, "The Spirit of God was a hovering thing (feminine) over the face of the waters." John has chosen to compare the hovering spirit to a dove soaring over (not onto) Jesus. *So he makes the baptism of Jesus the ideal, by the presence of the water, the Spirit, and The Firstborn Son.

If we ask why John used a dove as a symbol, perhaps Philo may assist us, for he says a good deal about the dove and the pigeon as emblems. For instance, he says,† "The Heaven is familiarly connected with flying birds, such as the pigeon and dove. * * * These two birds are emblematic of the divine attributes. * * * There are two (divine) Words. * * * The pigeon and dove resemble these. * * * The pigeon resembles speculation in natural science * * * the dove imitates what is intellectual and incorporeal."

The second part of John's preaching was a philosophy of the mode of salvation. The old theology had been a doctrine of sin against the person of God. It declared the need of atonement, penitence, and reform; and it believed that salvation was possible, because God is a Person. The new theology said salvation comes by him who condemns. It said, Hope in God, because his Son is come to earth. It presented a new doctrine, in which

---

*Notwithstanding the form of the description in *Matt. iii, 16*, it seems clear that John alone is authority for the statement of the Spirit's presence.

†*Questions and Answers, Book III, 3.* He says almost the same in the treatise *On The Heir of Divine Things, ch. 48.* See also *ch. 25.*

personal influence between the Persons of God, and personal relations between the Persons of God and of men, rose above all other ideas and theories and principles of philosophy and theology.

Then John added the crowning element of his doctrine, the element of atonement and redemption. As the Old Testament taught the need of reconciling influences between God and men, and taught the principles of confession, and submission, and profession, and added to these the education in the typical idea of personal mediation, John added the finish of all in declaring the personal Savior and the atonement.

Perhaps in the very year in which Philo* wrote, "I wonder at (or admire) most him who said, ' God will provide himself a lamb,'" John the Baptist cried, "Behold the Lamb of God who takes away the World's sin."

But, after calling Jesus "The Lamb of God," John gives no doctrine of the principles and methods of an atonement. Leaving that unexplained, he proclaims Jesus "The Son of God," coöperating with The Father, and giving eternal life to souls that trust him.

The gospel of John The Baptist is a philosophy of personal actions and of personal relations. The Son comes by arrangement with The Father; and souls, dead in sins, believing his assurances, receive new life from above, and testify their profession by the new symbolical rite, and by a life of obedience to the Son.

Few and meager as the recorded words of John The Baptist are, they contain all the basic principles of true philosophy of the personal relations between God and men.

*See page 182 of this book.

" He that cometh from above (*anothen*) is above all things. He that is out of the earth is out of the earth, and out of the earth (its facts, principles and modes of view) he speaks. He that comes out of Heaven testifies what he has seen and heard, and his (kind of) testimony no one (else) receives (power to bear). He who received his (kind of) testimony, has borne witness, as under seal, that he is The True God. He whom God sent speaks God's sayings, for the spirit (which he gives) he does not give out of a measure (as if it were a substance). The Father loves The Son, and has given all things by his hand. He who trusts on The Son has life eternal; but he who distrusts The Son shall not see life, but God's anger remains over him." *John III, 31–36.*

If, in reading the above citation, in the light of what we know of the Jewish logos doctrine (say of Philo and John The Apostle), we notice that it is all about words from Heaven, and testimony borne, first by Jesus, and then by his disciples, we are brought to the conviction that John The Baptist was accustomed to call Jesus "The Word of God;" but that the doctrine which he emphasized was the new doctrine, that the continuous living Word had brought life and light to Earth, that this ushered in " The Kingdom of Heaven," and that an era of testimony, of gospel or evangel, as a reign of The Christ, had begun.

We even further notice that these are the ideas which fill the Epistle of John The Apostle; and that with some others, which The Apostle connects with The Baptist, they may furnish the key to the interpretation of much of The Apocalypse.

Thus The Baptist stands to us, not only as a connec-

ting link between the old gospel and the new, but as an
epitomizer, a clew giver, a symbol maker. Around him
gather, in figure and metaphor, most significant suggestions. John The Apostle connects him with the symbolism of *Genesis i,* by calling him the first " Witness " of
that light which came in Christ for the World.

NOTE: Referring to note on page 183, we may say further,
in reference to the name " Lamb of God, that takes away the
world's sin," that it has many connections with other verses of
The New Testament, and that the name " The Lamb," is, in
The Apocalypse, the chief name of Christ, and that there it is
closely connected with the lights and days of the week of creation, and with the silence of the Sabbath, and with symbolical
language interpretive of Daniel's prophecies.

But it evidently has its origin in some broad and well-defined
conceptions and doctrines, familiarly spoken of by the Jews,
but not stated in wholeness anywhere. Saint Peter, writing
earlier than Saint John says, " The precious blood of Christ, as
of a lamb without blemish, and without spot, who was foreordained before the foundation of the world." See *I Peter i,
19, 20.*

In addition to what we say later, of these words, we may say
here, that the name " Ancient of Days " may mean " Older than
the days " (of creation), or may mean Splendor of lights; and
that the phrases, " The Son of Man came to the Ancient of
Days; and they brought him near before him," are in the original, and in the Greek, very puzzling to scholars. And both in
the Chaldee and the Greek one of the phrases suggests, if it
does not bear, the meaning, " He was old as the Ancient (or
splendor) of Days;" and the phrase, " Brought near," uses in
the Greek the word (*prosphero*), which is the common word
meaning to offer or sacrifice. This is the word used in Heb.
ix, 14, " Christ offered himself to God," and in Heb. ix, 28,
" Christ being offered," etc.

CHAPTER XI

PERSONALITY AND PHILOSOPHY IN THE NEW TESTAMENT

§ 1. ITS METAPHYSICS

Who does not sympathize with the sentiment which says, Let us not mingle with the words that come from Heaven to struggling souls, the hard problems of Earth, and the dark mysteries of philosophy? But if the New Testament is a book to tell men the nature of God and of souls, and of their relations to each other, it is not, and cannot be, a simple book; for these things are the essence of philosophy. They are in its profoundest depths.

If any soul does not take to itself a good, wise, and true philosophy, then a bad, foolish and false philosophy will seize and hold that soul. If the Bible does not deal with profoundest principles, and in a style that requires intelligence in its study, it never came from Heaven, and is useful neither for wise men nor for fools.

In dealing with facts and doctrines of the nature and relations of the persons of God and of men, the Bible became, and had to become a treatise on psychology. In fact that is the source of its power. It has moved men more than all other literature combined; it dominates the thinking of the World; it holds sway over millions who do not recognize it; and it does this because it is true to the facts of the nature and relations of God and men, and because it is, in literature, the only teacher of them.

If we ask how men can attain knowledge of God, and of their own nature and destinies, several, yet few, answers may seem to be reasonable.

We might say, first, that the cosmical philosophy is a revelation of these truths; meaning by cosmical philosophy such rational systems of belief as men acquire by exercising their Reasons on the facts of Nature and of experience. This is diverse and conflicting without limit, yet in general it is the one thing that we commonly call Common Sense, Reason, Truth, Intelligence, Philosophy, and Natural Religion.

Cosmical Philosophy.

Theoretically it may plausibly be said that men may attain some knowledge of divine things, and of some recondite things, through Reason. A perfect man, in favorable circumstances might do much; and in the course of ages men might advance to great attainments in wisdom, and even in knowledge of God.

But whether Reason can attain much or little divine wisdom by its own exercises, it can attain absolutely none without a correct idea of and a correct use of consciousness. Philosophy must be one of three processes. It must start in consciousness, and build up to a knowledge of God; or it must start with the principle of causation in God, and try to verify its convictions by psychology and conscience; or it must study God and consciousness at the same time, and try to bring them into one system.

Consciousness.

Men have carried all of these methods to the point of their exhaustion; and they have not been able *thereby* to secure either the most desirable knowledge of God or a complete theory of consciousness. Those who have exalted mind (*nous*), or intellect (*diánoia*), or Reason (*logismós*), or impersonal truth (*logos*), have all failed to settle on a basis for assured faith in anything; and have become propagandists of doubt, agnosticism and despair.

But what has the Bible done, and how has it done it? It began its doctrines with the first of first principles, getting it we will not say where, and it advanced in wisdom, on lines so true to God and to Nature, that it brought its students to points where, as we have seen in Philo's books, they said, Mind and intellect and Reason are true, so far as they are unbroken images of The Father, and so far as what man calls *logos* (reasonable) is the true law and word of personal God, asserting itself in souls.

It brought much of the thinking of the world to the point where consciousness had to be reckoned with; so that Philo and his class introduced and glorified conscience (*to suneidós*) and consciousness (*suneidesis*), and others introduced and glorified *gnōsis* (*rational conviction*), and New Platonists (so called) affirmed extatic union with God and truth.

When we advance from the Old Testament into the New, we find the intellectual development so advanced, and so true to Reason, that the word *suneidesis* for consciousness and conscience, has become a common word, an invaluable and necessary word, and occurring probably more *times than in all previous literature now known, Philo included.

Acts xxiii, 1; xxiv, 16; *Rom.* ii, 15; ix, 1; *I Cor.* viii, 7, 10, 12; x, 25, 27, 28, 29; *II Cor.* i, 12; iv, 2; v, 11; *I Tim.* i, 5, 9; iv, 2; *II Tim.* i, 3; *Tit.* i, 15; *Heb.* ix, 9, 14; x, 2, 22; xiii, 18; *I Pet.* ii, 19; iii, 16, 21.

The New Testament does not use the word *suneidôs*, which is really not quite scientifically nor philosophically the correct word; but it uses *suneidesis* to signify *intelligence (or understanding), conscience and consciousness.

But it may be asked, Did the Bible develop this use of the word *consciousness*, or did the Greek philosophies lead up to it?

We have shown that in the signification of *consciousness*, it was not much, if at all, known in Greek philosophy, and that Philo exhibits it as a common Jewish usage, growing out of the Hebrew theology or revelation, and especially connected with *inquiring of God*, in connection with the *logeion* and with spiritual or moral *conscience*, rather than *consciousness*. This might be called only a Philonic idea; but now something like it comes to us in the New Testament; and from one of the Apostles who is supposed to be least of all learned or metaphysical. Peter, mentioning baptism,† as connected with symbolism of salvation, says it is not a symbol of washing, but represents "The inquiry (or prayer, *eperôtēma*) of a good (i. e. wise) consciousness unto God."

How largely this training in the conception of the nature and use of the word *conscience* entered into Jewish philosophy, especially in connection with references to the inner sanctuary, may be seen in the *Epistle to the Hebrews;* for it is a key to the interpretation of a large part of that epistle. Of this line of thought we can here only give a suggestion by quotations.

"Consider the High Priest of our *homologia*. * * *‡

---

*It means *intelligence* or *understanding* in almost all passages.

†*I Peter*, iii, 21.

‡*Heb. iii, 1.* Philo also says "High Priest of the homologia," just after he has said, "The High Priest is the Divine Word,

* To-day, if ye shall hear his *voice*, harden not your hearts,
* * * †let us give diligence that no man fall after the
same manner of unbelief. ‡For the Word of God is
living and energetic, sharper than any two-edged sword,
and piercing even to the dividing asunder of soul and
spirit, and critical (*kritikós*) of the thoughts and notions
of the heart.   And there is no creature that is not manifest in his (or its) presence; but all things are bare and
open to the eyes of him, in relations with whom ‖ (*pros
hon*) we have (or know) The Word §(*hemin ho logos*).

¶"Christ, having come a High Priest, * * * entered
once for all into the holy place. * * * ††How much
more shall the blood of Christ cleanse your *consciousness*
(or moral intelligence) from dead works, to serve the

God's Firstborn Son." *On Dreams, Book I, ch. 38.* But *homologia* rarely, if ever, means confession. It usually means agreement (in word or thought).

* *Heb. iv, 7.*

† *Heb. iv, 11 to 14.*

‡ Philo says, "The High Priest is the Divine Word." *On
Fugitives, ch. 20.* "The undefiled High Priest, conscience
* * * a judge and conviction." *On Fugitives, ch. 21.* "God's
Word cuts through everything. Being sharpened to the finest
possible edge, it never ceases dividing, * * * dividing the soul
into the rational and the irrational part, speech into truth and
falsehood, and the perceptions into the comprehensible and the
incomprehensible." *On The Heir of Divine Things, ch. 26.*

‖ *Pros* means *in relations with.* "The logos was *pros Theon*
(in relations with God).

§ *Hemin ho logos* might mean, We have something to say,
or The Word comes to us. But here iv, 13, and v. 1 seem to
explain each other in regard to the word *pros ;* the *logos* in one,
and the High Priest in the other, being spoken of in the same
terms. Possibly here the phrase means, It is in relations to the
logos that we have *logos* (intelligent speech). Whether or not
this rendering would be consistent with the same phrase in
v, 11, is questionable.

¶ *Heb. ix, 11.*

†† *Heb. ix, 14.*

living God. * * * *Worshipers, if once cleansed, would have had no more *consciousness* of sins. But it is impossible that the blood of bulls and goats should take away sins. * * * †Having, therefore, boldness to enter into the holy place by the blood of Jesus, * * * let us draw near, with a truthful heart, in fullness of faith, having been sprinkled, as to our hearts, from bad *consciousness* (or understanding)."

If, now, we have been following true principles and correct reasoning in the preceding pages, we have found Limits of cosmical philosophy. that cosmical philosophy (or rational common sense) can attain much knowledge of God and of men, and of their relations to each other; and it might produce valuable books of philosophy and morals. But we have found that human philosophy has always gone astray in its highest aims. And this straying is inherently necessary in cosmical philosophy, because the seeker cannot attain complete truth unless he begins with correct knowledge of himself; and yet this preliminary necessity is what he has not, but is seeking as an end of his study. A philosophy that is in error in its beginnings never can eliminate its faults, nor attain its best ends.

Hence many philosophies (or rather, religions and ethical theories) have formulated moral principles and maxims that were excellent in all respects except one, viz, they contained no element of authority. They reached only principles of human utility. They could proclaim human interests, and even perceptions of the exaltedness and nobleness of virtue and beneficence; but they exhibit no Person who says *Must*, and who, in the

*Heb. x, 2 to 4.
† *Heb. x, 19 to 22.*

reciprocal and mutual relations of personal life, is Ruling Lord.

Hence, we have found that no philosophers, or rationalists, have found much truth, except those who have, directly or indirectly, derived their principles and chief elements of method from The Bible.

But we have found that The Bible itself demonstrates the need of something more than cosmical rationalism, and has itself derived its own truthfulness, as a teacher of philosophy, from its supplying that element. It, and it alone, has taught that the ends and values of life (and only in life are there any values), are neither intellectual nor cosmical; but are in the sentiments and experiences of what we call Spirits; and ultimately they are in the life-action of The Cause and Father as a person, in its relation to human spirits in their feelings and wills.

Hence, we find that, while The Bible has been the great leader of the world in intellectual philosophy, and its only leader in the establishment of religion as an authority and moral *force*, it has not done this on the lines of intellectualism alone, but has used and taught elements of a higher and truer philosophy.

We are thus brought to a second answer to our question, how men can attain knowledge of God, and of their own nature and destinies.

If we have, in preceding pages, followed correct lines, the highest and most intelligent personal life is that which has sense of the values of life in the Supernature of persons as spirits, Divine and human. This is, therefore, a philosophy which is not wholly cosmical, unless spirits are part of cosmical life, and are not only a part of it, but such a part that they can be described, and their life-action traced by cosmical reasoning.

Supernatural philosophy.

There is, therefore, necessary a super-cosmical philosophy, a spiritual philosophy, and this must not only exhibit something of the *nature* of spiritual personality, but must tell truthfully something of the life *actions* of spirits, their doings, their attainments, their wills, and their mutual and reciprocal relations to each other in living.

But this supernatural, or spiritual, philosophy must largely fail as a forecasting philosophy. It can estimate and appreciate values. It can recognize and appraise facts; but it cannot infallibly judge characters, nor foretell the movements of free wills, nor the force of loves and passions.

Hence the natural philosophy of the world has so much erred, because it has not been supernatural and spiritual; and the philosophy of The Bible has elevated the world because it was so largely true to the facts of the nature and lives of spirits, and of spiritual and moral forces.

The Bible has done more than this. It has been the leader in the declaration of the spiritual nature and reign of The Creator. It has been the first and the only describer of God, or of souls, in such descriptions as obtain the assent and admiration of wise and good minds.

The Bible has thus been what philosophy vainly tried to be, a revelation of the invisible. Aristotle tried to portray " The things after the physical things" (*tà metà tà physicà*); but his metaphysics are vain words; and his moral philosophy is only a judgment of the ethics (*ethica*, customs) of society.

The Bible is the true teacher of metaphysics, in that it has declared the undiscoverable, but reasonable, facts of the personality, nature (or character) and will of God, as they are related to the nature and life of men. It found men everywhere believing that men die and dissolve like the beasts, or that souls grovel in a gloomy world under the earth, cheerless and hopeless. It lifted that under-world into the light, and into and above the air. It made men know themselves children of God, born from above, and taught their eager hopes to look with exultant assurance into the broad space where are no coverings nor barriers.

It has made men know God as the perfection of personality, the Sovereign Will, the Complete Truth, the Absolute Power, the Infinite Goodness, the Only First Cause, the Father. He who takes into his soul the essons of the Bible, no longer walks the Earth a foundling. He stands in the presence of a majesty and glory and power awful and splendid; but he rests in the omnipotent hand, he looks into the beaming eyes; he hears the loving words; he homes near the heart of the all-mastering and all-ministering Father.

If in the preceding pages we have in the main followed correct lines, men needed a self-revelation of God. However much may be discoverable of God in his works and providence, it remains impossible that men should forecast his personal choices and performances. If they could do that, they would be Gods, and He would not.

Revelation of God and his Will.

Modern rationalism asserts that Reason can know God without a personal self-revelation by Him. To a certain extent this is true. It is true just so far as The Creator has made the relations between Himself and men such that they know Him in his self-revelation in Nature. And this is a great deal. But this was and is a self-revelation of God's person. If it is not that, it is not true, but is empty and illusory. Being originally a personal self-revelation, it may receive additions of similar personal self-revelations to any extent that The Creator may choose.

The Bible, and specially The New Testament, presents the only philosophical, consistent, and logical doctrine of the ways by which men can and do acquire knowledge of God's self, his truths, and his purposes (it being understood that there are no moral truths and purposes except those of God's Self). *First*, it exhibits God acting personally. *Second*, it exhibits God's revelation of himself as more spiritual than intellectual. *Third*, it declares such a doctrine of God's Spirit and men's spirits that it shows a sufficient (and the only) provision and method for The Creator to communicate to men the higher moral truths and his purposes.

Inspiration.

If their doctrine were not so detrimental, it would be amusing to note how some rationalists, denying everything that could give authority to moral principles, extol them as natural, and the best nature. The New Testament alone presents a rational and philosophical theory, in affirming that an exalted knowledge of God is attainable naturally; but that this is spiritual Nature; and that spirit Nature is communion or intercourse of one personal Spirit with another personal Spirit.

The New Testament exhibits the doctrine that, in this world of facts, in which spirits are the realest of facts, moral truth and God's purposes are communicable and communicated from God's Spirit Person to men's Spirit Persons. And this is the only philosophical theory possible. Any other theory, however superficially it may be plausible, leads on and down into empty darkness, until it drops into an abyss.

§ 2. THE DIVINE PERSON

While all the world except Jews worshiped either gross idols or idealizations of human beings greater in powers, but also often more wicked, cruel, and unjust than earth-born persons, the Jews worshiped an invisible God, whom they declared Creator of all things, exclusive Sovereign Lord of all men, Maker and Defender of moral law.

While an arrogant rationalism pervaded all educated society of the Pagans, and the philosophy of all beliefs was debated with masterly logic, the Jews calmly trusted conscience and the word of God, and argued that their philosophy was the essence of truth.

These conceptions of God and this philosophy the New Testament continues, and increases many fold their force, clearness, details, and relations to life. The God of the New Testament is The Cause, The Creator, The Father, The King, The Lord. He is a person, having loves, purposes, will, force, and agencies; and moral good and right have their origin and authority in the character and will of God.

But in the New Testament there is a great advance in the emphasis with which the personality is portrayed, and God is declared to have appeared in a Person who was both divine and human. This declaration is so positive, and so involves the moral teaching of the New Testament, that the new doctrine must either confound itself, or become the crown and finish of the Jewish theology.

The representation, in the New Testament, of the character of God is so well known that we need here only study, as a philosophy, the portrayal of the personality of God and the declarations that He is exhibited to us in the person of Jesus Christ.

We have seen how Philo, and the Jews generally, had, in consequence of their interpretation of Genesis I, used the name "Word of God" as the name of God when he comes into human view as Creator of the World and Father of men. This usage grew out of both their piety and their philosophy. But this philosophy, as we have seen, is Jewish, and quite different from Platonism. And this usage may be rationally justified.

There can be but two revelations of God, viz., his Person, and his word. In the absence of his visible Person, there can be no more perfect or precious revelation of him than his word. Rationalism everywhere is demonstrating this by trying to install words in human minds, in the place and with the authority of God. Speech is the physical form of truth or wisdom, and is the representative of the Author of truth to human intellects.

When Philo and other Jews represented "The Word of God" as a good name of Deity, first acting as Creator, and then as Teacher of the World, they were as reasonable as they were pious, and they were closer to the chief first principles of philosophy than any person had ever before come; for the first principles must be Creation by God—God acting by intelligent Will—God the sum and source of truth.

The first line of the theology of the New Testament is a restatement and enlargement of the beginning of the old one, somewhat as it had developed it-

The Creator
The Word
in Jesus.

self to, and had been paraphrased by, the best and wisest of the Jews. We quote the beginning of "The Gospel according to John."

"In firstness was The Word (*ho logos*). And The

Word was (or existed) in relations *with The God; and The Word was (a) God.   This (Word) was in firstness, in relations with The God.   All things came into being through Him (or it), and apart from Him (or it) became not one thing that did become.   In Him (or it) was life, and the life was the light of men."

"And The Word became flesh, and tented among us, and we beheld his glory, glory as of an only †Son from a Father—full of grace (favor) and truth."

In these sentences John recalls to view the first story of creation of matter, of light, and of life.   By using the definite article, and then omitting it before the word God, he makes about the same distinction that the Hebrew text makes in calling God "Elohim," and "Jehovah Elohim."   He makes the definite assertion that Jesus was a Person in God, and was the Creator of all things, all light and all life.   He connects the New Gospel with the Old Testament, and commends the first chapter of Genesis, and the philosophy which it teaches and which the Jews partially understood, by affirming that "The Word" is a good name for The Creator as a Person in God.

The Apostle John is not the only writer of the New Testament who refers to "The Word" as The Creator,

---

*The Greek which we translate "*In relations with,*" is *pros* followed by the accusative case.   It means much more than *with*.   *Pros ti* is the technical Greek term for the category *relation*.   Philo says "There are three kinds of Life.   The first is in relations with (*pros*) God, the second is *pros* creation, and the third is intermediate and mixed.   *   *   *   Moses brings forward as best the life that is *pros God.*"   *On The Heir of Divine Things, ch. 9.*

†The Greek word used here, *monogenēs* implies nothing of *begetting.*   See *Timaios Locrus,* who says "The universe is *monogenēs* (*only becoming*), but is ungenerated (*agennetos*)."   See also the end of Plato's *Timaios.*

and makes the idea a part of the gospel of Christ; recognizing him as Creator and The Word.

"Willing it He bore us, by the word of truth" (i.e. The Word and the truth, or the true word). *James I, 18.*

"Born again, through the living and abiding Word of God." *I. Peter I, 53.*

"Of old there were the heavens, and the earth composed (*sunestosa, systematized*) out (*ek*) from water, and through (or *by means of, dia*) water, by the Word of God." *II. Peter, III, 15.*

"In him (or by him) were created (*ektisthē*) all things in the heavens and upon the earth, things visible and invisible. * * * All things have been created through (*dia*) him, and relative (*eis*) to him. And he is before (*pro*) all things, and in him all things are systematized (*sunesteka*)." *Col. I, 16.*

"We understand that the worlds were framed by the word (*rhema*) of God." *Epistle to the Hebrews, xi, 3.*

Coming to names and representations of Jesus in the book of The Apocalypse (The Revelation), of which we must say more later, we find the following phrases:

(God) "signified it by his angel to his servant John (The Apostle), who bare witness of The Word of God, and of the testimony of (for) Jesus Christ." *I, 2, 9.*

" He is arrayed in a garment sprinkled with blood; and his name is called 'The Word of God.' * * * And out of his mouth proceedeth a sharp sword." *xix, 13.**

---

* This symbolism is explained by the language of *Heb. iv, 12.* "The Word of God is living, and active, and sharper than any two-edged sword, and piercing even to the dividing of soul and spirit, of joints and marrow, and living to discern the thoughts and intents of the heart. And there is no creature that is not manifest in his sight; but all things are naked and laid open before the eyes of him with whom we have to do." Compare this with Philo *On The Heir of Divine Things, ch.*

With these words the New Testament initiates its philosophy—a philosophy which is far more than a set of moral maxims.   It is a philosophy of the authority that is back of the precepts, making and enforcing them. It is a philosophy of God's personality, power, will, and purposes, as displayed in the person, the acts, and the institutions of him who was known as Jesus.   Let us then here somewhat observe this extraordinary person.

Whatever may be said or believed as to the divinity of Jesus, he is, as a man, foremost among the chief personages of the world.   In no other man have wisdom, purity, strength and goodness been so complete and so blended.   Jesus.   He lived above every weakness of humanity.   No appetite or passion held him in its power.   And yet, he was no recluse, but lived among the people.   Every best sentiment and sympathy of human life was exhibited in him.

He knew men, as no other knew them, in their woes, their wants, their powers, and their hopes.   He knew, as no other has known, their real needs, the springs of their better nature, the exalting forces of their best spiritual life.   He knew how to inaugurate a system, and proclaim a truth, which could capture the attention and win the faith of people of every race, of every prejudice and passion, of every degree of enlightenment or intellect; could supplant political and social systems of every kind; could reorganize society, and could largely convert religion from a philosophical theory into vital active life of righteousness and philanthropy.   For, if we schedule

26. "God's word cuts through everything; sharpened to the finest possible edge, it never ceases dividing all the objects of the outward senses, and when it has arrived at the indivisible atoms, it begins from them to divide those things which may be contemplated by the speculations of language."

the principles of Christianity, its doctrines and its forces, every one is found in the words of Jesus himself; and if all the Bible, except the words of Jesus, were destroyed, the system would still remain complete, symmetrical, powerful, covering the whole field of divine and human personalities and their relations.

He spoke, and the simplicity, significance and beauty of his diction became a model for the world. No other orator of the Earth has ever spoken so in words that were as living pictures. No other has so reached the heights and depths of truth, or the covered secrets of human souls and consciences. The thousands followed him, to listen, applaud and believe.

His life was a constant benefaction. The distressed, the poor, the sick, found in him tender sympathy, and received from him help, health and comfort. Even *the story* of his words and of his ministry holds such sway over innumerable millions, that they would die cheerfully for their love to him, and calmly for their trust in him. He seems to see nothing but people, and that these people need to be saved from sin and misery.

Without arrogance, he is an authority. Without passion, he rebuked the vices, sins and prejudices, even of the powerful of men. He shamed the inflamed ardor of contending sects, and the depravity of corrupt hearts. No hardship nor fear turned him from the set course and purpose of his life. He trembled neither before the wrath of the aristocrats of his race, nor under the cold and cruel eye of one of the worst of Roman governing soldiers. Such patient strength the world has never seen surpassed.

He has been the one man that has stood above criticism. He is the ideal of humanity. He has been, not a mere spectacle, but a power. He has touched every element of humanity to better it or to cheer it. He has erected principles of wisdom that have become sovereign in human minds, and has reconstructed rational philosophy.

He has none of the appearance of a deceiver of himself or of other men. If we cannot trust the goodness, the virtue, and the intelligence of Jesus Christ, then, in all the history of the world there has been no man whose honesty and wisdom could be trusted.

This Jesus claimed to be a Person of God, an exhibition of the personality of The Creator, and the Lord Sovereign of men, the Arbiter of the eternal destinies of all souls. *The claim was positive, persistent and uncompromising; although it was never brought forward except in honoring the supreme Father. He claimed that his word was the absolute truth, the very "Word of God." He claimed that he was "The Way, The Truth and The Life," and that the wrecked and helpless souls, the despairing souls, might confidently hope in him.

Jesus claimed to be God.

The Deity of Jesus was believed by his disciples; and became the basis of the system of doctrine of The New Testament. His declarations of the nature and law of God were accepted by Christ's followers because they trusted *him*. His assertions of the will and purposes of God were received as unquestionable truth from Heaven.

Jesus was believed to be God.

* "I and my Father are one," *John x, 30.*
"Before Abraham was, I am," *John viii, 58.*
"I came down from Heaven," *John vi, 38.*
"He that hath seen me hath seen The Father," *John xiv, 9.*
"All things that The Father hath are mine," *John xvi, 15.*
"I am the way, the truth, and the life," *John xiv, 6.*
"I am he" (The Messiah), *John iv, 25, 26.*

The *purposes* of God are, after all, the chief elements of moral systems and philosophy. The moral philosophies, which we say we devise from Reason, will always be found to be chiefly based on the deviser's idea of what The Creator is *doing*, or is *going to do*. However rational our systems may seem to be, because based on what we believe that God has already done, there will always be elements of uncertainty, caused by our sense that, in his personal nature, there are infinite possibilities of his will and actions, which can only be revealed to us by himself.

Hence the moral system of The New Testament, however rational or self-sustaining it may seem, rests chiefly on the authority of the declarations of God's will and purposes, that come to us from Jesus. And one of the curious facts in moral and philosophical history has been, and is, that multitudes of men who have not acknowledged the Divinity of Jesus, have accepted him as an infallible teacher of the otherwise unknowable and undiscoverable facts, and have formulated their principles and their hopes on his authority as a teacher.

However complete and rational The New Testament may be as a system of principles of moral science, it is more a declaration of God's purpose to save men from sin, and is a system of helps to the reformation and salvation of men; and this system stands or falls with the Deity of Jesus. And so the disciples saw it. The cry of Thomas, *"My Lord and my God," voices the central and controlling doctrine of The New Testament.

Had the Deity of Jesus been declared only by unlearned men, the world might call them credulous and deceived. But here are writers who plainly are familiar

*John xx, 28.

with the marvelously acute and complete reasonings of
their age; men whose literary ability is unsurpassed; men
trained to acutest criticism of principles and systems.
Here is Paul, matchless still in subtle analysis and skillful
synthesis of ideas.   Here is John, unrivaled in phrases
that hold souls entranced, as with the music of Heaven;
and he is master of a philosophy that, for profundity,
and scope, and coherence, has no competitor.*

Having declared God, The Creator, to be revealed in
his Word, and that Word incarnate in Jesus; and having
connected the old Scriptures about creation
with the new doctrine of Jesus, the Apostles, Jesus
The Light.
especially John, continue the same lines of
representation, by referring to the light which was the first
mentioned created thing, and by calling Jesus the source
of light, in the new display of the new creation and
kingdom.

They make a great deal of this representation.   They
make it as a principle of philosophy, and make it in such
metaphorical and rhetorical language as carries with it
conviction of its propriety, and brings a charm and cheer
along with the "Word of the kingdom."

They say such things as these, † "In him was life,
* * * and the life was the light of men. * * *
The light was the real, which, coming into the World,
illuminates all men."

‡ "God is light * . * * and the true light now
shineth."

‖ "The god of this world hath blinded the minds of

* Several of the Christian Greek writers of the first and second centuries ranked among the foremost philosophers and
scholars of their day—e. g. Clement, Justin and Origen.

†*John i, 4, 9.*

‡*I John, i, 5 ; ii, 8.*

‖*II Cor., iv, 4, 6.*

the unbelieving, that the glorious light of the gospel of Christ, who is the image of God, should not dawn. * * * God, who said Light shall shine out of darkness, hath shined in our hearts, to give the light of the knowledge of the glory of God, in the face of Jesus Christ."

And Jesus himself said,* "I am the light of the world," and †"I am come a light into the world." He called the holy or pious people ‡"Sons of the light," and the Apostles, preaching of new spiritual birth, and of Sonship from God, and using baptism as the symbol of the new birth, said also,‖ "Walk as children of light," and ¶"Ye all are Sons of light and day," and §"Every good gift is from above (ánothen), descending from the Father of the lights. * * * Willing it he begat us by The Word of truth (or True Word)."

The Apostle John seems to intimate** that, in the first preaching of The Baptist and of Jesus, much was said about light with The Living Word. To this conception not only the importance of light in science and in the story of creation contributed, but also the naturalness of the metaphor of truth (or proclamation) as light, and also the many sayings in The Old Testament about light in truth.

We might gather together many sayings of the Apostles, coupling the Word and the light, which seem to have a reference to phrases of The Old Testament.

*John viii, 12; ix, 5.

†John xii, 46.

‡Luke xvi, 8.

‖Eph. v, 8.

¶I Thess. v, 5.

§James i, 17. He seems to indicate a habit of associating birth, father, light, word of God, will of God, ánothen, and throws light on John i, 3, 5, 13; iii, 7.

**John i, 1 to 14.

And when we add to these the remarkable passage from Philo, which we have quoted on page 182, connecting light in God with " The Word " and " The Lamb," and add the phrases of and about The Baptist, connecting " The Word," " The Light," and " The Lamb of God," and also the phrases in John's Apocalypse about light, such for instance as *" The lamp thereof is The Lamb," we are led to believe that a line of representation in The Old Testament had trained and taught the students of The Scriptures, for a culmination, in which the Word, the Life, the Lamb, and the Light are combined; and all this combination, this conception of glory and promise, and beneficence, the Apostles, with all their earnestness and all their enthusiasm, even with their worship of Most High God, bring as an investiture to the name of Jesus.

Having now noticed the beginning of the New Testament's representation of The Creator, and its declaration that Jesus is the incarnation of a person of God, we may proceed to observe the other names given to him. We shall find each of these connected with a special set of representations and doctrines; but we shall also find them so blended into a conception of one person, that he is often said to perform under one name the functions of that character, and those of one or more others. Names of Jesus.

We have shown that in the Old Testament there was nothing more prominent than the name Jahoh, and that in the Greek and Syriac versions the words that mean Lord (*kurios* in Greek, *mar* in Syriac) had entirely taken its place, and occur thousands of times. There was no other name which Jesus as Jehovah, or Lord.

*XXI, 23.

meant to the Jews "The Creator and Moral Ruler" as the title Lord did.*   And yet this name was given to Jesus by his disciples, and was accepted and approved by him.†

The name of Him who brought the Hebrews out of Egypt, of Him who said, "Thou shalt have no other Gods before me," of Him who was worshiped in the "Holy of Holies," became the common title of Jesus.

These names which we have now noticed, Creator, God, Word, Light, Life, and Lord, are brought to Jesus out of the most ancient Scriptures, and out of the first principles of philosophy.   But there is also another line of description and of titles, a line that issues out of that spiritual enlightenment which we call " Prophecy."

Under the administration of a personal God, aiming at the enlightenment, welfare and salvation of men, reve-

Jesus in prophecy.

lations, or discoveries of truths, and forecasts of events, are at least possible.   Since Man is God's Child, and in God's likeness, and since truth is one connected and interwoven system, it seems to be the plan of The Father that, in the knowledge of divine things, " The path of the just shall be as the sunlight, shining more and more unto the midday brightness." (*Prov. iv, 18.*)

With many haltings and mistakes, Reason instructed by the truth of God advances along the pathway of light; and Reason prejudiced and misled turns into by-paths and wildernesses.   So there arises among many peoples

*This fact was so well known that when, in the reign of Caligula, the Alexandrian mob was robbing and murdering Jews, their mocking cry was *Mar* or *Mari* (*My Lord*).   See Philo *Against Flaccus*, ch. 6.

†"Ye call me Master and Lord.   And ye say well, for I am." *John xiii, 13.*

a literature that is well called " Prophetic "; for prophecy is speaking for God. It is the language of the soul's conception of God, his works and his ways. It is the utterance of its best philosophy and hopes.

It may be something more than this, even a true spiritual enlightenment, from the very presence and act of God. It may be even more than this, even a revelation of the personal purposes of God. Indeed any true revelation, from personal communion of God with men, is almost necessarily interwoven with forecasts of his purposes, and with intimations of the ends in which his principles and types must result.

Around these best facts, principles and forecasts, is constructed the best literature of all peoples, filled with their philosophy, theology, culture and rhetoric. It may be irrational and even absurd; but it can never be ridiculous, because it is the earnest intensity of souls.

In the Old Testament are many forecasts which have had wonderful realizations in facts. Others, before the birth of Jesus, aroused in the minds of pious Jews expectations of momentous events. Among these prophecies, those of Daniel and Isaiah had especially caused the Jews to look for the near advent of an extraordinary man.

As we study the names given to Jesus, and the characters ascribed to him, we find many of these so originating in the prophecies of Daniel, and so connected therewith, that it is well to quote here at some length from his book.

"I beheld till thrones were placed, and an (or the) Ancient* of days did sit. His raiment was white as snow, and the hair of his head like pure wool. His

---

*The phrase, "Ancient of days," is used nowhere else; and the proper translation is very doubtful. It might be translated,

throne was fiery flames, and the wheels thereof (or his circles) burning fire. A fiery stream issued and came forth from before him. * * * The judgment was set, and the books were opened, * * * and, behold, there came with the clouds of heaven one like a son of a man; and he came even to the "Ancient of days;" and they brought him near before him. And there was given to him dominion, and glory, and a kingdom, that all the peoples, nations and languages should serve him. His dominion is an eternal dominion which shall not pass away, and his kingdom that which shall not be destroyed." * * *

" I beheld, and the same horn made war with the holy ones, and prevailed against them until the Ancient of days came, and a decision (or judgment) for the holy ones of the Most High was given, and the time came that the holy ones possessed the kingdom. * * * And the kingdom, and the dominion, and the greatness of the kingdoms under the whole heaven, shall be given to the people of the holy ones of the Most High. His kingdom is an eternal kingdom, and all dominions shall serve and obey him." *Ch. vii.*

A Splendid One of days, or A Splendour of days (or, the days), or. He who is old as the days (or older than the days). There is much reason for thinking that the name means the same as that which Daniel in *chap. ix, 27,* calls *suntéleia kairoû,* and elsewhere, especially in *chap. xii,* describes by many different words and phrases, and which Christ called *suntéleia toû aiônos* (which means the consummation, or extremity, of time).

We shall see, later, (pages 239, 241, 249, 253) reasons for believing that, in the three mentions of the *Ancient of days,* Daniel presents three different epochs, which John in The Apocalypse represents separately, in large detail, and which in *Rev. i, 19,* are called " Things thou *hast* seen, things that *are,* and things that *shall be.*"

"And he (Gabriel) said, I am come to make Thee skillful of understanding * * * therefore understand the vision.   Seventy sevens are decreed upon thy people, and upon thy holy city, to finish transgression, and to make an end of sins, and to make atonement for iniquities, and to bring in everlasting righteousness, and to seal up vision and prophecy, and to anoint a most holy place.   Know, therefore, and discern, that from the going forth of the commandment to restore and to build Jerusalem, unto The Anointed, The Prince, shall be seven sevens; and (in or after) three score and two sevens it shall be rebuilt.   * * *   And after the three score and two sevens shall The Anointed be cut off, and shall have nothing; and the people of the Prince, that shall come, shall destroy the city and the sanctuary."   *IX, 22 to 27.**

"At that time thy people shall be delivered, every one that shall be found written in the book.   And many of the sleepers of earth dust shall awake, some to everlasting life, and some to shame and everlasting contempt.   And they that be wise shall shine as the brightness of the sky, and they that turn many to righteousness, as the stars forever (or, as the eternal stars).   But, thou, Daniel, shut up the words, and seal the book until the time of the consummation."   *Ch. xii, 1 to 4.*

"How long shall it be to the end of these wonders? * * *   It shall be for a time, two times, and an half. And when they have made an end of breaking in pieces the power of the holy people, all these things shall be accomplished."   *Ch. xii, 7.*

*The proper translation of vv. 26, 27, is doubtful. For Jesus' interpretation, see page 232. " And shall have nothing" (In our older version " But not for himself"), is in Hebrew, "And not for him (or to him)."   The interpretation of Jesus seems to be "He shall (be set at naught." See *Mark ix, 12,* and *I Cor. ii, 6.*

These prophesies had caused the Jews to expect the establishment on Earth of a kingdom of The Most High God of Heaven, ruled by an "Anointed One," a "Prince," a "Son of God," and a "Son of Man." It should be a kingdom of all races, but a people made wise and holy, who should "Shine as lights in the world."

As soon as The Baptist began to preach, these Jewish expectations concentrated around him. The burden of his preaching was "The kingdom of The Heavens is coming," and it demands righteousness. The people asked him, "Art thou The Anointed?" He answered, No! and proclaimed Jesus "The Son of God."

Forthwith the names "Son of God," and "The Anointed" (In Hebrew *Mashiah*, in Syriac *Meshicho*, in Greek, *Christos*) became the common names of Jesus. The people saluted him as King, and expected him to establish himself as head of the kingdom of The Heavens. They asked him about the time and nature of the kingdom. He accepted the titles, and made the kingdom of God (or of Heaven) a frequent theme. His assumption of the titles "The Anointed" and "King" became the cause of deadly hostility to him, and the title King was the mocking inscription on his cross. Thoughts of the kingdom of God (or of Heaven) occupied the minds of The Baptist, and Christ, and the Apostles. Jesus said,* "Since the days of John The Baptist, the kingdom of The Heavens is attacked, and the violent assault it;" and †"Since then, the kingdom of The Heavens is proclaimed, and everyone is violent against it." Doubtless

Matt. xi, 12.
†*Luke, xvi, 6.*

there was great moral power in John's preaching about a moral kingdom; but the force of the preaching was in what he said of "The Son," and of Him "That cometh from Heaven," and of "The Bridegroom," as a person.

The kingdom of The Heavens was the theme that brought the eager disciples to Jesus *asking "Wilt thou at this time restore the kingdom to Israel?"

That the name "Kingdom of God" (and of Heaven) is a suggestion from the prophecy of Daniel, and that the approbation of Jesus and the Apostles is thus put on the prophecy of Daniel as a word from God, and that the prophecy of Daniel is the source of many of the titles of Jesus, seems clear.

Not only the name Christ (*Mashiah, Anointed*), but the companion name "Son of God," seems to have this origin.   Four† verses of John's Gospel may seem to suggest that this name comes to us out of the doctrine that Christ is "The Word" and The Creator.   But even this suggestion is modified by the ‡contexts, and all the instances of the use of the name "Son of God" are closely connected with the representation of Jesus as "The Anointed," and as King of "The kingdom of Heaven." It has no similarity to, or apparent connection with, Philo's ideas of "The Word" as "The Firstbegotten Son of God."

But if the name "Son of God" has its suggestion more from the prophecies than from the philosophy in the Bible, it must conform to that true philosophy, if the New Testament is true.   It must represent properly

*Acts, i, 6.
†Chap. i, 14, 18, 34, iii, 16 to 18.
‡John, i, 49; xi, 27; xx, 31.

some fact of the Divine Nature of Jesus. The mystery of the Divine Nature of Christ the Bible does not attempt to explain. It leaves The Christ as undescribed as Jehovah. And it makes no suggestion of a description, or explanation, in the name "Son of God." The declarations of the Deity of Jesus, and the suggestions of the nature of it, are quite independent of the name Son, and are made in direct and positive assertions in other connections. It is the man Jesus Christ of whom it is said the He is "Son of God," and "Only Son," (*monogenēs*), and God, and "In him dwells the fullness of God bodily."

The name "Son of God" is the companion name to the title which Jesus always used for himself, "Son of Man." To us it has an inestimable philosophical value; for as given to Jesus, the God and Man, or both Christ and Lord, it affirms God's fatherhood to men, makes the most emphatic representation of his personality and activity in the world, and adds to our conception of The Deity precisely the elements which make our conscience recognize The Creator as of right our moral Lord.

On the lips of Jesus, one of the chief doctrines is the fatherhood of The Creator to Him and to us, which he constantly urges as a law and motive and inspiration of moral life. Nearly forty times in Matthew's Gospel, and more than fifty in John's, He calls God our Father, or his Father, or both. Taught by the tongue of Jesus, men have learned to say, as they say no other words, "OUR FATHER, WHO ART IN HEAVEN," and perhaps there are no other words of Jesus which hold us quite so close to him as the words, "I ASCEND TO MY FATHER AND YOUR FATHER."

While the disciples called Jesus "The Son of God," he called himself constantly "The Son of Man." The use of this name seems clearly connected with the prophecies of Daniel. We have seen that, in the vision of Daniel, the Prince, to whom the holy and glorious kingdom was given, appeared like a "Son of a man," *Bar Enosh.*

These prophecies of Daniel are largely written in a dialect then called Chaldee, later called Aramaic, and now called Syriac, and much like the dialect in which we have the Aramaic version of the whole Bible. In these dialects there is a common compound word, *barnosh* or *barnosho,* equivalent to *manson,* which is used generally instead of the word *man.* But this is not the title of Jesus.

In Daniel the name is not so contracted, but is made in the longer form which means "Son of a man," or "Son of Man," and emphasizes the sonship. The name which Jesus took to himself is the long and emphatic phrase (in Greek *Ho Huios toû Anthropou,* in Syriac *Bareh d'Nosho*), which means The Son of Mankind.

In the emphatic manner with which he did everything, Jesus applied to himself the name "The Son of Mankind" and the prophecies of Daniel respecting the Kingdom of Heaven, using the phrases of Daniel, or others so akin that the reference and connection are unmistakable. He said, "The Son of Man shall come in the glory of The Father." *Matt. xvi, 27.*

—"shall send out his angels." *Matt. xiii, 41.*

—"shall sit in the throne of his glory." *Matt. xix, 28.*

—"shall come in the clouds of Heaven." *Matt. xxiv, 30.*

—"shall sit at the right hand of power." *Matt. xxvi, 64.*

—to whom "all judgment is committed." *John v, 22 to 27.*

—"is Lord even of the Sabbath day." *Luke vi, 5.*

—"has power on Earth to forgive sins." *Mark ii, 10.*

—"is come to seek and to save the lost." *Matt. xviii, 11.*

"All things written by the prophets shall be accomplished to the Son of Man." *Luke xviii, 31.*

"The Prince of the World is coming, and in me he has nothing." *John xiv, 30. Dan. ix, 26.*

"Now shall the Prince of this World be judged." *John xii, 31. Dan. ix, 26.*

"The Prince of this World is judged." *John xvi, 11. Dan. ix, 26.*

Sometimes Jesus speaks of himself as the subject of prophecy, and evidently refers to Daniel, e. g. The puzzling phrases of *Dan. *ix, 26, 27,* "And shall have nothing in me, and The people of the Prince," etc., may be referred to in *John xiv, 30,* "The Prince of this World cometh, and has nothing in me (perhaps *sets me at naught*);" and in *Mark ix, 12,* "It is written of The Son of Man that he should suffer many things, and be set at naught;" and in *Matt. xxvi, 24,* "The Son of Man goeth, as is written of him;" and *Luke xvii, 25,* "He must suffer many things and be rejected by this generation."

At length, he said to the disciples, "Unto you it is given to know the mysteries of †The kingdom of The

---

* See page 227, note.

† Daniel says, "The God of The Heavens shall set up a kingdom." In Matthew's Gospel it is always called "The kingdom of the Heavens." In the other Gospels it is "The kingdom of God."

Heavens. Every writer instructed about The kingdom of The Heavens is like a householder who brings out of his store old things and new" (of present and future). *Matt. xiii, 11, 52.* Then, in a discourse of word-pictures, he explains the nature and the establishment of this kingdom.

He explains that the kingdom is one of truth and of character—that it is to be gradually established by the preaching of the word from soul to soul, as leaven works—and that it will spread amid difficulties, as wheat grows; but will surpass its small beginning, as a tree surpasses its seed.

But to declare himself "The Anointed," and "The Son of God," and "The Son of Mankind," and the realizer of Daniel's prophecies, was at once to raise and to shock the hopes of the disciples. They, and many other Jews, looked for an immediate, splendid, and powerful display of royalty and divinity. They had learned from Daniel to expect that, at a set time, The Anointed Son of God would come in the clouds of heaven with the angels, and then at once establish a dominant kingdom of Israel.

Daniel had called the period, towards which his prophecies were directed, by phrases which the common Greek Bible translated into *suntéleia kairoû* (ix, 27; i. e., consummation of time), and *kairós suntelelas* (xii, 4, 9; i. e., time of consummation), and *suntéleia hemerôn* (xii, 13; i. e., consummation of days). The word *suntéleia* means, not *end* or *cessation*, but *completeness*, or *perfection*.

Fullness of time. Advent of The Anointed.

The words of Jesus in general, and especially the thirteenth chapter of Matthew, following probably the habit of that day, had changed these phrases of Daniel

into *suntéleia toû aiônos* (consummation of the age, or of
the period, or of time), and had led the disciples to
understand that the establishment of the kingdom of
God, at the fullness of time, would be after another
coming of Jesus in glory.

At last, when the end of Christ's earthly life was
near, the disciples prayed him to tell them " What shall
be the sign of thy coming, and of the consummation of
time?" Then, in a long discourse (*Matt. xxiv. and xxv*),
which he distinctly says is a reference to, and explanation of, Daniel's prophecies, and in which he uses many
of Daniel's words and phrases, he explains that the kingdom and the advent have different times.   He explains
that the kingdom was initiated in that generation, and
that, as his kingdom, it would progress towards supremacy, until he should come to reign in his personal glory.

He seems to authorize us to interpret Daniel's phrases
by his, and his by Daniel's.   Hence we may understand
many of the words and phrases of both to be symbolical,
perhaps representing moral, rather than physical, or his-
torical, events, and portraying the operation of moral
forces, and the effects of principles, in the conflict of
truth with error, and of righteousness with sin.

While we shall have occasion in other pages to recur
to these representations of the kingdom of God, and the
coming of The Christ, we may now pass to the observation of other names and representations of Jesus.

At the beginning of the public life of Jesus something
caused The Baptist to call him " The Lamb
of God, who takes away the World's sin."
The antecedents of this name are not
easily, if at all, traceable.   Lambs had a conspicuous
place in those types which, in the Mosaic institutions,

Jesus The
Lamb of
God.

taught the principles of the divine government. But types are not prophecies; and there is no evidence that any type was understood to forecast later events. The types were illustrations of principles; but the ultimate scope of those principles would be beyond human vision. Hence a sacrificial lamb could only to a very limited extent be suggestive of a perfect atonement, or of a personal redeemer.

Referring to our notes on pages 183 and 202, and to our quotations from Daniel, on pages 225 and 226, we may say that under the peculiar phraseology of *Daniel*, and especially of *Chapter VII, 13*, there seems to lie the full conception of The Son of God and of Man, as a Lamb, before the foundation of the world, silent and sacrificed. The words of this verse are very ambiguous, and have puzzled all translators.

We show hereafter, (See pages 249 to 250), reasons for believing that *Daniel vii, 13*, is explained by Revelation xii, 1 to 5, and is a tableau of events that preceded creation, and of others that preceded the advent of Christ. The name Ancient (or Splendour) of days (or lights, See *Gen. i, 5,*) is a representation of something older than creation. Saint John, in passages corresponding to Daniel's, calls The Son of Man a Lamb, and describes him in words like Daniel's, that have some resemblance to a description of a lamb.

We may say further, of the puzzling words of *Daniel vii, 13*, that the Greek version merges two phrases in one, and so adds to the reasons for believing, as we do, that the verse means, " He equalled, or reached, or was old as, The Ancient of Days." And the Greek version also uses in its translation of the phrase " They brought him near before him," the word *phosphero*, which is the Greek word commonly meaning *to offer* or *sacrifice*.

As we come later to the study of The Apocalypse, we will find there (See page 246) a silence in heaven at a point in the visions (*Chap. VIII, 1,*) where the representations of the Lamb opening the mysterious book of life, correspond to Daniel's words about the same book of silent mystery, and where also, in the correspondences of the Apocalypse, there is a suggestion of the Sabbath silence, after The Word, on six days, had created.

And when we come, as we shall, to reasons for thinking that, in Rev. xii to xx, one of the beasts that aid the Serpent, (The Dragon, The Devil) is symbolized by the name Cain, we may be reminded of the phrase, "Blood that speaks better than Abel's (*Heb. XII, 24,*) and we may be confirmed in the belief that The Lamb, older than creation, silent, self-sacrificing, the opposite of The Serpent and his beasts, was a widely accepted conception among the Hebrews ; and was a large element in the doctrines of Christ and the Apostles.

Among the names and representations of Jesus, those of The Apostle John are the most numerous, varied, and remarkable. Together they constitute the most wonderful portrayal of God, in relation to the world, which exists in any literature, whether it be considered as to its philosophy, rhetoric, symbolism, or prophesy. These are in three writings, making a trilogy, with many relations of coherence and mutual explanation. These are *The Gospel, The First Epistle,* and *The Apocalypse* (or *The Book of The Revelation*).

John's trilogy.

The *Gospel of John* exhibits Jesus as The Word of God, The Creator, The Only Son of God, The Life, The Light. He records more than the other disciples, the personal acts, and the most philosophical sayings of Jesus, such as the birth from above and of spirit, the spiritual water, the eternal life, spiritual worship, spiritual food, The Advocate, and the virtue of love.

The *First Epistle* exhibits Jesus as "The Word of Life," "The Light," "The Son of God," "The Advocate," and presents, as no other book does, the part which the blood of Jesus bears in the salvation of men.

The Gospel and the Epistle of John present to us the facts and principles on which may be formed a theology, delineating the nature of God and of men, The Gospel the law and ways of God, the salvation and and Epistle blessedness of the revived children of God, of John. and, in general, a coherent and rational philosophy. They deal with the past and the present. They appeal to conscience and reason, and to the purest and noblest of the sentiments and springs of action in men. And for this they hold a place, in the minds and hearts of millions, which the more superficial and simpler words and phrases of other gospels and epistles cannot fill. It is in going to the profoundest depths, and in rising to the supreme heights, that they carry the hosts of exultant and confident souls.

The "*Apocalypse*" (*Book of The Revelation*) is the most remarkable book in the literature of prophecy. Its emblems and metaphors exhaust the best resources of rhetoric. They are the appear- The Apoc-alypse. ances and names of God, the thrones of kings, the skies and space, the sun and stars, the mountains, seas, rivers and islands, the infinite ages of the past and the future, the array and battles of armies, the most blessed joys and most awful agonies of souls, the convulsions of Nature, and the life of Heaven.

An analytical survey of *The Apocalypse* reveals the following facts. Its general character is a repetition and amplification of the messianic prophecies of Daniel. The prophecies, figures, and symbols, are much like Daniel's, and the number and sequence are the same as his. As he reiterates (vii, 16, 21, 23; viii, 26; ix, 24 to 27; xi, 2; xii, 1, 2, 7, 10), for the purpose of explaining and enlarging, so *The Apocalypse* exhibits one general spectacle, which is arranged in seven tableaux, reiterating, enlarging, and explaining either the general conception or some special parts.

On this essential structure, there is laid a rhetorical dress, which is largely derived from the books of Isaiah and Zechariah; more than forty of the most distinctive conceptions, figures, and phrases, being drawn from these two books. (See *Appendix*.)

There is also some correspondence with *Ezekiel*, as to Spirit (see *Appendix*), a throne, and a man on it (i, 26, 27; x, 1), its circles and eyes (i, 18), and rainbow (i, 28). There is a book (ii, 10), and it is eaten (iii, 1, 3). There is a proclamation of an end (vii, 1).

In this composite structure there is incorporated a considerable body of imagery derived from the first four chapters of *Genesis*. This fact is so conspicuous in the last half of the book that *The Apocalypse* might well be entitled *Paradise Regained*, or *Eden Redeemed*. There is also incorporated a general recognition of the Mosaic institutions, under the names *Moses* and *The Temple*.

It is the most artistically constructed book in *The Bible*. It exhibits a cluster of spectacular tableaux. Certain features are present in all the tableaux, and others reappear after long sections, so that the book is in general one spectacle. It seems plain that *The Apocalypse* is not a prophecy of events and of history, which to Saint John were future; but is a symbolical display of principles, and of the purposes and methods of God's moral government, and is especially a demonstration of salvation by Christ, and of this as begun before creation.

These spectacular representations are found to be in seven grand divisions, each of which is introductory to a set of promises, which are interspersed from *chapter vi* to the end of the book. These sets of promises, even thus introduced, enter somewhat abruptly, are connected with others less relevant to the scenes portrayed, and have an appearance of an artificial correspondence with some lines of thought that are not in the depicted tableaux, many of which correspond with phrases of *Genesis, Isaiah,* and *Zechariah.*

The second and third chapters contain also a set of seven promises, or sets of promises. These are put as messages to churches, but are in fact personal promises to individual souls. They are messages of the seven (i. e. all, or the one) spirits of God, to seven (i. e. all) churches. Each begins with the phrase, " For (not *to*) the Angel of the church of ——, Write." These Angels are called *Spirits,* and are also (i, 4; iv, 5; v, 6) represented symbolically as stars, lamps, and eyes. These seven letters are in their phrases, considered alone, quite abrupt, incoherent, and inexplicable; but when the sets of figures and promises in the letters are compared with the seven sets interspersed in the book, the two sets are found to correspond with each other; *but the order, or sequence, of the seven in chapters ii, iii, is the reverse of that of the seven interspersed in the rest of the book.*

This correspondence by inversion seems to be part of a general plan, by which "First and last," "Beginning and end," are set together, not merely in phrases, but in the larger representations, all of which have the effect to make the book a grand exhibition of God's sovereign rule as one plan, complete in its beginning, providing for human salvation before sin began, and including the reversal of all moral disorder by "The Lamb slain before the foundation of the world."

The second and third chapters furnish another clue to the whole book; for the seven promises are addressed "To him who conquers." In this they are like Saint John's First Epistle, wherein he says, "Ye have conquered the Evil One," "Whatsoever is begotten of God conquers the world. And this, our faith, is the victory which conquers the world."

The second and third chapters being guides, and the key-word in them being *conquers*, the whole book bears the character of a pageant of victory in God's "Conflict of The Ages." All the principles of truth and philosophy, all the forces of good and evil, are exhibited in symbols, and in them, and over them, is the presence and power of the personal Lord.

And, grand and mighty as are the conflict and the victory, they are not for the glory of God alone, but for "The saints of the Most High God," and for each saint. No book of The Bible is more the book of the individual person. It is the book in which our Lord comes nearest to his disciple, and says, I and Thou will fight this battle, and win it.

The number *seven* is used with names of more than fifteen things. To a Jew it always suggests the days of creation, and symbolizes completeness.

Daniel's sevens and half sevens reappear.   Instead of his "Ancient of the Days," there are The Creator, and the sevens which suggest the creative days.

From our analysis, we infer that the apparent design of *The Apocalypse* is,

1.   To explain much of older Scripture, and to exhibit the wonderful harmonies of the Hebrew book and its theology.

2.   To glorify Christ, under many names, as Saviour and triumphant Lord.

3.   To declare the constant presence of Christ in the world, and to explain the prophecies about his presence.

4.   To declare the assurance of the end in the beginning.

5.   To declare the immortality of human souls, and the bliss of souls saved by Christ.

6.   To magnify revelation by inspiration, and to indicate something of its nature and methods.

We now attempt a more detailed, but concise, analysis.

Chapter I verses 1 to 9 are a declaratory prelude, ascribing to Jesus Christ many of the names, attributes, and deeds which are detailed and illustrated later.

Verses 10 to 20 represent The Son of Man very much as *Daniel vii* represents "The Ancient of Days," and his throne.   He has also the two-edged sword proceeding out of his mouth, apparently signifying that He is "The Word of God."   (See page 216.)

He names seven churches as receivers of his messages, which are communicated by seven spirits, Angels of the churches, also represented as seven stars, set on seven golden lamp-stands.

Chapters II and III we introduce elsewhere, in sections corresponding with other parts of the book.

Chapter IV seems to be a correspondence with *Daniel, vii, 13, 14*. We have in *Daniel vii* two spectacles. So in *Rev. i and iv* we have two, which are phases of the same one, and are like Daniel's two phases of one. But instead of " Ancient (or Splendor, or Splendid) of days," we have a splendid person saluted as Lord God, Almighty. Instead of " The Son of Man " we have "Lord, Our God, Who didst create all things." Instead of " Ancient of days," we have seven lamps of fire, which are spirits of God.

Chapter V continues the spectacle of *Chapter IV*, very much as in *Daniel, vii, 22 to 27,* continue *Dan. vii, 13, 14*. As in Daniel there was a promise that a decision should be given for the holy ones of The Most High, and that the kingdom should be theirs, so here the promise is to people of every tribe, race, tongue, and nation. The seven spirits are prepared to go *to all the earth*. But now, and from this point continuously, the name of The Lord is " The Lamb of God." In the hand of Him that sat on the throne was a book which no one but The Lamb could open. This book is mentioned many times later, as " The Lamb's Book of Life," and is a prominent feature of the whole Apocalypse from this point to the end, as a similar book is in Daniel. The representations respecting this book show it not merely as a list of the redeemed, but much more as containing the principles of God's government of life from the creation to the end.

It must be noticed that the three tableaux in *Chapters I, IV* and *V,* are three representations of the same thing in general; and that four and twenty Elders who are present in *Chapter IV*, are also present in *V, VII, XI, XIV, XIX,* and there is thus a unity of time in all the book of The Apocalypse, making it bear the character of a representation of principles, and of the past and present, more than a forecast of events to come in the then future time.

Chapter VI.   At this point there seems to begin the opening out into details of the "Book of Life."   Here begin series and groups of spectacles and panoramic movements, sometimes successive, but quite as often in synchronous groups, and sometimes even turning the view back into the eternity before the creation of the world.

First, The Lamb breaks six seals of the book, and causes six spectacles.   As God in six divisions of his work called "Days," prepared the Earth for his Sabbath, which yet is the time of human history, so here are six spectacles of the operation of divine forces.   At the breaking of each seal there is a vision of awful woe.   Disorders and wreck of every kind rage in tumult.   Nature is in convulsions and ruin, and men are in misery and terror.

This is an awful spectacle of moral chaos.   All the scenes are held in a certain relation to The Lamb, who breaks the seals, and the wicked men's fear, after the sixth seal is broken, is fear of Him.   There are bright features in the spectacles, for there are saved souls clothed in white, singing the praises of God and The Lamb.

Have we not here a spectacular representation of the principles of moral government, of the havoc which sin works, and of its relation to God, and of the terrors of conscience?   All this is plainly a preparation for a gladder and hopeful vision after the breaking of the seventh seal.

We are reminded of the six days of creation before the Sabbath, but still more of .the first day's chaos, be-

fore The Creator said, " Let there be light.' This tableau
is much like Christ's parable of " The Tares."

Chapter VII.· There seems to be in this chapter not
an advance movement, but rather a consummation spectacle. It depicts the best phases of the results of the
old conditions, and a host saved out of the great tribulation. It is like the seventh tableau in Christ's wonderful thirteenth chapter of *Matthew,* and like the finishing
of his discourse in *Matthew xxiv, xxv.* It has analogies
with the seventh day of creation. There is to be no
more sun created. There is to be water of life; but,
instead of a hovering Spirit, there is now the Lamb
leading to the fountain. There is also correspondence
with *Daniel viii,* where he says, " The vision of evenings
and mornings, which hath been told, is true." *Chapter
vii, 16, 17,* is also almost a quotation of *Isaiah xlix,
10 to 13.*

The first verse of *Chapter VIII* evidently belongs
with the preceding chapter. "When he opened the
seventh seal there followed a silence in heaven about the
space of half an hour." This completes a correspondence with the seven days of creation. The Sabbath of
God has come; in one sense a rest, but a life-work of
infinite power. It exhibits a host saved out of the great
tribulation. There are a hundred and forty-four thousand of the children of Israel, and a vaster number out
of all races, ascribing their salvation to " The Lamb."

Besides the other indications that at *chapter viii, 1,*
the first grand spectacle closes, here occurs another, in
the fact of the correspondence of the figures and symbols
here with those of the message written for The Spirit to
the seventh church in *Rev. iii, 14-22.*

Rev. iv to viii, 1.	*Rev. iii.*
iv, 11. Angels cry, "Thou hast created all things. For thy pleasure they exist, and were created."	14. He is "The Beginning (*Arché*) of creation."
v, vi. Good and wicked separate.	15. Hot and cold souls.
vi, 15. Rich men cower.	17. Some rich are naked.
vi, 11; vii, 9, 14. White robes.	18. "Buy white robes."
vi, 15. Consciences wake.	18. "Get eye salve." "Are blind."
vi, 9, 11; vii, 14. Tribulation.	19. "I chasten."
v, 13; vii, 15, 17. Lamb's throne.	20. "I am set with my Father in his throne."
v, 15. Judah's Lion conquers.	21. "Even as I conquered."
v. 10. Hath made us kings.	21. "Shall sit on my throne."
vii, 15. Are before the throne.	21. "I will come to him."
vii, 12. Angels cry "Amen."	14. He is called "The Amen."
vii, 16, 17. Lamb shall feed them.	20. "Shall sup with me."
vii, 17. Shall wipe away tears.	18. "Anoint eyes."

1 { ... } 7

Chapter VIII, 2, begins a new group of tableaux which, as living pictures, pass before the same thrones and presence that had witnessed the other spectacles. But the structure of the conception, or composition, is changed. The group is larger, more balanced and artificial. Parts are suspended till others are introduced. There is a peculiar arbitrary numbering of three woes (ix, 12; xi, 14;), which reminds us of the abrupt enumeration of the days in *Genesis i.*

The central feature of this group is the result of the blowing of a seventh trumpet (xi, 15). The correspondences with *Daniel ix, 24 to 27; xii, 1 to 4*, and *7 to 13*, are close, and there are correspondences with *Genesis ii, iii.* A climax or crisis is announced in *Chapter X, 7.* "There shall be time no longer; but in the days of the voice of the seventh angel, when he is about to sound, then is completed the mystery of God according to the gospel which He declared to his servants the prophets. *Chapters vii to viii, 1*, seem to describe the "Things that have been," as they resulted in the things "That (at that day) are." Now apparently begins a representation of the things (principles and facts) that were and that are, as a preparation for "The things that shall be."

The section which begins at *VIII, 2*, is itself divided into three sections, or groups, of spectacles. There is one sub-section embracing *VIII, 2*, to *IX, 12.* It is a spectacle of woe, and may be presumed to represent the world in its sins. A feature of it is (*IX, 1 to 12*) woe that comes out of the abyss, the King of which is called "Apollyon" (destroyer). We are reminded of *Genesis iii, 1*, and the serpent.

A section beginning at *IX, 13*, exhibits four angels at the river Euphrates, reminding us again of *Genesis ii* and the four rivers, of which the Euphrates was one.

These, and the other sub-sections, group themselves around the indicated crisis. This is represented, as in Daniel, by various symbols of half a seven. We are compelled, by the conjunction of many indications, to recognize that the design of this section beginning at *VIII, 2*, is to represent the life and death of Jesus as the central crucial point of the aspect of God's moral kingdom. We now survey the features of this section.

Chapter VIII, 2 to IX, 12, as we have before said, is a spectacle of woe wrought by sin. *Chapter IX, 13 to XI, 14*, depicts other woes, personal, social, and national. These are the second woe. Into the latter part of this sub-section is introduced a display of the opposite forces, the forces of righteousness and of God's kingdom. And there, distinctly, are introduced the symbols of the half-seven, and the analogies with Daniel's half-seven, and with the advent of The Messiah as he describes it.

This inserted portrayal begins with *Chapter X, 1*. An angel announces the end of (the) time. He has a book which is both sweet and bitter, when John eats it. Is this like life? He announces the consummation of the mystery of prophecy. This sub-section in *Chapter XI* presents emblems in marked resemblance to those of *Genesis ii*.

Instead of Eden, there is God's temple, and its court. There are two trees, which are also called " Lampstands " and "Witnesses" for God. As witnesses they have mouths, from which issues fire against their enemies. A beast which comes out of the abyss (but whose coming is not really described till *Chapter XIII, 1*), and who is the earthly colleague and servant of "The Serpent, the Devil," and seems to be a symbol of all sin, fights them after they have prophesied twelve hundred and sixty days (three and a half years), and kills them. Their dead bodies are gazed on in the streets till the end of the last half of the week (or seven). Then they revive and ascend to heaven.

During the second half-seven, or forty-two months, the nations trample on the holy city. The scene is called Sodom and Egypt, and the place "Where their Lord was crucified."

As we survey the other sub-sections of this great section (beginning at *VIII, 2*) we shall see a strong corre-

spondence with prophecies in the last three chapters of
Daniel. The two trees have a correspondence with the
two trees in Eden, and also are the same as *Zech. iv, 3,
11, 12, 14,* and also have a correspondence, in *Daniel ix,
24,* with "Vision and Prophecy" which are "sealed up"
at the end of the seventy weeks; or possibly with (ix, 27)
the "Oblation and Sacrifice," which cease for a half-
seven.

This inserted portrayal of hopefulness and power for
good (beginning ·at x, 1) is the place where, if our
understanding of the general structure of The Apocalypse
is correct, we would expect to find emblems, and figures,
and prophecies, corresponding with the next to the last
set in *Chapter III.* And this is what we have:

Chapter XI.	*Chapter III.*
1, 7, 19. Temple opened in heaven.	7. David's key. Door opened.
19. Ark of *covenant.*	7. The Holy and True.
3, 10, 18. Witnesses.	8. Kept my word.
7. Satan's beast.	9. Synagog of Satan.
15. Christ's kingdom.	11. I come quickly.
18. Time to judge.	10. Trial of the Earth.
18. Time of reward.	11. Thy crown.
1, 19. Saints in temple.	12. Saints pillars in temple.
15, 17. Names, Anointed; Lord; Lord God; Almighty; He who is and was.	12. Will write names of God and my new name.

2 { ... } 6

Chapter XII begins another distinct sub-section, apparently not a new event, nor a sequence in time, following what has preceded; but a new simultaneous symbolic spectacle of the principles and facts of God's moral kingdom, in the center of which is set Christ's life and death on Earth. It seems to represent " The things that have been," and those that are, as they prepare the way for those that shall be.

A woman is seen in Heaven, arrayed in the sun, moon and zodiac constellations. She bears a Man-child, who is to rule the nations with a rod of iron. He is taken up to God's throne. There is war *in Heaven.* A dragon who is said to be "The Old Serpent," and "The Devil," and "Satan," and "The Deceiver of the whole world," is cast out of Heaven, and comes to the Earth. The kingdom of God and The Messiah is proclaimed.

A voice in Heaven proclaims that the saints conquer because of the blood of The Lamb. It cries, "Rejoice, O Heavens! Woe for the Earth, because the devil is gone down unto you!" The woman is persecuted by the devil, but she is preserved for twelve hundred and sixty days (v, 6). She is nourished in a wilderness for three and a half periods (v, 14), while the devil makes war on her children who are on earth. After this, the woman is no more mentioned.

This spectacle bears the appearance of representing in symbols Daniel's vision of The Ancient of Days and The Son of Man, and also the chief principles of *Genesis i, ii.* The scene is *in Heaven* at first. It recognizes, under the names "Dragon," "Serpent," "Devil," and "Satan," the Accuser or Adversary. If we turn to *Gen. i, 1, 2* and notice that there God's Spirit is, in the Hebrew, described as a feminine thing brooding or hovering, although the word *spirit* is of neuter gender in Hebrew, have we not reason for thinking that this woman symbolizes God's Spirit, or his creative purpose?·

Comparing what is here said of the man-child with what Daniel, in his corresponding passage (*Dan. vii, 13*), says of the "Son of Man," and with what Saint John says of Christ as ruling with a rod of iron (*Rev. xix, 15*), must we not understand that the man-child is the Son of God and of Man?

Have we not here a representation of the declaration in eternity, in Heaven, of God's purpose to create men, and of the moral objections, and of the inexplicable evil Spirit, and then of the provision in God's Son for human salvation? In Daniel's corresponding section, the time is said to be seventy sevens, representing perhaps eternity and time; then sixty-two sevens, representing perhaps eternity before Satan's contention; then perhaps seven sevens for that contention, and then one seven for the duration of human moral history, and this latter seven divided, as to its moral aspect, into two halves, by the birth or life of Jesus.

Chapter XIII. A beast having seven heads and ten horns (symbols of consummate intelligence and great power) comes out of the sea, as the earth itself had come. Satan and this beast combine for forty-two months (half of seven years) to mislead men.

A second beast having only two horns comes out of the earth. He associates himself with the first beast, aids him in seducing the people, makes an image of the first beast, and puts the brand mark of the first beast on the people. This second beast is later called "The False Prophet," or else the "Image of the beast" is so called. (See xvi, 13; xix, 20; xx, 20.)

Probably no passage of the Bible has been seized by interpreters with more unscientific, prejudiced and unreasoning methods.   And yet we have quite evident guide marks for an interpretation; for, *first*, the agreement of Daniel and John places this reign of Satan, the beasts, and the False Prophet, in the half-seven before Christ's life and death, but reaching to that period; and *second*, the clews of correspondence in *Rev. ii, 12-18* give us the name Balaam for the false prophet, and the name Nikolaitans for the wickedness; and, *third*, a guide is given in xiii, 16-18, where it said that the beast is associated with a brand mark, and the number of his name is six hundred and sixty-six.

Following these guiding lines we find that the name Balaam (Hebrew for Lord of People) is the same as Nikolaos (Greek for Conquer People).   The name Balaam was always held in abhorrence by the Jews.   At the Christian Era, however, there was a large body of people who held the doctrine that almost everything in Hebraism must be reversed; that Satan, the Serpent, was a deliverer of men, that Adam fell forward, that sin was moral freedom, and that Cain was to be glorified.   These doctrines were so widespread, and so firmly fixed, that Satan-worshipers remain to this day in Mesopotamia.

This shocking doctrine John calls "The doctrine of the Nikolaitans," and the messages of *Rev. ii* speak of it with special abhorrence.   The histories of Gnosticism call the Balaamites also Cainites, or else there were two schools having similar doctrines.   History and Scripture inform us that the Hebrews abhorred the names of Cain and Balaam, as synonyms for the two great forms of wickedness, the violent and the seductive.   Saint Peter (*II. Peter, ii., 15-22*) condemns the Balaamites, and Saint Jude (verse 11) speaks of Cain and Balaam together as leaders in sin. ·In *Numbers xxiv, 21-22*, we see the name Cain given by Balaam to one of his associate heathen tribes, which is to be destroyed, and which he bewails. Cain seems to be a symbol of all gross, bestial wickedness; and Balaam is a symbol of ostentatious and intellectual antagonism to God.

If we take the name Cain as it is spelled in Hebrew and Syriac, and write it in Greek letters, we have Χάιεν (Chaïen). And, if we count the numerical value of these Greek letters, we have 600+1+10+5+50=666. The lesson is, that false religion leads to the old bestiality, (*Numbers xxv, 1, 9; xxxi, 16; Revelations ii, 14*), and the mark of Cain.

Chapter XIV is one of the chapters which help to the conviction that The Apocalypse is made up rather of spectacular representations of the principles and general features of "The Kingdom of God," than of descriptions of events and their sequence in time. It constitutes in itself a complete tableau, exhibiting the good results of the conditions described in Chapters xii, xiii, and it therefore belongs to the group of tableaux beginning with Chapter xii. If, therefore, our analysis of The Apocalypse, according to the keys heretofore suggested, is correct, we should, in the blessings here promised to the saints, find a correspondence with the fifth message to the churches. And precisely this we do find.

Like several other chapters, this chapter xiv exhibits the hosts of saved souls. There are here the same saints of Israel and of Gentiles that were shown in Chapter vii. Here are shown the judgments on the Balaamites who have just been described, and on Babylon which is about to be portrayed. Here is the harvest of God, and the general judgment.

Here is introduced with some abruptness, but, in this, with much similarity to Daniel's phrases and methods, the declaration of human immortality. *Daniel xii, 2, 3,* says, "Thy people shall be delivered; every one that shall be found written in the book. And many sleepers of earth-dust shall awake; some to everlasting life, and some to shame and everlasting contempt, etc." Saint John, by The Spirit, says here, "Blessed are the dead who die in the Lord, from this time. Yes! Says the Spirit, while (or when) they shall rest from their troubles; for their works (or deeds) accompany them." Both of these cited passages explain or supplement *Daniel vii. 27,* and *ix. 24-27.*

This Chapter xiv seems to be a companion picture to Chapter xx, representing the same principles or facts, viz., the final judgment, the salvation of the saints, and the immortality of all human beings. Here we reach an assurance that our analysis of this book is, at least in its general features, correct, and that one of its great purposes is to make resplendent our assurance of immortality, and to show the blessedness of the saints in the triumph of The Lord's kingdom. The doctrine of immortality, and of holy bliss and glory, are declared in the first chapters; but the portrayal of the principles and processes is carried forward and developed progressively until the consummation of glory and bliss is reached in the end of the book. And to make this unity of theme, and to exhibit these ideas at the beginning of the book, the assurances and promises, that follow these processes of development, have been carried to the beginning of the book by the reversed set of messages to the churches.

Here occurs the third correspondence of promises:

Chapter XIV.	*Chapter III.*
6, 8, 9, 15, 17, 18, 19. Angels sent.	1. He has seven spirits.
1, 3. 144,000 Saints.	1. Hast a few names.
3. Multitudes ruined.	1. Art dead.
5, 12. Faithful witnesses.	3. Faithful witnesses.
7. Hour of judgment coming.	3. I will come.
4, 5. The undefiled.	4. Undefiled, in white.
4, 12. Blessed d e a d. With Lamb.	5. Will not blot name. Will confess name.

(3 ... 5)

Chapter XV continues the vision of the transition from the old dispensation (or covenant, Dan. ix, 27) to the new. The host of the saved sing (as in vii, 10 to 12) a "Song of the Lamb," but also the "Song of Moses."

We seem also here to have the beginning of a new parallel with Daniel's prophecy.

Daniel says, " Even unto the consummation, and that determined, shall wrath be *poured out* upon the desolator," (*ix, 27*, in revised version English). " The people of the prince that shall come shall destroy (desolate) the city and the sanctuary; and his end shall be with a flood; and, even unto the end, shall be war. Desolations are determined," (*ix, 26*).

This chapter (*Rev. xv*) says now, " Seven golden bowls, full of the wrath of God, were given to seven angels, (i. e., all the power of God was arrayed against all wickedness), and God's temple stands closed while the seven plagues are *poured* on the Earth," (v, 8).

Chapters XVI, XVII, XVIII describe the contrast and conflict of sin and righteousness. The chief form of abomination is figured as a debauched city, called Babylon, called also a sensual woman. This gross wickedness is universal. The city is on seven (i. e., all) mountains (xvii, 9), and on waters, which are said to be "Peoples, and multitudes, and nations, and tongues."

Chapters XIX to XXII exhibit the spectacles of the blessedness and the magnificence of the *triumph* of Christ and his people. They show close correspondence with the latter parts of the prophecies of Daniel, and with the idea of a fourth, or sunrise, day, and with the reversal of the sin of Eden, and with the mercy shown to Adam and Eve, and with the tree of life and its flashing light. These do not seem to portray successive movements of events and of time; but rather principles, forces and facts that exist together, and that began to exist when Jesus came to Earth.

The pageant grows in glory as a reign of the personal Lord, in and with his people, until at last it is a full display of his personal presence and exaltation and benevolent supremacy. In the tableau of *chapter xix* there is the vindication of God in a display of the kingdom of Jesus. Sin is crushed, but in righteousness, justice and love. Jesus is presented as the solution of all moral mysteries. He is exhibited as God, Jah, The Lord our God, The Almighty, The Lamb, The Faithful and True, The Word of God, King of Kings, Lord of Lords, The Amen, He who has a secret name, and He who in righteousness judges and makes war.

This display in *Chapter XIX* has its point of strong

illumination, where "The Word of God" (as a sword), as a truth, triumphs over the false prophet and all deceptions, and as a Person overwhelms the persons of the rebellious and the vile. The beast that came out of the sea (xiii, 1) and the one that came out of the earth (xiii, 11), if he is the False Prophet, Sensuality, and all their adherents, meet a ruin figured as a swallowing up in a volcano; and the rest of the wicked perish before the truth and its Author.

Chapter XX. presents the climax of the reversal of the picture given in *Chapter XII.* Satan, himself, the dragon and old serpent, reaches the limit of his efforts and of his permitted sway. In contrast with the death which followed his work in Eden, there is exhibited *first* (vv. 1 to 6) a spectacle of the sainted dead. *These are priests of God and of Christ; and, as priests go into the sacred sanctuary, these are living and reigning with Christ, for the indefinite period of a thousand years, in Heaven.*

The *second* part of the spectacle exhibits the last judgment. The souls that have lived in heaven with Christ, and those that have been hidden away in Death, and Hades (i. e., in an undescribed condition), with the two beasts (and the pretended prophet), all come to judgment. Satan makes a last desperate effort against the bliss of the saints, and to hold the wicked in ruin. The Book of Life becomes the rule of judging. Death and Hades (the grave, or unseen world) have no more place and work, because the end of the earthly living has come. And the souls of those not written in the Book of Life ("of the Lamb") disappear from view, as the Devil, and beasts, and false prophet had gone. This is the second Death (that in Eden being the first).

Chapters XXI, XXII, present the spectacle of the cul·

mination of God's purposes, and moral reign, and of the glory and bliss of the saints with Christ.   Creation, and the symbols and figures of the first chapters of *Genesis* are reëxhibited in triumph.   There are new heavens and earth.   Instead of God present to one pair in Eden, " He shall dwell with them" (xxi, 3).   There is water again, the water of life (xxi, 7; xxii, 1).   There is " The Tree of Life " (xxii, 2, 14).   There is a woman—not the ambitious and rebellious woman of Eden, but a saved host becoming The Bride of Christ.

There are now no more evenings (xxii, 5).   One eternal day has succeeded the seven.   No more created light or sun is needed, for The Lamb is the light, and " The Lord God shall give them light " (xxii, 5), and He is "The Morning Star."

As, in the rest of the book, the sections that exhibit the bliss and glory of saved souls are correspondent to the messages and promises in Chapters II, III, in reverse order, so here the last four sections and correspondences are found.

xix, 1 to 16.	*ii, 18 to 29.*
The wanton woman is denounced.	Jezebel a wanton and prophetess is named.
The rider on the horse has eyes as a flame.	The son of God, the promiser, has eyes as a flame.
Out of his mouth goes a sharp sword (see Heb. iv, 12).	He searches reins and hearts.
He will rule with a rod of iron the nations.	He will rule with a rod of iron, and give authority over the nations.
The consummation in the marriage of The Lamb is announced as near.	Keep my works *to the end.*

4   4

xix, 12 to end.	*ii, 12 to 17.*	
The beast and false prophet are overwhelmed, after serving Satan. An angel invites to God's supper. Christ named in thirteen ways (see page 243). One name is secret. The sword of his mouth is mentioned.	Balaam and the Nikolaitans are named. This church lives near Satan's throne. Manna is promised. They shall have Christ's new name. The sword of his mouth is mentioned.	3
5		

xx, xxi.	*ii, 8 to 16.*	
The book of life opened. Souls are judged. Saints *reign* as priests with Christ 1,000 years, and then forever. The second death buries Satan and his followers. There is a new sky and earth. The Creator is "The Beginning and the End," and Alpha and Omega.	Suffering from false Jews and Satan, "That ye may be tried." He that conquers shall receive the crown of life. He that conquers shall not be hurt by the second death. The promiser calls himself "The First and the Last."	2
6		

xxii, 2.	*ii, 1 to 7.*	
The tree of life is exhibited.	The tree cf life is promised.	1
7		

Besides the spectacles and promises which we have now enumerated, "The Book of The Apocalypse" (or The Uncovering) has a few verses of an introduction, and a few of peroration. In these there is chiefly a glow of spiritual vision and joy; and the cause of this is an expectation of Christ's presence. The names of Christ, that in all the book are mentioned in connection with his appearances and performances, are here clustered.

With these names, the chief representation is of the presence of Christ. One promise and hope rise above all other things. That promise and hope declare that He will soon be more visible, and will reign in power and glory.

St. John says plainly that this representation is the purpose of the book. Not only in many other ways does he say this, but he dwells on the words *witness* and *testimony* of (i.e. *about*) Jesus. He makes us hear an Angel say, "The testimony of (or *witnessing about*) Jesus, is the spirit (essence, or purpose) of prophecy," (xix, 10). Noticeably something of this kind comes in in connection with the seven sets of displays of his presence and promises throughout the book after *Chapter III.*

The prelude and the peroration emphasize the promise that he will be seen quickly (i, 1; ii, 15, 16; xxii, 6, 7, 12, 20). The whole book exhibits him present alike in Heaven and on the Earth, ever working, conquering and reigning. The Christian world would have been richer in cheer and hope, if it had always translated the word *parousia presence* instead of *coming.* That is the word which our Lord and the Apostles used so much in speaking of his personal reign; and it means *presence.*

The book of The Apocalypse is "The Uncovering" of the fact of our Lord's personal presence always in the moral history of men. It is shown before creation, in the whole of earthly history, and in the *aionios* (eternal) life of the saved hosts. In the conflicts and triumphs of the kingdom, The Lord and his people are together, and the victory is theirs in common. When his people close their eyes in death, they are with him in a *millennium* of

Advents or presence of Christ.

glory and bliss (*Chap. xx.*), and surround his throne in joy (Chapters, i, iv, v, xiv, xix,). And when the whole drama is enacted, and there are no more conflicts or judgments, then all shall see Him, and He shall reign in person with the saints forever. The light that dawned at creation, and the fire that flashed at the gate of the garden in Eden, will have become the dazzling effulgence of his presence.

In *Matt. xxiv, xxv,* our Lord said that one of his advents, or presences, would be immediate; and it was so, in the initiation of his reign. In *Rev. xxii, 12,* He says, "I come swiftly" (or suddenly), using a word, (*tachu*) which rarely means *soon* in time, but rather means a quick manner of coming. The whole book is a display of quick comings; but the last three chapters, having seen the end of The Lord's conquests, and having displayed the millennium of the deceased saints, and the judgment of all souls, exhibit the perpetual blessedness and glory of Christ and his people. The Lord, who at first sat on a distant throne, and sent out messenger angels, and ruled by armies, is with his people. An eternal festival has begun, and The Lord has taken his "Bride."

When we have finished the study of The Apocalypse we do not feel that it is merely an artificial conception, or a dramatic display of Saint John's theories, or of his interpretation of older prophecies. While it is the grandest picturesque representation of the kingdom of Christ and the joy of the saints, it is also the fact, and a wonderful and admirable one, that similar ideas are expressed by other writers of The New Testament. Some of them appear even in Philo. They are a part of the unity of

Apocalyptic ideas elsewhere.

"The Faith."   We are constrained to believe that, not
only those parts which are like Daniel's words, but many
others, were foreshadowed and prepared by the older
Scriptures, and had become definite expectations, and
that these, in radiant pictures, with much detail, had
been given by Jesus to the Apostles, and had become
the common hope of the church.

So Saint Paul comprises in short passages many of
the characters of Christ, and characteristics of his personal
reign, e. g.   "Giving thanks unto The Father, who has
made us meet to be partakers of the inheritance of the
saints in the light, * * * and has translated us into the
kingdom of his dear Son, * * * Who is the image of
the invisible God.   Because in (or by) Him were created
all things in the heavens and on earth. * * * All
things were created through Him and for Him.   And
He is before all things, and all things are constituted
(systematized) in (or by) Him.   And He is the head of
the body, the church.   He is The Beginning, Firstborn
from the dead."—*Colossians I, 12 to 17.*

So *The Epistle to The Hebrews* says, "God has spoken
to us in his Son * * * through whom he made the
worlds; who, being a ray (*apaugasma*) of his glory, and
a copy of his real being (*hypostasis*), and carrying all
things by his word of power, sat at the right hand
of the magnificence in the high places. * * * When
He again bringeth The Firstborn into the world he
saith, 'Let all the Angels of God worship Him,' Who
maketh his angels winds, and his ministers a flame of
fire; but of the Son he saith, 'Thy throne, O God, be
forever and ever. * * *   Thou Lord, in the beginning
hast laid the foundations of the earth, and the heavens

are works of thy hands. They shall perish, but Thou
continuest,' " etc.* *Heb. I.*

So the Apostles write not only of the *parousia* (presence) of Christ, but of his appearance (*epipháneia, display*
or *manifestation*).

" Christ Jesus, who shall judge the living and the
dead, at his *manifestation* and kingdom. * * * The time
of my departure is come. * * * For the rest (or future)
there lies waiting (*apokeitai*) the crown of righteousness,
which The Lord, the righteous Judge, shall give me at
that day; and not only to me, but also to all them that
have loved his manifestation (*epipháneia*)." *II Tim. iv,
1 to 8.*

" Blessed is the man who endures trying; for, when
he has been approved, he will receive the *crown of life
which He promised* to those who love him. * * *."
James i, 12.

"Where is the promise of his *presence?* for, from the
day that the fathers fell asleep, all things continue as
they were from the beginning of the creation. * * *
But one day is with the Lord as a thousand years, and a
thousand years as one day. * * * But the day of
the Lord will come as a thief, in which the heavens shall
pass away. * * * What manner of persons ought ye
to be, in all holy living and piety, looking for and earnestly desiring the manifestation of God's day. * * *

*The reader can find in Philo's treatise *On Noah's Planta-
tion, Book II, ch. xii,* a passage bearing a remarkable resemblance to this in words and phrases, and also much like Paul's
above cited. Here occur the words *God, creation, ray, copy,
glory, hands of God, word, king, worlds, high, heavenly.* This
illustrates the ideas that had come out of the Hebraic education
and inspiration; but it only treats of the inheritance of the
saints, and gives no suggestion of an expectation or conception
of a Messiah.

According to his promise we look for a new heavens and a new earth, in which righteousness dwells." *II Pet. iii, 4 to 13.*

§ 3.   MIRACLES OF JESUS.

In studying, as a philosophy, the representations which are made of Jesus, the miracles which are declared to have been performed by him must be carefully considered. If they are authenticated, his divinity is confirmed. If they are discredited, a shock is given to all faith in the New Testament and its teachings. Primarily, some principles of rational philosophy seem to discredit the miracles, and to demand that they shall be accepted only after severe scrutiny of the evidence and of the principles involved. The objections brought against the credibility of the miracles of Jesus are entitled to a respectful hearing.

But over against such objections there stand certain facts and principles that are impregnable. Rational philosophy, which has some rights of domination in all thinking, is a science of relations. Their credibility. Hence it must take hold of the study of miracles as purely a discussion of the relations of the personal God to his own purposes in respect to his creatures. Now the ethical, moral, or doctrinal value of any religion depends on the authority which it recognizes as making and maintaining the moral laws. It is not as a system of moral maxims that Christianity competes with philosophies; but it competes with them insofar as it points to the authority that is behind the maxims, and that makes them to be laws.

The doctrinal and moral system of The New Testament rests on the evidences of the Divinity of Jesus, and stands or falls with them. And if they fall, nothing stands. The tremendous importance of the salvation of untold millions of souls, and of the happiness of the World, constitutes a rational ground for believing that, if he was Divine, credible evidences would have been given to prove his Divinity. But no proof could be given except performance of divine acts. The only evidence that a person is what he professes to be is the fact that he can do, and does perform, acts which that person alone can do.

We have said in our philosophical discussions that there are no facts except concrete ones, and there is no knowledge of persons except as to their doings. Christianity has for its chief excellence the fact that it penetrates through all words and phrases, and *goes to the person of God in his doings.* And, in Christianity, all authority of God, in all moral law, is so bound up with *the authority of Jesus as Divine,* that, if he is not demonstrated as God, the whole system of morality is wrecked. Infidels understand this so well that strenuous efforts are made to impugn the credibility of the miracles of Jesus.

One objection tries to array itself in the dress of Science, and to come to us with the prestige of learning and of established facts. But it is a bubble, and its rainbow hues are, as in all bubbles, due to its thinness. Science, in its own sphere, is magnificent; and it goes, as it were, hand in hand with Christianity; for all knowledge is based on Science; and without it there can be no philosophy or theology.

Scientific objection.

But Science is nothing but a classification of observations. It knows nothing but things. It works in the narrow realm of the senses. This is not to say that scientific men are not brainy, nor that they do not bring to the aid of Science the highest intelligence and intellectual work. But they seek only facts, and they glory in this search. Scientific men recognize that theorizing, and going outside of the lines of observation, have been destructive of Science, loading it with unbearable burdens, and holding it back from truth. And yet many of them are just as ready as ever to go out of the lines of Science, and to set up their theories, and to claim for them the sanction of Science.

He, however, who argues from things to causes and principles, does so as a philosopher, and not as a scientist, whether he affirms or denies. And he who assumes to philosophize, while professedly confining himself to Science, has confessed himself narrow.

Science demonstrates that Nature is a magnificent system, operating by forces that never change. But Science discovers nothing about moral or intellectual causes and purposes. It discovers what things are, but not why they are.

But if men, on the ground of scientific knowledge, affirm that "The First Cause" cannot act in other ways, or that He is trameled by his own created works, or that He has no ends which are unattainable through material forces, these are trying to be philosophers, while they are impertinent to their Creator. They must drop the pretense of Science; for they are as men who would fly in the dress of a diver.

Science, pure and simple, cannot touch the problem of miracles, because it cannot even approach ultimate causes, and cannot even investigate the problem of Will. What can it say about Beings with free Will, or about the ways in which a personal God may meet the exigencies involved in the moral life and intellectual life of persons who are free but finite?

Philosophical, or so-called rational, objections to miracles are based on an assumption that the objector knows all about God, his purposes, his pow-
ers, and his methods, and knows that he has no powers which are not in matter, and no aims or methods which he has not already set in opera-tion. In this assumption the objector really abandons philosophy; for philosophy is a science of personality and of free agents.

Any philosophical logic which could demonstrate that God could not, or would not, act except in the methods of matter, would demonstrate that God never did create anything. Who that sees that there is a personal Cause of the universe, operating for free-willed beings, can say that God would not attain grand ends by personal acts, and on short lines? Who can say that personal per-formances of God may not be the normal manner of his operation, or that, wonderful as God's patience is, his impatience may not be grander and supreme?

There are several objections offered against the credi-bility of miracles, that are called practical and philo-
sophical, and would have great force if they were not in fact counter to real philosophy. The first of these alleges that the miracles are incredible, because the object supposed to be sought is insufficient to justify such extraordinary procedures. This objection implies that there is something deroga-tory to God, as Creator, in miracles by personal agency. But if the miracles are for the purpose of demonstrating the personality of God, and if that demonstration is immensely valuable in establishing the personal authority

of God, and in uncovering some of the mysteries of spiritual being, are they not reasonable and worthy of God?

If they assist purposes of infinite beneficence, and if they help to transform religion from a theory into a life, by making The Lord assume his personal place as dominant Master in the soul, are they not reasonable and worthy of God? Who knows the value of God's purposes? Who knows the worth of his own soul? Who knows the value of the hosts of souls that have lived, or now live, or are to come?

The second practical objection to the credibility of the miracles says that they were unnecessary for the alleged object. This is only another form of the idea that God can have no aims which Nature cannot secure. Over against this pretension we may set the almost universal, and much more philosophical, sentiment, that God does not do enough personally, and that he ought to interfere constantly, persistently and powerfully, to persuade men of his personal reign, if that is the truth that must be enforced in order that free-willed beings may be saved. *Second practical objection.*

What was, is, and will always be necessary, is *the authority* of God in the hearts of men; and if this authority is to be exercised by Jesus, then the demonstration of his authority made necessary the performance of acts which only God could do.

The third practical objection to the credibility of miracles attacks their authenticity, and does this in a most specious way. It does not deny that there is much evidence of the occurrence of the miracles; but it says that miracles are so improbable, that it is more likely that the evidence is false or mistaken, than that the miracles did occur. *Third practical objection.*

When this is the argument of the ignoramus, we may disregard it. Everything is improbable to a fool. But this plea against miracles has been used by many of the most learned and acute minds. Some of these, however, and among these, we think, its first propounder, have admitted that it is a trick, and that it has no force, except against those persons who have erected for themselves the theory that God is unable to act as a person. It seems to have been first put forth as a sarcastic mockery of Christians who held too rigid theories of God's unchangeableness.

It is simply an attempt to divert attention from some great principles, and to install as principles a mass of notions for which there is no defense. If, however, God is personal, and if Jesus saves men by his personal performances, and if men need evidences of his Divinity, then the probability of his performing miracles is easily greater than the improbability of evidence.

Few facts of history so ancient are better verified than those related of Jesus. Christianity made its first, and a great progress, because of the testimony of the then living witnesses. And it was not established in an ignorant or a credulous age, nor among an ignorant or thoughtless people. In fact, the most common objections to Christianity now current are as nothing to the acuteness, the rationality, and the vehemence against which it made head and established itself. And its great advance in the first and second centuries, when the traditions of Jesus were preserved in only second or third hands, was among learned scholars, professed philosophers, and keen logicians.

§4.   SPIRIT OF GOD.

We come now to the New Testament's doctrine as to God's essential being, or, if we may use the word, the *substance* of his person.   We shall find that no subject more imperatively demands philosophical treatment, and none is of more serious practical moment to human beings, because it involves the questions How can, and how does God affect and control souls? and What is a human soul?

If we go back to facts and principles of ontology, we must observe that no Being can affect, in any way, any other Being who is not, in some respect, of the same order or kind of being.   Some kind of sameness of relation must exist, either between the Beings, or between them and some other Being or system.

In the physical world there are many relations of all things to each other, because of their relations to a common Cause, and to his Will as incorporated in Nature. But if this is all the relation existing between men and their Creator, our philosophy cannot rise above materialism, just as many persons say that it does not.   We have, however, found in ourselves a system of what we call Moral Life, a system of sentiments, of sense of values and worth, of vital experiences, of relations to ends and purposes.   And this is the whole glory and preciousness of life, having power to destroy or to increase even physical enjoyment.   (See Chap. iv., §§ 3 and 4.)

This moral conscience and sentiment cannot be part of the material world, nor even of the utilities in the relations of men to each other.   It is a part of soul-nature and soul-life.   And yet everything in and about it is a relation.   A relation to what?   A relation to its

Cause. Then it is a relation of community and reciprocity with the Cause of souls, in respect of values and experiences. And if it is this, it is more, very much more; for it must be some community and reciprocity in the ways of attaining those moral ends and values, and of sharing in the sympathies of such joys, and in the ways of mutual influence and help. (See page 68.)

Every philosophy of the World, except the biblical, ignores or denies these principles. The Hebrew Bible suggests them, and leads far towards a full recognition of them. The New Testament, and it alone, brings forward a philosophy of these principles that is full, coherent, and sufficient.

This philosophical declaration of a community of essential being between God and men, and of relations and influences because of that community, is what gives to The Bible its character. The whole New Testament is constructed on the declaration that God exercises moral law over men only because of an essential commonness of being, and that He influences and controls moral beings through the agencies existing in that community. This declaration appears in multitudes of sentences, that have become to us so familiar that we have ceased to notice how philosophical they are.

Such sentences are those that speak of God as our Father, and as Spirit, and as acting spiritually, and such sentences as these. "In him was life, and the life was the light of men." "This is life eternal, to know Thee, the only true God." "We love Him because He first loved us."

The scope of this book forbids our adducing the multitude of texts bearing on these facts and principles, and compels us to epitomize the New Testament's doctrine of God's Being, of Spirit, and of spiritual agency.

It begins with the declaration* by Jesus, "God is (a) spirit, and they that worship Him must worship Him in (their) spirit." The philosophical scope of this declaration is immeasurable. So long as God is a Spirit. men started from their lower and material-istic knowledge towards a conception of God's essence, their ideas of Him were necessarily materialistic, and spirit could only seem to be a kind of matter. And men had always done that; and to the most of the Jews *spirit* meant matter (air).

With this one sentence, Jesus reversed all philosophy, and carried it to its highest level. When it was said, "God is spirit," a definition† of spirit was made which did not degrade our idea of God, but made God, who is known in his doings and character, and causativeness, the ideal of spirit. Then, in biblical language, the word *spirit* lost its meaning of *wind* and *breath*, and God's personal Being became the standard of its definition. The word became divested of all physical or materialistic meaning, and became a symbol and name of that inde-scribable essential Being, in which, and by which, the life of God is localized, and can and does come into rela-tions of action and influence with other personal Beings.

The second part of the New Testament's doctrine of Divine Spirit teaches that, in the There is a person in Being of God, there is one personality, whose God who is essential nature is such that He is known to The Holy Spirit. us especially in the character, attributes and activities of spirit.

*John iv, 24. The Greek here does not say A Spirit. The Greek language has no "Indefinite Article."

†See page 293.

We have observed, in preceding pages, that in moral
Beings there are powers of force, intelligence and sentiment, and that it is impossible for us to conceive how
these three kinds of power can be the same in essence,
or issue from one kind of *being*. We know that they
do cohere in the unity of a person, and that they *must*
cohere into one personality, if that Person is to be moral;
but nevertheless Reason recognizes their diversity in
kind and in action. (See page 64.)

The trinity of human personality may be little analogous to the Trinity in God; but it furnishes to us an
argument for the possibility of a triplex unity
in God, which may be His perfection and
glory. We have observed in preceding
pages, that Reason even suggests that God's felicity may
require a plurality of personalities in Himself. (Page 84.)

The Holy
Trinity.

The New Testament attempts a portrayal of the psychology of God and of men, as no other book or philosopher does. It makes declarations based on this psychology, respecting God's person and nature and actions.
These declarations either establish this psychology as a
true system of philosophy, or they are, as a whole, a
system of superstition, untruths and folly.

In our analysis of a human person, and in our statement of the categories of personality, we recognized
that there is a part of a person which we called spirit,
or spiritual, and of which the chief characteristics are,
that in it are the sentiments, the best values and ends of
life, and the moral relations of persons. It is of such a
nature that, notwithstanding the fact that the thoughtless
of the World, and often the great thinkers, may and do
sometimes so conceive human personality, that a man's
forceful being, or his intellectual being, seems to be his

person, yet when we take into our view this spirit being, it seems to us at once that this is a whole man, and that in this are all his glory and his joys. (See page 67.)

Somewhat so The New Testament sets in our view God The Cause, God The Son, and God The Spirit, as three personalities, having distinguishable characteristics and functions, and as having relations of personality, not only toward us, but toward each other. The New Testament does not uncover the mysteries, either of Deity or of personality; but, in addition to all that rational philosophy affirms in regard to God's being. The New Testament exhibits his nature and actions as a Spirit so prominently, that The Spirit God is second to neither of the other Persons in God.

To this Person of God The New Testament gives a special name, "The Holy Spirit." In saying this we come to a point where there is needed the most intelligent care in the use of language, but where a great deal of common talk is unintelligent and even unintelligible. As there are many significations of the word *spirit*, so there are many phrases in which the relations are such that a spirit may be called The Spirit. And as all kinds of adjectives may be used with the word *spirit*, so the word *holy* may be used with the name "The Spirit" in all of its meanings.

The name "The Holy Spirit" serves as a name of that Person of God who is known to us as "The Spirit;" but it also properly designates that spirit which is his essence; and with equal justness it designates his agency when we call that *spirit*, or his influence when we call that *spirit*, or that which he implants in soul when we call that *spirit*, or the spirit of a human person when that is sanctified. Hence, in a great number of sentences in The New Testament, the name "The Holy Spirit" does not mean the Person of God, nor a Person in God; and to treat it as if it has such a meaning in these sentences is to make language incoherent and irrational.

The New Testament having said that God's nature is the definition and description or ideal of spirit, and that there is a Person in God who acts wholly as a spirit, next teaches that "The Holy Spirit of God" comes into many relations with human spirits, operates in and on them by spiritual agency, which itself is called "The Holy Spirit," and imparts an influence which is also called "The Holy Spirit," and produces in souls a result which is also called "The Holy Spirit," or "The Spirit Holy."

The Holy Spirit as influence and agency.

There is thus in The New Testament, as there is nowhere else, a full and rational psychology and moral science. There is here that coherence and sequence, in the doctrine of spiritual being, which is demanded by rational philosophy. The omission of any one element would wreck the system; and it is the omission of one or more features of the sequence, that has involved the word *spirit* in other religious systems, in superstition and irrationality. If Christians would keep clearly in view this coherence and sequence, and would remember that the use of the word *spirit*, in one of its meanings, rationally implies its just relation to the other meanings, they would less often be led, by their fear of disparaging God's person, into saying things about "The Holy Spirit," which are unintelligent, and are in fact disparaging to Him.

Before leaving the observation of The New Testament's doctrine of God's Spirit, we may observe a few of the classes of ideas respecting it which The New Testament exhibits. But many texts we may better study later, when we come to the study of human spirits and their relation to God's Spirit.

Before the birth of Jesus, it was announced * that, "That which is conceived is out of Holy Spirit," and † "Holy Spirit shall come upon thee," and ‡ Mary "Was found with child out of Holy Spirit." In none of these sentences is the word *the* used.   Birth of Jesus from Holy Spirit.

The apparent intention is to declare that Jesus, as to his earthly being, is not merely of material substance, nor is he, in merely the ordinary manner of men, "Born of spirit," but, extraordinarily, his spiritual being is of God's Spirit. The suggestions of the origin of Jesus, and of the personality of "The Holy Spirit," are here remote and indefinite. The declaration of the spiritual nature of his soul is direct and emphatic.

There is a saying by John The Baptist which has naturally been of great interest to Christians. He said,‖ "He (Jesus) shall baptize you with Holy Spirit and with fire." Jesus also said, § "Ye shall be baptized with Holy Spirit before many days."   Baptism with (or in) Holy Spirit.

Baptism with Holy Spirit is not mentioned again. Neither John nor Jesus said *The* Spirit. We have shown ¶ that baptism is emblematic of our creation from material

* *Matt. i, 20.*
† *Luke i, 35.*
‡ *Matt. i, 18.*
‖ *Matt. iii, 11 ; Mark i, 8 ; Luke iii, 16 ; John i, 33.*
§ *Acts i, 5.*
¶ See page 196.

elements, and has reference to *Genesis i, 2.* It seems evident that the sentences cited above were designed to complete the emblemism of baptism; and that they, also, have reference to *Genesis i;* and that they do not refer to an action by The Holy Spirit as a Person; but they refer specially to something done by Jesus, and refer remotely to baptism as symbolizing that, in the new installation as children of God, our body, soul, and spirit profess the fatherhood of God.

In Genesis i, water, spirit, and light are prominent as chief elements in the creation of personal being. The Apostle John shows how Hebrew philosophy had occupied itself with this idea, when he says, "There are three that bear witness, the spirit, the water, and the blood, and the three are unto the one (or make unity)." Moses said, "The blood is the soul (or life)." John said, "The life was the light of men." The prevalence of such phrases, and such ideas, makes it clear that John's meaning was, that Jesus would make baptism a complete symbol of a new creation of a person.

The New Testament has much to say about Holy Spirit as given, and as a giver. Gifts of spirit, or of spiritual character and power, and gifts bestowed by The Spirit of God, are the Christian's treasure. These are what make Christianity more than a system of morality, and different from every other religion or philosophy. And these furnish an explanation of the progress and power of Christianity in the world.

The gift of The Holy Spirit.

The texts that refer to gifts of spirit, and by The Holy Spirit, we cannot here discuss. There is no subject that needs more careful treatment; and there is perhaps none that is more often treated carelessly and irrationally.   It is intelligible, simple, and philosophical, if we keep in mind the fact that the word *spirit* has many meanings, but that they together constitute a coherent chain of ideas, beginning at God's Spirit personality, and ending in results of character and power in human spirits.

Probably by far the larger number of mentions* of the word *spirit* in The New Testament have reference to human spirits, or to spiritual agencies, influences, and effects; but all of these would be unmeaning phrases if there were not, at the head of the sequence, a Spirit Person of God.   Hence the fear which many persons feel, that they may fail to honor God's Spirit, if they do not recognize His Person wherever the word *spirit* occurs, is a needless fear.   Hence, also, the phrase, "Full of the Holy Spirit," means "Full of a spirit that is holy"; but it implies that ultimately that personal spirit in a man has its start from the personal Spirit of God.

Few texts of The Bible have been studied with more anxiety than the words of Jesus, "He that shall blaspheme against The Holy Spirit has never forgiveness, but is guilty of an eternal sin."† If we understand this to mean that, he who derides and rejects such a purity and rightness of his spirit as God's Spirit aims to produce in him, elects to be eternally guilty, we have a doctrine which accords with the principles of moral philosophy.   It is a most momentous and awful fact; but it is only the reverse side of that possibility of salvation, which begins in the Spirit of God, and becomes a sanctified spirit in men.

*The phrase, "Have the spirit of Christ" (*Rom. viii, 9*), must mean, "Have a disposition like Christ's," just as "Have the mind of Christ" (I Cor. ii, 16) means "Have ideas like Christ's"; but it also implies that God's spirit is the cause of that disposition.

† Compare also *Mark iii, 29; Matt. xii, 31; Luke xii, 10.*

Even The Old Testament had almost made clear the same principle; for Philo says: * " Is not everlasting life a fleeing for refuge to The Living God? And is not flight from his presence death? There are no wicked actions which we can say are done through God's Will; but they are done only through our own will. Whosoever, therefore, accuses, not himself, but God, as the cause of his offense, let him be punished, being deprived of that refuge to the altar which tends to salvation and security, and which is meant for suppliants only. To pronounce The Deity the cause of evil, is a spot which is hard to cure, or rather, which is altogether incurable."

There are some other words of Jesus, respecting The Holy Spirit, which have great importance, and require special study. They are as follows:

The Paraklete "Spirit of Truth," and "The Holy Spirit."
" I will pray the (my) Father, and He will give you another Paraklete, to be with you forever, The Spirit of Truth, which the world cannot receive; for it neither observes nor knows it. Ye know it, for it stays among you, and is in you. * * * The Paraklete, The Holy Spirit, which the (my) Father will send in my name, he† (The Paraklete) shall teach you all things, and shall remind you of all that I said to you." *John xiv, 16, 26.*

"When The Paraklete is come, whom I will send unto you from the (my) Father, The Spirit of Truth, which proceeds from (the presence of) the Father, he† (The Paraklete) shall testify about me." *John xv, 26.*

On Fugitives, chap. xv.

†We say " He," but in the Greek the masculine is used here only because *parákletos* is a masculine noun. It has no relation to the question of the personality of the Paraklete. So also we use the neuter form, as the Greek does, with the word *spirit*, because *pneuma* is neuter even when it may mean a person.

"It is expedient for you for me to go away; for if I go not away the Paraklete will not come to you.   But if I go, I will send him to you.   And when he is come, he will *convict* the world about sin, and righteousness, and judgment; about sin, because they do not trust me; about righteousness, because I am going to my Father, and ye will see me no longer; about judgment, because the Prince of this world has been judged (or condemned). * * *   When that (Paraklete) is come, The Spirit of Truth, he will lead you to all truth; for not from himself will he speak, but he will speak what he hears, and will declare to you the things that come." *John xvi, 7 to 13.*

In these words of Jesus there is a most precious doctrine; and it is an epitome of the philosophy of spirit, in the widest scope, and in many of its most remarkable details.

First, it affirms that there is A Spirit, truthful and holy, who assumes the part of an Advocate,—who does a peculiar work, which is not done otherwise by God,— who came from the side of The Father when Jesus returned thither,—who is not perceived nor known by the unbelieving world.

Second. He does spiritual work—leads to truth—*convicts* (or convinces) spirits of spiritual facts and relations —reaches men's spiritual consciousness and consciences.

We have in previous pages *noted many facts which are conducive to an understanding of these words of Jesus, and of their place in the great system of doctrine.

We have seen †that the word *parákletos*, means *arbitrator*, or *advocate*.   This is its meaning in *I John*

*See pages 133, 174, 189.
†See page 174.

ii, 1, the only other place in The Bible where it occurs.
It cannot mean *comforter.* If it were made from the
verb *parakaléo* in its signification *to comfort,* it might
mean *a person comforted;* but only **paraklétor* and †*para-
kalōn* could mean a comforter. We have noted ‡that in
the Greek version of The Old Testament *parakaléo* represents the Hebrew *iakach,* which means *to be right, to
convict,* and to *arbitrate.* We have noted ‖that Philo
shows that "The breastplate of judgment (*hhoshen
mishpat*), with its *urim* and *thummim* (lights and truth),
was associated with a recognition of conscience and
conviction, and was called in Greek *The logeion* and *The
Parákletos,* meaning an *Arbitrator.*

If we now observe the words of Jesus, we find that
he intimates that the work of a Paraklete is twofold,
first, to convict and spiritually instruct; *second,* to arbitrate, or mediate. As, under the ancient covenant, the
High Priest was a Paraklete for the people, and the *logeion*
was a Paraklete for the Priest with God (when the Priest
was representing the people), and as Philo and others
extend these ideas, and spiritualize the conception, making conscience a Paraklete, so Jesus approves all these
ideas, and adds precisely that one which completes their
system. He promises a work of The Holy Spirit, a
Person of God, who shall bring into human spirits conviction and truth, and shall complete the arbitration,
or mediation, between sinners and God.

*This is the word used in the Greek version of *Job xiv, 2.*
†This is the word used in the Greek version of *Psalm
lxix, 22.*
‡See page 174.
‖See pages 174 and 175. See Philo *On Animals Fit for
Sacrifice, ch. xi.*

§ 5. HUMAN PERSON

We have observed, in the first part of this book, that a truthful conception of our Self must be the beginning and foundation of our whole system of knowledge. The philosophies of God and of men must be one philosophy. A clash between the two, or an irrational element anywhere along the line, wrecks, or at least shakes, all belief. We saw many so-called philosophies ending in skepticism, in regard alike to God' and to Nature, because their theories of human nature and human powers were destructive. Indeed, in all philosophy, there is nothing more perilous than a theory of the human person.

Does The New Testament dare to enter this field strewn with the wounded, and the graves, of minds and hearts that entered it full of the pride and hope of high endeavor? Does it dare to tread the perilous heights, and hang over invisible depths? It had to do both of these, or perish early, imbecile and scorned.

It dares do this. And it comes ·with no timid or wavering tread. It comes like an embassy of an irresistible dominion. It holds high its banners emblazoned with its principles. It sounds the trumpets with its proclamations. It sends forward heralds, with authority and commands. It sends, too, soft-voiced ministers, who cheer the fearful hearts. It sends bearers of swords who challenge the forces of the world; and with them are philosophers ready to meet any argument, or theory, or system of men.

We have seen *that The New Testament lays the foundation of its philosophy of human nature in recog-

*See page 204,

nizing the sphere and authority of consciousness and conscience, and that in this it has preceded and guided the learned world. We shall also see that, in the rest of its doctrine of human personality, it introduces just the principles and doctrines which complete a rational philosophy of human nature, and with it a rational theology, in one coherent and harmonious system of truth.

First. The philosophy of The New Testament has a clear and rational doctrine of the physical nature of men. It reiterates the doctrine of *Genesis i*, which declares man not a product of matter, but a body of matter vitalized by God. It gives to this a new emphasis, by making the symbol of it, baptism, the organizing and emblematic ordinance of the new system of faith. (See page 196.)

Human bodies.

It is not afraid of materialism. It points to water as a reminder of men's creation out of the matter of Nature, but it points to it as also a memorial of inertness and death. It makes the symbolic ordinance emblematic of that principle of causation which is the fundamental and conductive principle in philosophy; but it does this by pointing to matter as only material, which a sovereign personal power has endowed, and of which a wise and revered scripture had said, "In the beginning God created, * * * and God divided the waters," etc.

Birth from water. Baptism.

The old Scripture had not saved the Jews from false ideas and materialistic conceptions. Matter was invested with a certain sanctity to them, because God made it. Spirit was to them vaguely like breath and etherial air. Spirits were ghostlike, and resurrection was revival of the old body. Yet a wise direction, and the essence of truth, were in the Old Scripture, and it had done a great work of education for the Jews; hence Philo says:* "The elements, earth and water, may almost be said to utter distinct words, and to say, We are the essence of your bodies." Hence, also, when Jesus said† to Nicodemus, "Unless a man is born of water and of spirit, too," etc., he said, "Art thou a Presider in Israel, and understandest not these things?"

To these first principles The New Testament adds a clear and philosophical statement of the moral distinction between the bodily Self, and the spirit Self, and between nature in the body, and will in the spirit of a man. The discussion of this topic, by Saint Paul, in *Romans vii*, is a masterwork of philosophical acumen.‡

At a time when no other religion or philosophy in the World occupied itself with really fundamental principles or philosophy, Moses, claiming divine direction, suggested the distinction between mind, matter, and spirit. He saw that, in philosophy, there is an important place to be held by the elements that are intermediary, and helpful, between material bodies and their spirits.

Blood, Soul.

Then he instituted a perpetual protest against materialism, by saying,‖ "The soul is in the blood." If this had been the whole of his doctrine, it would have been crude materialism; but, even so, it should have had the front rank, as science, with the theories that magnify, and almost deify, protoplasm and molecular forces; for it starts with the ultimate and supreme vehicle and agent of life, and with this vitalized and pregnant with forces,

On Those Who Offer Sacrifices, Chap. ii.
† *John iii, 5.*
‡ See pages hereafter.
‖ *Leviticus xvii, 11.*

and with those directed purposes which now we call laws. (See page 51).

But this was not his whole doctrine. Before this, was the doctrine that, " Jehovah breathed into him the breath of life, and he became a living soul."   Hence, although the conceptions of Moses and the Jews* were faulty, blood was to them water plus spirit, and was the medium by which spirit vitalized every part of the bodies of men. And this doctrine was reiterated, and enforced † with ordinances that invested blood with a halo of sanctity, teaching men to treat all blood reverently, and to use blood in the most significant and far-reaching ordinances, with which the souls of men penitent came to the worship of their Creator and Father.

Out of this Mosaic doctrine, of the nature of blood, comes the significance ‡ of the Mosaic sacrifices of animals, the emblems of atonements, and the symbols of forgiveness.   It is no secondary and superficial doctrine, but one of measureless importance.   And this line of philosophy The New Testament follows, in its references to the Mosaic ordinances, and in its representations of the nature of Jesus, and the atonement by him.

It makes blood the emblem of the humanity of Jesus. The fact that he had it, as we shall say more at length

---

* Philo says, " Blood is the substance (*ousia*) of the soul; not of the mental and rational life, but of that which exists in relation to the senses." *On Special Laws, Book IV, chap. 10.* See also, *Questions and Solutions, ii, 59;* and *On Who Is Heir of Divine Things, chaps. 11, 12, 13.*

† It was so emphasized that it still governs the Jews everywhere in respect to the slaughtering and eating of animals.

Philo says, " Moses would not have spoken of the blood as occupying the most important place in the body, unless he was making reference to a very necessary and comprehensive principle." *On The Worse Plotting Against The Better, chaps. 22, 23, 25.*

‡ See pages 131 and 163.

hereafter, completed his preparation for being a Savior; and the fact that he and it died, completed the earthly part of redemption.   That Apostle who was the philosopher of the twelve, and who said most about "The Word," and "Spirit," and "Sons of God," and "Birth from above," most clearly saw the philosophical import of "Water and blood."   Out of this comes perhaps his saying that one of the soldiers pierced the side of Jesus, "And there came forth blood and water."   This is the significance of John's saying, "This Jesus Anointed is He that came by water and blood: not in (or with) the water only; but in the water, and in the blood.   And it is the spirit that beareth witness; because the spirit is the truth.   For there are three that testify, the spirit, and the water, and the blood, and the three are unto the one (or the one thing, or unity)." *

Second.   The New Testament recognizes just such a spiritual element in men, and just such an origin of that element, as philosophy approves.   We have observed, in preceding pages, that it gives the name *spirit* to God's Spirit Being, and to the influence of that Spirit, and to the Spirit Being of a man, and to the nature or disposition of that personal spirit.

Birth from above,— from God— from spirit.

A large part, probably the larger part, of the verses of The New Testament in which the word *spirit* is used, have reference to human spirits.   This is true of many verses in which a hasty reader supposes that God's personal Spirit is mentioned, but which, by that supposition, are divested of intelligible meaning.   For illustration we cite a few such verses.   Such is the second chapter of *I Corinthians*, a most powerful exposition of the nature of spiritual wisdom.

I John, v. 8.

Such is *Rom. viii, 23, 26, 27.* "Ourselves, who have the first fruit of the spirit, even we, ourselves, groan in ourselves, waiting for the installation as Sons, the redemption of our bodies, * * * In like manner also, the (our) spirit comes to the help of our feebleness. For, what we may properly pray for, we do not understand; but itself the (our) spirit helpfully intervenes with unuttered groans. And he that searches hearts knows what is the disposition of the (our) spirit, that according to God it intervenes on behalf of saints." Perhaps we cannot comment on this passage in a better way than by citing Philo, who says, in reference to *Gen. iii, 16, and Exod. ii, 23:* "Groaning is a violent and intense pain. It is of a twofold nature. * * * As soon as vice is dead, the man who sees God and his way groans, * * * When the evil disposition is dead, the soul groans over the committed sins. Wherefore, also, it cries out to the Sovereign, beseeching that it may not be again perverted, nor attain an imperfect end." *On Allegories of The Sacred Laws, Book III, chs. 70, 71, 75.*

"God breathed into Man from above (*ánothen*) something of his own divine nature. And that divine nature stamped its impress on the (man's) invisible soul. * * * One part of our soul is endowed with utterance * * * and that part alone has formed a conception of God. * * * God does not reject his suppliants, especially when, groaning at the Egyptian deeds and passions, they cry to him in sincerity and truth. * * * We bewail and groan over ourselves * * * and the law, taking pity on our lamentations, gently receives our suppliant souls." *On The Worse Plotting Against The Better, ch. 25.*

For The New Testament's exposition of the nature of human spirit, we must go chiefly and first to words of

Jesus in *John iii, 3–9.*   Nicodemus, a "President of a Synagogue," had come to him with questions, evidently about the nature of the baptism of repentance, and its symbolism of birth. Jesus repeated the doctrine to him, saying, " I say to you emphatically, positively (Amen! Amen!), whoever (or, if any one) is not born from above (*ánothen*) cannot see the Kingdom of God."

Spirit in
John iii, 3–9.

The word *ánothen* means both *from above* and *again.* We have observed * that Philo uses it a great many times in the signification *from above*, in declaring that human spirits are born *from above*, from Divine Spirit, and that some wise men are inspired from above. Philo's doctrine, being derived from *Genesis*, which it was the business of Nicodemus to expound to " The Congregation," was doubtless familiar to Nicodemus; but he did not see that this had any relation to another birth, although Philo had pretty nearly a doctrine of a second literal spiritual birth from above.

Jesus reiterates to him, " I say to you emphatically, positively, whoever is not born of water and spirit cannot enter into the kingdom of God.   That which is born out of the flesh is flesh; and that which is born out of the spirit is spirit.   Do not wonder because I said to you, ' Ye must be born from above.'   The wind blows where it will, and thou hearest its voice, and knowest not whence it comes and whither it goes. So is every one that is born out of the spirit."

In this discourse, Jesus seems not merely to reiterate the doctrine that men must come into a new spiritual

* See page 165. Compare *James i, 17, 18.* " Every bestowal, and every perfect gift, is from above (*ánothen*), and cometh down from the Father of Lights, * * * for He bore us by the Word of Truth."

state; but he lays a foundation and defense for that doctrine. He says, in effect: If men are not both from Earth and from Heaven, they are not capable of having a part in the kingdom of God which I am to establish. Only what is of spirit can be spiritual. You cannot trace out spirit and the spiritual life; but the birth from water cannot make men moral beings, and is not all the life that men have. Birth of all human spirits from above, from God, out of spirit, is the foundation of all spiritual philosophy, and makes possible the whole system of divine spiritual effects, and new spiritual conditions, for those spirits of men who have blessed places in the kingdom of The Son of God.

From the first principles, thus proclaimed, The New Testament becomes a wonderful treatise on human spiritual life. God's Spirit and men's spirits, and the living agencies and influences that, from God's Spirit, act on human spirits, to change* them "From glory to glory as by The Spirit of The Lord"—these are among its chief themes. Probably in more than a hundred places, the glory, illumination, and blessedness of human spirits, from the ministries of God's Spirit, are spoken of. This makes The New Testament a book of cheer and of moral power, and a philosophy for all time and all men.

This makes, the writings not less of Peter and Jude, than of John and Paul, glow with a heavenly light. This gleams in The Epistle to the Hebrews, where God is called† "Father of Spirits," and where there is mention of‡ "Spirits of just men made perfect, and of‖ "The

* II Cor. iii. 18.
† Heb. xii, 9.
‡ Heb. xii, 23.
‖ Heb. iv, 12.

Word that discriminates souls and spirits," and of "Eternal Spirit," through whom, or which, Christ offered himself to God.*

But perhaps it is Paul who most clearly states the doctrines as philosophy. He says: "A psychical man does not receive the things of God's Spirit; for they are folly to him, and he cannot understand, because they are spiritually discerned. But he who is spiritual discerns all things, but is himself discerned by no one." *1 Cor. ii, 14.* Paul also perceives the relation of spirit-life to immortality, and says, "It is sown a psychical (or soul-ish) body. It is raised a spiritual (*pneumatic*, i. e., adapted to spirit) body. If there is a psychical body, there is also a spiritual." *1 Cor. xv, 42.*

Among the sentences of The New Testament are some of the Apostle John, many of them being sayings of Jesus, which indicate that Jesus said a great deal about spirit as a gift of God, and about those ideas of which baptism is a symbol. He said much to make water an emblem; but it was water quickened into life by Spirit. So he uses the word *water* as a symbol of spirit in connection with life; and the phrase "Water of life" remained in the mind of John, emblematic of life from the Spirit of God. For example, he said, "Whosoever drinketh of the water that I shall give him shall never thirst; but the water that I shall give him shall become in him a well of water, springing up into eternal life." *John iv, 14.*

Again he said, "He that believeth on me, as the Scripture hath said, out of his belly† shall flow rivers of living water." John adds, "This spake he of the spirit

---

Heb. ix, 14.

†The word translated *belly* (*koilia*) often means *heart.*

which they that believed on him were to receive. For
the spirit was not yet (given)." *John vii, 38, 39.* Jesus
seems to use here some old phraseology and ideas, but
makes them the occasion for saying that he is himself
the source of spiritual life. We may compare some
words of Philo, who says: " The face is irrigated, as from
a fountain, from the dominant part of the soul; making
the visual spirit reach the eyes, that for hearing reach
the ears, etc."*

Jesus seems here to refer to *The Song of Solomon, iv,
15,* "Thou art a fountain of gardens, a well of living
waters, and flowing streams from Lebanon." He probably cites from some paraphrase or commentary. The
name Lebanon, which is Greek, is made from the
Hebrew word *laban, white,* and without the Greek final
syllable is in Arabic and some Syriac dialects *liban,*
which is in form the same as the Syriac words, " Our
heart."

Let us now resurvey some of the differences between
the doctrine of spirit in The New Testament, and that of
other philosophies.

There were beliefs about spirits, among Egyptians,
Greeks, Romans, and others; but these had no element
of real philosophy, because they had no definite ideas of
causation, or of the relations of beings. The Oriental
beliefs, as a class, were forms of monistic pantheism.
They had, it is true, recognitions of personalities and
antagonistic forces; but, as philosophies, their fundamental belief was of an universal, or single, essence or
substance, in which force, intelligence, and moral character, had their source and being. They were and are
materialism, refined, disguised, and colored.

* *On Fugitives, chap. 32.*

In the mingling ideas of the East and the West, there had germinated the beginnings of ruder monistic pantheisms. In fact, material science, restless, forceful, but uncertain of itself, was pushing to the front. It had made a strong leap forward in Aristotle's works. It had been a large factor in the skepticism which followed Platonism. In Philo's time it had become so advanced that he almost reached* a clear description of the digestion of food, and of the circulation of the blood, enormous factors in materialism.

With pretensions of science and philosophy, monistic pantheism enslaved all theories of Nature and Spirit, and held them, and largely still holds them, with a grip of steel under a smooth and cushioned glove.

All philosophies of this kind have the essential fault, that they have no logical, rational, or scientific, explanation or statement of causation, or of the activities of Beings, and yet are very pronounced in some declarations about the activities and relations of Beings. Their essential weakness they try to hide, by diverting attention to logical puzzles with the words *being, essence,* and *substance,* and by euphemistic, but empty, phrases.

These philosophies we may divide into general classes, according as they are more or less crudely materialistic.

One class makes matter its God; although it claims to honor only subtle forces, invisible agencies, and recondite laws. It, after all is said, refuses to separate force from substance. It has no conception of personality in The First Cause, because it confounds character with substance. It affirms that force, and character, and intelligence, are imparted by The First Cause, by its giving or

*On Animals Fit for Sacrifice, chap. 7.

subdividing its substance. It knows souls only as parts of the universal being, having their intelligence and character as part of their substance. It has no real philosophy, because it has no idea of causation, no belief of any wisdom, no basis for morality in any authority.

Another class is represented in Philo. It acknowledges one universal *substance*—causative of life, intelligence, and sentiments of morality—but calls it Spirit and God, or part of God. But this is still a refined, materialistic, and monistic pantheism; for it affirms that intelligence, character, and sentiments, are inherent in the *substance*, and are imparted by bestowal of part of that substance. This also has no real philosophy, because it has no real recognition of causation, or of moral relativity, nor any intelligible theory of intelligence.

Other classes deny the imputation of materialism. They affirm the existence of Universal Being, causative, intelligent, and good; but they hide it with veils and painted screens. They divert attention with phrases about Unity, Universality, and all the witching words of philosophy, which mean something or nothing, as you please. But, however fine-phrased these theories of being are, they are radically materialistic and pantheistic, in that they have no definite ideas of causation, or of intelligence, or of morality. After all is said, their philosophy is a doctrine that all that is best in men is a part of the Universal Being, having intelligence in its *substance*, and returnable perhaps, who knows? to absorption in that substance. This, no matter what its phrases and pretensions may be, is an abandonment and negation of philosophy.

Against all these theories, The New Testament comes with a doctrine that is a real philosophy, because it de-

fines the being of God, and that of men, and their relations to each other.   It defines God by his doings and
his character, in his personality, and then says, "He is
(a) spirit."   In this definition there is no thought of
substance, or of materialism.   In this definition the conception of a spirit comes, not from below, nor from
matter, *but from above, and from the nature and vitality
of the Supreme Being as a person.

In such spirit-being, there are conceivable, personality, force, character, and relations, that are not substantial, and causation that antedates and outreaches matter.
In this are possibilities of moral relations of God and
men; because in it are true fatherhood and childship,
constituted by a relation of causation and likeness, with
complete personal selfness.

When it is said, "God is a spirit," and this is accepted
as defining the word *spirit*, it is not thereby said all
Spirit is God, any more than to say, "Man is a spirit,"
is to say Spirit is man.   It is just saying, Spirit, as
essence, is divine, and is common to God and men, but
not to men as animals and material.   It is placing spirit
above mind and nearer God, rather than at the bottom of
the scale, under mind, and in the flesh and blood.

To say, "God is a spirit," is to open up glimpses of
wonderful and glorious, if unexplorable, possibilities in
personal beings and in life.   It is to say that we have
gained a conception, or a word, which contains in itself
some parts, if not the whole, of all that is common to
God and men, and of the relations of God and men,
and of the influences and acts of God in men.

With the doctrine "that God is Spirit," there came
the full declaration that God is "Father of Spirits," and

*See page 271.

the proclamation of the fatherhood of God became chief among the utterances of Jesus; because without it the rest were unintelligible, if not meaningless. Then the declaration that "God created man in his own likeness" became a proclamation of the dignity and blessedness of God's children. Then he, whom men called "Son of God," but who loved better to call himself "Son of Man," taught the children of men to say* "Our Father who art in heaven," "Pray to the (your) Father who is in secret," "Glorify your Father who is in heaven."†

A new language and a new philosophy came to the Earth when Jesus said,‡ "That ye may be the children of your Father. * * * Be ye perfect, even as your Father"; and‖ "One is your Father, who is in heaven"; and§ "It is your Father's good pleasure to give you the kingdom." And that proclamation had wonderful power and persuasiveness when the Apostles took it up, and said,¶ "Behold, what manner of love the (our) Father hath bestowed on us, that we should be called the children of God; and we are, * * * beloved, we are now children of God."

The Gospel calls God's children "Heirs" (*kleronomones*). It summons the children home, to the Father's home, and to the Father's heart. And the child hears, because it is born to the language and the hearing of heaven; and it answers, because it has the nature of a heaven-born spirit; and it goes to the Father's breast because, and only because, there is its home.

Matt. vi, 6, 18.
†*Matt. v, 16.*
‡*Matt. v, 45, 48.*
‖*Matt. xxiii, 9.*
§*Luke xii, 32.*
¶*I John iii, 1, 2.*

In this it confirms to us that philosophy which we have outlined in the first part of this book. It draws a sharp line, but an impassable gulf, between, on the one side, such philosophies as build on materialistic conceptions, or verbal logic, or such words as *substance* and *being* and *essence*, and, on the other side, its own philosophy, which builds on *doing*, and on spiritual causation, and on character and relations. It builds on the facts of that *spirit-being* of which God is the ideal and the source, a being which is inconceivable as a thing, indefinable as a word, but known in its power, character, and relations.*

This doctrine of the fatherhood of God, and childship of human beings, involves the philosophy of several matters, which we may well stop to survey. Such are immortality, rightness, and the adoption (or installation) as children of God.

We have shown, we think, in the first part of this book,† that certain principles of moral science carry an argument for the immortality of human souls. These principles are as follows: Human spirits are, in some vital way, children of God's Spirit. They are moral beings, and under God's moral law, because they, by virtue of this spiritual kinship, are parts of the same moral system of relations. This system requires a future judgment and an immortal life for its own completeness.

Immortality.

These principles are precisely those which Jesus and The New Testament affirm. And these they supplement by such an array of declarations and principles that the doctrine of human personal immortality is involved in

---

*Or, in the language of categories, "*quality*, *modality*, and *relations*."

†See page 68.

the beginning, end, and whole structure of Christian
beliefs.

It was pronounced at the first word of the Gospel, in
baptism, which, in effect, said: "God, who once formed
bodies from water, and vitalized them by his Spirit, will
raise the dead bodies again, and demands that also their
spirits, whose moral alienation is a death, shall be
revived to pure spiritual life."   We do not need to cite,
and have not space to quote, many texts to detail these
doctrines.   They are the core of Christ's talk to Nicodemus.   That they were common ideas with the Disciples, appears from such sayings as Paul's in *I Cor. xv,
29.*   "What will they do (effect) who are baptized on
behalf of the (their) dead bodies, if in fact (*hólōs*) dead
bodies are not raised; and why are they baptized on their
behalf?"

Jesus found the Jews imbued with a belief tnat the
dead will rise, and that there will be a judgment of
spirits.   These beliefs had come to them as a branch, or
a fruit, of the tree of the Old Testament's words and
spirit.   These beliefs Jesus approved, and he wrought
them into the body, and every part, of his system of
truth.   The declaration that He was Himself constituted
Judge of spirits, and bestower of the new and best spiritual life, was made a central and effulgent doctrine in
the Gospel of Jesus and of the Apostles.*

Jesus and the Apostles seem to have been even more
intent on the philosophy of immortality than on the
mere fact of it.   It was the relation of immortality to

*On resurrection.   See *John v, 28, 29; vi, 39, 50, 54; xvii,
2, 3; Rom. vi, 8; viii, 11; I Cor. xv; I Thes. iv, 15; II
Cor. v, 1.*
On judgment.   See *Matt. xiii, 30. 41, 49; John v, 22, 27;
Rom. ii, 16; II Tim. iv, 1; I Pet. iv, 5; Rev. xx, 12.*

righteousness, and to happiness, that chiefly occupied them.   The life towards which they pointed was holy life; and the terrible death was sin.

It is these references to fundamental principles that obscure somewhat the declarations of immortality or the resurrection; but the recognition and statement of these principles by Jesus make him stand forth foremost of philosophers.   Some of these recognitions are in Jesus' doctrine of spirit and of the reformed spiritual life, as we have already noted it.   Others reach the utmost scope of philosophical vision into the connections and relations of Divine Being to Human Being.

Such are these: "I am the resurrection and the life. He that believeth on me though he die, yet shall he live. And whosoever liveth and believeth on me shall never die." *John xi, 25.*

"It is the will of my Father that every one that beholdeth the Son, and believeth on him, should have eternal life; and I will raise him up at the last day." *John vi, 40.*

No philosopher of the World has so declared the principles of the philosophy of moral life, as a connection of life, and a mutual and reciprocal relation, as Jesus has done in such sentences as these, and others in *John xvii.*

"This is the eternal life,* to know Thee, the only true God, and him whom Thou didst send, Jesus Anointed." *John xvii, 3.*

"As the Father hath life in himself, even so gave He to the Son also to have life in himself.   And He gave

---

Hina ginōskōsi, commonly translated, "That they might know," is the modern Greek *infinitive mode.* This form of the infinitive is very common in The New Testament.

him authority to execute judgment, *because he is the Son of Man.*" *John v, 27.*

"As I live because of the Father, so he that eateth* me, he also shall live because of me. * * * The (your) spirit is what makes (you) alive. The flesh helps not at all." *John vi, 57-63.*

"I am the way, and the truth, and the life. No man comes to The Father except through me." *John xiv, 6.*

In our survey of The Apocalypse, and of the apocalyptic sayings which seem to have had derivation from Jesus,† we saw Daniel's prophecies of immortality confirmed and enlarged. We saw the millenium of the deceased saints, and the eternal fate of the wicked impenitent. We saw endless glory and bliss of Christ and his people, assured not only in The Apocalypse, but in many, and indeed all, the promises, or prophecies, of Christ and the Apostles.

So, the doctrine of the immortality of human·spirits glows in all The New Testament, as a line of golden light, establishing an authority, and reason, for moral law, exhilarating human life, and turning hope and faith to the eternal presence of The Lord with his immortal Bride.

§6.   HUMAN RIGHTNESS

We said also (page 295) that the doctrine of God's fatherhood involves the philosophy of human rightness. By *rightness* we mean an idea which every human being has in some form. But to explain it is to plunge into the depths of philosophy. We may say that it is excellence of personal being and happiness. But is that all?

---

* Compare *John iv, 34,* "My food is doing the will of him that sent me."

†See pages 253, 256.

What have Reason and Conscience to say about the matter? They bring into the problem divine elements. They ask, What are the aims, ideals, and rights, of The First Cause, The Creator? and, What are the disturbing elements in life? They ask, Which is best for men, rightness or happiness? and, Can happiness be attained except by rightness? What theme of greater interest can engage a mortal man?

The philosophy of The New Testament, in this matter, is complete, as no other is. It studies the aim of human life from two view-points, and with two ideals: those of The Creator, and those of the man himself. Finding men puzzled with the questions, How much of human excellence is in character, and how much in actions of men? and, How much of the ideal, or law, is the character, and how much the Will of God? it offers solutions of these problems, by presenting the only array of principles, which can be combined in one harmonious and satisfying system. *The aim.*

⁓Finding multitudes of persons believing that happiness is the natural right of men, and that it should be conferred on all men, by Nature or God, or whatever other Power the men may believe to be supreme, The New Testament adduces the sufficient, and only, principles of the philosophy of happiness.

We need only recapitulate here the chief principles of this philosophy; for it is that which occupies the foregoing pages of this book. They are: Causation by personal God,—The rights of the Creator, by virtue of causation,—The spirit-being of God, having loves, will, and all excellences of character,—The ideal result, sought by God's will, being what his wisdom, nature, and love, intelligently pursue,—Man is God's creature,

and is therefore rightly subject to his absolute will,—
Man is spirit, from God's Spirit, and is therefore capable
of such harmony with God as to find perfect happiness
in God's will,—Man is God's child, and is therefore of
the one system of life in which all things of human life
are mutually related, and related to God,—Man is
endowed with such intellectual and moral consciousness
that he knows the demands of God's will, as both a law
from God's authority, and an excellence from God's
character,—Man's happiness can be found only in his
conformity to what God's intelligent will demands, and
his loving Spirit desires,—Man's disturbing element,
and wrecking force, is his free will, without which, however, he would not be a spirit, nor God's Child, nor a
moral being, nor capable of any of that exalted and
exquisite pleasure which God's purposes design for him,
—Individuals are members of a system, in which the
free will of other persons, the intelligence of all, and
the processes of Nature have place,—Men must be freely
like God in character, and be obedient to his will, or be
miserable and cause misery to others.

Among these principles, there are certain ones which
have the most near and direct relation to human rightness, and are therefore to be specially observed in this
connection.

Human Nature has always chafed under the authority
of God's will.   Nature in petty ways, in sensual lines, in
passionate courses, has always been more enticing to
men than God's will in the larger view, the greater plan,
and the higher ways.   Greatness and goodness come by
endeavor and by victory.   If this were not so, all things
would be alike contemptible, or detestable.

Even philosophy and theology have shrunk from

declaring that God's will is the cause of his law, and so the ideal of the aims of human life.   Men wise and good and sweet, perhaps *because* they were good and sweet, have rather said, Holiness is self-existent, and God's character and loves are the cause of his law, and human rightness is in character and sentiments.   Even some theologians whose expositions are, as a whole, grand and noble, exhibit the holiness of God as something more causative of his law than his pure will is.

The New Testament rises above all narrow and imperfect views, and harmonizes all the good elements in all these ideas.   First, it presents to us God, the Cause; strong in power, authority, and will; worship-worthy because he is Almighty and The Cause.   When it has done this, and so has maintained his rights to order both the World and Man, and to make his will the standard of excellence, then it magnifies the spirit-excellence of God, and its likeness in men, and extols the goodness and holiness of his will, as we know these in their harmony with all the best nature of men.

We repeat that, The New Testament portrays God's will, giving commands for the activities or doings of men.

Conductive philosophy has led us to God known as a person, known in his doings.   It has shown that all known life is action, and that what we call *qualities* and *character* are not existent apart from activities, but are names for relativities of actions.   So the person and the holiness of God may be partially compared to the forces of Nature and to light.   The forces work, however covered the material may be, and in the darkness.   When the light rises over the field of work, it is radiant with beauty and glory, and some processes of the forces are

aided, and some are hindered. But if the light itself
does anything, it has the power to do because it is, to
that degree, a force, in the same class with the other
physical forces; and not because it makes beauty or
reveals operations.

So the philosophy of The New Testament presents
God's holiness as an excellence of his being, and always
displayed in his will and his acts; but it keeps
God's Will
the law.
always foremost, as authority, and as law and
guide for men, God's personal indescribable
being, in which intelligence, power, and holy character
join together to make what we call Will. Or, we may
say, The New Testament magnifies God's holiness, as
indicative of the kind of his will; but does not let it
obscure our view of his person and his rights, as All-
wise, and All-mighty, and The Creator.

Conductive philosophy has also shown us that *human*
excellence is in men's *doings.* Character is sometimes
glorious; but character is known only in acts, for philosophy* knows no life except the activities. So also The
New Testament reaches the fundamental principles, and
tears away the flimsy delusions, with which we persuade
ourselves that sentiments in us can excuse the lack of
obedience. The New Testament magnifies obedience to
God, and glorifies service of The Lord.

Jesus taught fundamental principles when he said,
"Pray ye, Our Father! Thy kingdom come! Thy Will
be done. Not every one that says unto me, Lord, shall
enter into the kingdom of Heaven; but he that does the
Will of my Father." *Matt. vii, 21.*

"Whosoever shall do God's Will is my Brother."

*See page 38.

Mark iii, 35.   St. Paul says, "The mystery of his Will, according to the good pleasure which He hath purposed in himself,   *   *   *   Who worketh all things after the counsel of his own Will." *Eph. i, 9, 11.*

"We do not cease to pray that ye might be filled with the knowledge of his Will, in all wisdom and spiritual understanding." *Col. i, 9.*

As to the nature of sin, the Apostles say—

"Where there is not a law, neither is there a transgression." *Rom. iv, 15.*

"Not the hearers of a law are justified in their relation to God; but the obeyers of a law shall be justified." *Rom. ii, 13, 14, 15.*

"Because, in consequence of facts of law, 'All flesh shall be not justified' in his presence; for through law is knowledge of sin." *Rom. iii, 19, 20.*

"Is the law sin?   No!   But I would not have recognized sin except through a law.   For, also, I would not have understood covetousness if the law had not said, 'Thou shalt not covet.'   But sin, taking start through the commandment, operated in me all covetousness; for apart from a law sin is dead." *Rom. vii, 7, 8, 9.*

St. John says: "Every one who performs (*poieî*) sin, performs also unlawful doing (*anomia*); and sin is unlawful doing (or lawlessness)." *I John iii, 4.*

As to the nature of human rightness, as being active obedience, Jesus says: "My Father is working, up to the present time, and I am working." *John v, 17.*   "We must work the works of him that sent me." *John ix, 4.*   "The things which proceed out of the mouth come forth out of the heart, and they defile the man." *Matt. xv, 18, 20.*   In this last paragraph, Jesus does indeed indicate that sins take character from the heart; but he none the less declares that it is the doings of a man that defile him.*

The Apostle James, also, has written of this matter, in a way that is eminently practical, yet reaches to fundamental principles. He begins by recognizing the value of character, and the tests of it; but he also sees that life is doing, and rightness is obedience. He says: "Be ye doers of the word, and not hearers only, deluding yourselves. * * * He that looketh into the perfect law, that of liberty, and continueth, being not a hearer that forgetteth, but a doer that worketh, this man shall be blessed in his doing." *James i, 22, 25.*

"So do as men that are to be judged by a law of liberty. * * * Faith, if it have not works, is dead in itself. * * * Faith, apart from works, is barren. * * * By works was faith made perfect. * * * Faith, apart from works, is dead." *James ii, 12, 17, 20, 26.*

We repeat, then, that The New Testament doctrine of human excellence starts from the Will and law of God respecting human actions. Sometimes when we chafe under authority, even of our Creator, and rebel against the idea that righteousness is a matter of God's *Will*, we glow with admiration of the conception that both divine

---

*It may interest some readers to compare Christ's profundity of philosophy with Aristotle. See *Ethics I, i, 1 ; Metaphysics VIII, 6 to end of Book VIII. Also Book X, chap. 9, and Book XI, chap. 5 to 7.* Aristotle makes a careful study of energy (*energeia*), as it is involved in both knowing and the virtues. Among other excellent things, he says: "To be ignorant that by energizing on every subject the habitual dispositions are produced, shows a man to be stupid." *Ethics III, 5, 12.* Philo says: "Moses makes the utterer responsible for whatever goes out through the mouth, because the act of speaking is one which is in our own power." *On the Change of Scripture Names, chap. xlii.*

and human excellence are in character and loves. We abhor the idea of mechanical, servile, and perfunctory rightness; but the idea of being like God, in character and sentiments, appears to us magnificent.

The philosophy of The New Testament justifies and teaches these ideas and sentiments; but it does this without disturbance of these other principles which we have recognized. It brings the principles, on both lines, together, in such ways that each exalts and strengthens the other.

It recognizes that, as we have affirmed in our survey of the principles of philosophy, a Will cannot want anything but acts. A Will is itself an activity, and it calls for activities. The idea that a Will, or a law, can call for anything but activities, is fundamentally unphilosophical, irrational, and absurd. We have said also, that all our general conceptions come to us in facts, things, and events, and would not exist without the facts, things and events. We have said that life is unknowable except as activities of concrete things.

We have seen that consciousness knows* nothing but active facts, events and things, and knows no causation by The Creator except by his cosmical Will. We have seen† that our moral consciousness, or conscience, knows things, facts, and events as having ends, values, relations to the loves of God, and relations to his plans for human beings, and that conscience takes note of our attitude and sentiments towards the Will of The . Creator for cosmical things. Hence The New Testament teaches a true philosophy, in teaching that human rightness is what conforms to the rights of The Creator as The

*See page 38.
†See page 55.

Cause, and that his rights are to execute his Will respecting all the life-activities of human beings.

But this is a partial and one-sided view, an intellectual and cosmical view. Supplementing, illuminating, and coloring this, The New Testament presents, as the aim of God for men (and as the excellence of human beings), personal nobility of being.

Personal nobility.

It does this by that philosophy of spirit-being which we have detailed. According to this, the Will of God, as to what is moral in personal relations, is itself the utterance of his Spirit; and our Will, our obedience, in moral relations are matters of our spirit-being.

The conception of moral nobility and performance, which The New Testament sets before us, is so wise, complete, and exalted, that any attempt to detail it in descriptions, or by citation of texts, would dim its luster, and detract from its glory. Spirit-life, as it is pictured in ideal in The New Testament, is the consummate conception of excellence and happiness.

It is an ideal of Man in God's image,—Man God's child,—Man a Spirit,—Man's nobility an obedience, but a free and glad obedience, of a spirit living its best nature, in response to, and in sympathy with, the Spirit of The Father. It is an ideal of a double glory,—the glory of exalted being and performance,—and of a living temple of a present God.

This free glory stands forth, in the words of Christ, in such sentences as these:

"If ye abide in my word * * * the truth shall make you free. * * * If The Son shall make you free; ye shall be free indeed." *John viii, 31, 36.*

" He that believes on me, the doings that I do, will he do also." *John xiv, 12.*

"If a man love me, he will keep my word; and my Father will love him; and we will come to him, and make our abode with him." *John xiv, 23.* See also *John xv, 5; xvii, 16, 22.*

In this connection, The New Testament grapples with, and elucidates, the problem of the moral character of the physical life and acts of our bodies. It does this with a thoroughness of philosophical science, and psychological exactness, not elsewhere in literature attempted or approached.

How human souls, in their deepest experiences, agonize with this problem; sometimes glowing with the splendor of a lofty ideal; sometimes singing in conscience the peans of victory; sometimes bowing in the humiliation of defeat and shame!

The principles of The New Testament in this matter are these, viz.: Every act of a human being has a relation to the person's conformity to God's ideal for him, or to his obedience to, or attitude towards, God person, or to the welfare of other beings, and is therefore a moral relation. But it is not thus far a moral act of the person, but only an occasion for a moral act. When, towards this occasion or relation, the person's spiritual Will acts, or refuses to act, there is a moral act and moral state of this person.* A human person is, therefore, under laws of physical Nature that seek his good; but which are also alternative laws, punitive and destructive, "Laws of sin and death." In this " Body of sin and death," the real Man, the true Self, fights his battles, wins his victories, rules as a King, or stands as a

*See page 99.

holy temple of the Spirit of God, when the spirit is quick with the spiritual life from The Father.

The statement of this philosophical doctrine is chiefly the work of St. Paul, although its elements are in the principles enunciated by Jesus. Some of his words we quote without comment, except by exercising some liberty of translation and suggestion.

" I buffet my body, and bring it to service; lest, in any way, after having preached to others, I myself become blamable." *I Cor. ix, 27.*

" Ye are not in the flesh, but in the (your) spirit, if God's Spirit dwells in you. * * * If Christ is in you, (although) the body is dead by its relation to sin, yet the (your) spirit is life by its relation to righteousness." *Rom. viii, 9.*

" When we were in the flesh (i. e., were fleshly), the sinful experiences, which were through the law, wrought in our members, to bring forth fruit to death. But now, we have been discharged from that law, * * * so that we serve in newness of the (our) spirit, and not in old-ness of the letter. * * * I would not have understood sin except through the law. * * * Sin, finding occasion, wrought in me, through the commandment, all manner of desire; for apart from the law sin is dead. And I was alive apart from the law (or when not confronted by a law); but when the statute came (to my knowledge), sin came to action, and I (morally) died.

"So the law is holy, and the commandment holy, and righteous and good. * * * But sin, that it might be shown to be sin, by working death to me through that which is good (i. e. naturally, when out of moral relations) did become deadly. * * * We know that the (divine) law is spiritual; but I (regarded in the wholeness of my being) am bound to my flesh, sold under sin. For what I am performing I do not (fully) understand; for, not what I will to do, do I perform; but I perform what I (in my spirit) hate. * * * So, in that case, it is not I (my spirit-self) that perform it; but sin (animalness) that has dwelling in me. * * * I delight, with my inward man, in God's law; but I see a different law in my members, warring against the law of my mind, and bringing me into captivity (this is not, however, obedience) to the law of sin (i. e. sinfulness) in my members."

"Wretched (am) I, a man! Who shall deliver me out of this body, this body of death? I thank God, through Jesus Christ our Lord! So then I, Self, with my mind, am subservient to God's law; but with my flesh to the law of sin (or for sin)." *Rom. vii.*

We cannot suppose that St. Paul in this chapter is bewailing a special infirmity of his own. He is not wailing at all; but singing a song of triumph. He is stating principles of moral philosophy, as they relate to human beings on Earth, and he is glorifying the power of a person's spirit to rule the body.

And St. Paul continues, in the next chapter, the declaration of the advancing nobility of God's children, when their bodies serve their spirits, and their spirits, freely, in the nature of children of God, respond to God's, The Creator's, Will.

"The law of the spirit (and) of life, in Christ Jesus, made me free from the law of sin and of death, * * * that the righteous end of the law might be made full in us, who walk not according to flesh, but according to spirit. * * * The thought (or *animus*, or disposition, *phrónēma*) of the (our or any) flesh is death; but that of

the (our or any) spirit is life and peace. * * * Ye are
not in flesh, but in spirit, if spirit of God dwells in you.
* * * And if Christ is in you, the (your) body is dead,
on account of sinfulness, but the (your) spirit is life, on
account of righteousness. But if the Spirit of him that
raised up Jesus from the dead (ones) dwelleth in you, he
that raised up Christ Jesus shall also make alive your
mortal bodies, through his Spirit dwelling in you. * * *
As many as are led by Spirit of God, they are Sons of
God. * * * And ye received (a) spirit of installation
as Sons, by which we cry Abba (Syriac for The Father),
The (our) Father. The (received) Spirit bears witness
with our spirit that we are Children of God."

"I reckon that the experiences of the present time are
trifling in comparison with the glory which is going to
be revealed in (or to) us. For the (our) created part's
eager watching is waiting for the uncovering (*apocalypsis*)
of God's Sons. For the (our) created part was subjected
to vainness, not voluntarily, but on account of the Sub-
jecter, in connection with a hope that the (our) created
part itself shall be released from the bondage of corruption, into the liberty of God's children."

"For we know that all the (our) created part joins in
groaning * and travailing until now. And not only is
this true, but also we (our real, or whole, or best) Selves,
having the initiation (or first fruits) of the (our) spirit,
even we Selves, in ourselves, do groan, awaiting the (our)
installation as Sons, the redemption of our body (or our
redemption of the body). * * * And we know that
to those who love God, and who are called according to
his purpose, all things (parts) coöperate towards (a or
their) good (or goodness, or a good result). Because,

* In reference to groaning of our spirit. See page 286.

those whom he forethought he also predefined (to be) of like form with the image of his Son, that He might be firstborn among many brothers." *Rom. viii.*

Again, in a few words, St. Paul declares the principles, that sin is not the bodily act, but the spiritual; but that the acts are wished because the spirit does act in them; and that moral excellence comes through coöperation of the Divine Spirit and the human spirit.

" Every sin which a man may do is apart (separate) from the (his) body. But the fornicator sins against his body. Or know ye not that our body is a temple of the Holy Spirit which is in us, which ye have from God, and ye are not your own? Glorify God, therefore, in your body."

"The body is for The Lord, and The Lord for the body. * * * Know ye not that your bodies are Christ's members? * * * He that is attached to The Lord is one spirit."*

St. Paul also repeats the same doctrines, that the body is deathly, and burdensome, but the spirit of the man can rule it.

" Wherefore, that I may not be too exalted, there was given me, by (or to, or for) my flesh, a stake, an angel (messenger) of Satan (or an adversary), to buffet me. On behalf of this (fact) I thrice besought The Lord that it (the body? or the stake?) may separate from me. And he said to me, My grace suffices for you." *II Cor. xii*, *7, 8, 9.*

What a splendid ideal, what a complete and perfected ideal, of personal nobility of human beings, is thus exhibited to us in The New Testament! In our previous survey of the categories of human person,† we found

* *I Cor. 13 to 20.* † See page 72.

that the ideal of man, which is philosophically constructed, exhibits him first as sound, pure, and vigorous in body, mind, and spirit; then, as in spirit, worshipful, obedient, and loving to his Creator and Father; then, because of both excellence of nature, and of relations established by the Creator and Father of all, as loving, just, and helpful, to his fellow-men.

Such is the New Testament's ideal; presented to us, not alone in moral maxims, but with such influences and helps as kindle a love for the ideal, a devotion to its Author, and an ardor of glad obedience in the relations of life in society. Other religions have the moral maxims; but as they lack love and obedience to The Creator, they fail in practical power. The ideal of humanity, in the New Testament, comes to us accompanied by motives and forces that give it vigorous effect.

The first part of the ideal we have seen in the words of St. Paul. To these many more might be added. It begins in words of Christ himself.

" Be ye complete, as your Father in Heaven is complete." *Matt. v, 48.*

" If thine hand or thy foot makes thee stumble, cut it off, and throw it away." *Matt. v, 29.*

Then it stands out, magnificent, in the whole New Testament; not alone in laws and prohibitions, but in the glorification of spiritual life, and in the exhibition of Jesus for the ideal, and of close relations with God for the sources of power, a power in which the freeness of the human Self is glorified.

" The Lord is The Spirit. And where the Spirit of The Lord is, liberty is. But, we all, with an uncovered face, mirroring the Lord's glory, are transformed, in reference to that image, from a glory to (another higher) glory, in that way in which (it comes) from The Lord, The Spirit." *II Cor. iii, 18.*

"Practice* fully the salvation (or health, or saved state) of yourselves, for God is He who energizes in (or among) you, both in respect to his willing and to his doing, on behalf of benevolence (or kind intent)." *Phil. ii, 12.*

But the ideal is too perfect and grand to be actualized in any one man except Jesus, and so the New Testament presents it as an ideal to be fully realized only in the race of mankind.

"Unto a construction of Christ's body, until we attain, all together, unto the unity of the trust and of the comprehension of God's Son, unto a man complete, unto a measure of maturity of Christ's fullness." *Eph. iv, 13.*

The second part of the ideal man, his rightness towards his Maker and Father, is the chief matter and topic of the whole Bible. Creation and its rights, Fatherhood and its relations, Sonship and its duties and privileges, Spirit and its influences and helps,—these elements of true moral philosophy, are the glory and power of the Bible. Jesus, repeating it from Moses, puts it into these few words,—"This is the first and great commandment. "Thou shalt love The Lord, Thy God, with all thy heart, and with all thy soul, and with all thy reason (*diánoia*), and with all thy force."†

And the Apostle John, sums the essence of all the principles, in these words, "We love him because he first loved us." *I John iv, 19.*

The third part of the ideal, helpfulness to one's

---

* *Ergazomai* is the Greek word from which, through Latin, we get the word *exercise.*

† *Matt. xxii, 37 : Mark xii, 30 : Luke x, 27.*

fellow-men, is so great a part of the lessons and exhortations of The New Testament, that everybody knows it, and it invests Christianity with an unique glory. Other religions may have the maxims, but Christianity alone has its spirit and practice.

Its principle Jesus quotes from The Old Testament.* "Thou shalt love thy neighbor as thyself." And then, from him, the Gospel and its spirit went out, an instruction about love, and a ministry in love.

"Whosoever does not practice righteousness is not from God, neither he who does not love his brother. * * * We know that we have passed out of death into life because we love the (our) brothers. He who does not love stays in death." *I John iii, 10, 14.*

"Every one that loves is begotten of God, and knows God. * * * Hereby do we know that we love God's children, when we love God, and do his commandments." *I John ix, 1, 2.*

What a World this would be, if the Christian ideal were actualized! Imagination cannot construct an adequate description of the glory and blessedness of society, in which all persons should be pure, thoughtful, instructed, and active ; in which all persons should be obedient to their Maker's Will, sympathetic with and responsive to his Spirit, holding Him as the object of their highest love,—and in which all souls were bound together by justice, love, and common aims, and by devotion to a common Creator's plan, and a common Father's desires and universal love.

When justice shall be more than a theory,—when sympathy shall be a vital bond,—when ministry shall

*Lev. xix, 18 : Matt. xix, 19 : xxii, 39 : Mark xii, 31 : Luke x, 27.

be earnest and self-sacrificing,—when Society shall both defend the rights of individuals, and secure the happiness of the masses,—when the thoughts and labors of all men combine to aim to understand the plans of The Maker, and the loves of The Father, and to join the lives of all in one flow of family life, then there will be philosophy made actual,—the life of The Father and his Will being answered in the lives of the children, who are controlled but free,—taught and wise,—serviceable but happy,—self-sphered, but sphered also in God and in humanity.   Then The Father will be known in his children; and the children will know their Selves, in knowing The Father, and in responding as spirit-persons to the wisdom of the divine mind, to the movements of divine force and law, and to the sympathies of the Father's loves.

§ 7.   SALVATION OF MEN

After the plan of God, and his Will for the good and glory of his children, are recognized by us, it remains true that the ideal has not become actual. Disobedience, misery, and unlikeness to God, are in some form an universal spectacle.   Shall we therefore conclude that our philosophy is wrong, and abandon it ?   That would be childish, if not idiotic.   Let us rather note the principles of sin and misery, observe their place in the beneficent plan, and ask if there is not also a provision of remedy, which crowns and glorifies the system.

We have observed that the plan and Will of The Creator and Father have constituted a system, and in the nature of things (i. e. of life and being) could not make anything else but a system, that vast, intricate, and interwoven system, which philosophy recognizes.   This system has personal God

Freewill is the disturber.

for its Cause and Head, Spirit-being for its vitality in moral relations, men with free wills for its material or subjects, and moral law for its governing principles. So far as we can see, no part of this system can be changed without the wreck or annihilation of the whole.

The free Will of men is the disturbing element; but without it there can be no moral glory, no goodness, no childship of God. A system that could not let men sin, could not make them holy; for there could be neither holiness nor happiness in such a system. Not a single element of the greatness, and glory, and bliss, of men could enter into such a system.

Nothing can be more irrational than to blame The Creator for the wickedness of men, or to doubt the personal nature of God because men are wicked. If there was to be a system of life in which men should be good in freeness, good in Will, moral beings—and a system in which souls could progress in goodness, grow in moral excellence, advance in moral strength and spiritual power and glory, that system had to include free Will of souls, with all the risks of sin, of degradation, of wreck of souls by other souls. It had to be perilous or nothing.

We stand appalled at the spectacle of souls ruined, lives made miserable, by acts of other men, of parents, and of society. But here also calm Reason says, There could not be a system in which man should help man, and in which man's chief work for God should be in helping other men, without having, in that way of good, this awful way of woe.

And so, with free Will in all men, free Will controlling thought, study, labor, amusement, and devotedness—free Will towards God,—free Will towards men,—free Will of One crossed and beset by the free Will of all,—free

Will as to ideals crushed down into a struggling, tem-
porizing, feeble Will in respect to what is allowable or
attainable,—the ideal of the system is only partially actualized, and its consummation dawns only far away.

But our philosophy, and only this philosophy of The
Bible, sees hope, and ground for trust. The end proposed cannot fail. Somehow, sometime, the end shall
glorify the plan; the results shall justify all the doings;
and the system, which works in love and aims at happiness, shall crown itself with the garlands of triumph; and
a countless host of glad children of God shall rejoice in
the glory and blessedness of the vast family of The
Father.

Christianity is the one philosophy which comes forward to rescue the wrecked souls, and presents a gospel
of salvation, wonderfully harmonizing with the principles
of Reason. The Old Testament has, indeed, the same
principles; but Christianity brings more light and
help.

In the first part of this book (page 94) we have outlined the hopes which philosophy entertains of the salvation of sinners, and the principles which Reason conceives to be included in any possible plan of salvation.
We now examine the doctrine of salvation presented by
The New Testament, and inquire how far and how well
it accords with rational philosophy. In its general features this doctrine is as follows:

Before the creation of the world a provision was made
for such a salvation of sinners as should justify creation,
and conform to and exhibit the infinite love Outline of
of God. This provision included certain acts the plan of
to be performed, in due time, by that same salvation.
Personality in God, who was Creator and Moral Lord,

and by that other Personality in God, who is Father of Spirits, and is spiritual agency.

This provision became at last operative in time by the incarnation of The Creator, and through operations of The Spirit. Through these, justice was honored, divine indignation allayed, human minds instructed, human good Will revived, human love and trust turned again to God, and human spirits brought into life harmonious with God's.

So much has already been noted in this book respect ing this philosophy of God, that in this connection we need only survey the two topics called commonly *atonement* and *regeneration*.

The reconciliation of men with God our English tongue calls atonement. The word is made from *tone*, and is the same as attunement, or harmoniza- Atonement. tion. The verb *atone* was of later origin, and derived from this noun. The Hebrew uses, in describing the reconciliation, a word that means *covering;* and the Greek uses a word that means *reconciliation* or *propitiation*.

The theme, The Attunement, is one worthy of the pen of The Archangel. It is a theme that comes like the rising of a new sun, bearing gladness and life in its beams. If this sun is eclipsed, or sets again, the dead World must "Swing blind and blackening in the moonless air."

We have shown (page 104) that it is an axiom of moral philosophy that God would not have begun crea-

Began before the creation.

tion unless, in advance, provision was made to meet the evils of freewill in men, provide a salvation, and harmonize the existence of sin and misery with God's justice and love.

That such a provision actually was made is declared,* and first declared, by Jesus; and evidently this was a prominent feature in his teaching; for it is repeated by John,† Peter,‡ Paul,‖ and The Epistle to the Hebrews.§

The reconciliation is represented as having been effected by a Mediator;¶ and this Mediator is declared to have been, before creation, "The Lord God," "The Creator" of men, "The Moral Ruler," "The Word of God," and later "The Man Christ Jesus."

It is probably natural that, commonly, we should take most note of the mediation in time, and of the human mediator; but philosophy takes perhaps more note of the provision that was before time. It sees, perhaps, less importance in the things done later, than in the principles on which those acts could be done, and by which the acts could be effective.

The provision of mediation before creation must present itself to us, chiefly, as a matter of intentions in God. But, as the creation of men was the act of that Personality in God who was to be Moral Lord, and of that other Personality who is Father of Spirits of men, philosophy has to regard the

Atonement a personal influence.

---

*"Inherit the kingdom prepared for you from the foundation of the world." *Matt. xxv, 34.*

†"The Lamb slain from the foundation of the world." *Rev. xiii, 8.*

"Written in the 'Book of Life' from the foundation of the world." *Rev. xvii, 8.*

‡(Christ) "was foreknown before the foundation of the world." *I Pet. i, 20.*

‖ (God) "chose us in Him (Christ) before the foundation of the world." *Eph. i, 4.*

"Which God foreordained before the worlds, unto our glory." *I Cor. ii, 7.*

§"The works were finished from the foundation of the world." *Heb. iv, 3.*

¶*I Tim. ii, 5; Heb. viii, 6; ix, 15, xii, 24.*

provision before creation as, chiefly, a matter of personal relations between the Persons of Triune God.   It stands before us, chiefly, as a matter of personal influence between the Persons of Deity.   If the creation originated in divine love, as philosophy says that it did, and if it was made possible, as philosophy says that it was, by the harmony of purpose and sentiment between the Persons of Deity, then the atonement was largely a matter of personal relations of sentiment, and of that influence of person on person, which accompanies personal life as a glory and joy.

This does not imply that nothing was *done* for atonement.   It rather implies that a great deal was done.   That was done which only persons can do.   That was done which is precious between persons, and which has its value from the fact that it is a personal act.   That was done which only those persons could do, and which had its value from the personalities, and from the relations and sentiments, mutual and reciprocal, of the persons.

The atonement before creation must be conceived, not as a bargain or traffic, not as an unwilling concession wrung from a reluctant person by persuasion, promises, performances, and placations.   It must be conceived as a system, initiated in absolute harmony and coöperation of all the powers, all the persons, all the sentiments of Deity.

Perhaps a sufficiently near approach to a philosophical statement, of the principles of an atonement before creation, is made, if we say that the provision is incorporated in the system initiated by God, but not in that material part which we call " Nature."   It remained a part of the system of personal life, personal relations, moral relations,

that go with the created system, almost like a soul. We
shall understand them, when we fully understand causation, and the rights and perpetual relations that go with
it. Now we can say that it is not in substance, nor in
the essence of spirit; but it is part of the inscrutable
mystery of personal life, and chiefly of the life of The
First Cause.

When we survey, with a reference to the salvation of
men, the principles involved in the philosophy   Vicarious-
of causation, they stand to us in a second   ness.
aspect, quite apart from that which we observed when
we studied the principles of causation with reference to
rights of the Creator in the creature, and the duties of
the creature to the Creator. The word *duty* becomes
more glorified, and signifies a relation of the Creator to
his creatures, a relation of moral obligation, assumed
voluntarily, but perpetually, in the act of creating moral
beings.

In our survey of the outlines of psychology and
philosophy, in the first (see page 77) part of this book,
we made some observations respecting the mutuality and
reciprocity of the relations of a Cause to his creatures,
and respecting the perpetuity of these relations, and respecting the resulting relations of all beings in the system of one creation, to each other. When we further
survey these principles of relativity, and apply them to
the problems of the philosophy of salvation, their scope
widens immensely and gloriously.

Who can define all moral principles? Who can speak
of them without obscuring them? Who can depict the
glories, even of his own conscience, without reducing
them, like a lusterless painting of sun? We confuse and
degrade our ideas of moral being, even more than we do

our definitions of physical things. But God and true philosophy keep separate the things that are distinct; as He keeps ever apart the spectrum hues, which we see as white light or blended tints. And He keeps subtly connected the principles that to us are distinct; even as he joins, between the earth and the sky, the flashing fluid, which we can only force to leap a finger's span.

So, when we survey the principles of the philosophy of causation (which is really the philosophy of ontology or being), we find our ideas tending, in one direction, towards a doctrine that all things are one identical being or essence, and, in an opposite direction, towards an exaggeration of the distinctness, or separation, of the Creator and his creatures. But between these lies the whole system of moral science ; and in this system there inheres, as its glory and power, a principle which we call "Vicariousness."

Vicariousness is the name which we give to the voluntary assumption, by one free being, of the place of another being, in some one or more of his relations. Vicariousness is not, and cannot become, identification or absorption of being. It is and remains a relation, and a voluntary one. A vicariousness, therefore, cannot absolutely annul an old relation, nor absolutely create a wholly new relation. It can occur only in a system where it is made possible by the relations established by its Creator in the act of causation. And it is only possible, as a mutual relation, between two beings who are prepared for such a relation by the inherent nature of the principles of the system.

Vicariousness is, therefore, not unification, but community, not absorption, but place-taking. And it is only possible in respect to beings who have, to some extent, either likeness of nature, or likeness of relation to the Creator, or to his system of created things.

Vicariousness enters, in an immeasurable degree, into all the relations, both social and moral, of all spiritual beings in the created system. It enters into the principles of moral obligations between man and man. It gives life to love; for liking is being like, and love is a liking which is become a vital and controlling force. Vicariousness is the basis of all rights of transfer of property, or of influence, between men. It is inherent in the basis of government and authority. And somehow, somewhere, there lies in it the justification of that tremendous fact, the power of men to affect the lives and destinies of others, in the family, in society, and in the State.

Vicariousness is the spring of personal influence, and of the gentle but mighty power that moves kind grace, sweet pity, and strong helpfulness. It is a binding tie of the Universe of living spirits, and transforms its aspect, from that of a mass of matter, to a brotherhood, a family, a spirit host. It is the force in leadership, and quickens the thrill of all sympathies. Call it community, and we recognize it as one of the most fundamental principles, and most precious facts.

Vicariousness is also a basis of our self-transforming power, our power to accept ideals, and other persons as ideals, or as leaders, representatives, and sovereigns of our souls. It is the nearest thing to a self-creating power.

Such principles, we are philosophically compelled to believe, are inherent in the moral system of creation. In a moral system of related personal beings (and there is, and can be, no other sort of moralities) every act and relation is a moral responsibility. Such responsibilities The

Vicariousness before the creation.

Creator assumes in creating. Responsibility is itself a
a certain vicariousness. The Creator assumes, before
creation, a certain moral obligation (*i. e.* relation) of
vicariousness.

In these principles we see the Creator of men assuming a medial position between The Divine Unity and
men, so that He assumes for men, his creatures, a
vicarious position before the Godhead, and assumes
before men a vicarious position as representing all
Deity. In this vicariousness, men were not in The
Creator ; but, as free personalities, they were represented
by Him before all Deity.

We thus recognize that, before creation, a provision
for an atonement for sin had its initiation, in the
relations of The Creator of men, and The Father of
spirits, to men and to the All God. This is not a figment
of theology, but a declaration of philosophy. It consists of engagements voluntarily assumed by the Creator,
engagements towards God and towards men. And in
these engagements, or provisions, personal relations
and influence of the Persons of The Trinity appear to
be the chief elements.

When, however, we survey the philosophy of atonement, as related to the lives of human beings, and to
time, that which is *done* to effect it becomes
of immeasurable importance. Man needed
to be saved from his acts, and in his acts, and
from the effects of his acts; and for this much must be
done.

Atonement
in time.

If nothing had to be *done* to satisfy the justice of
God, and to allay his righteous indignation against the
wicked, then that justice and indignation are figments
of imagination or of false logic. A system that was

complete in its life-performances, before it began, was impossible; and the idea of it is pantheistic. A moral government or system cannot be anything but personal activities, on both the divine and the human sides.

A part of this doing must be done by God; for, if sin can be escaped, or rectified, or atoned for, by acts of the sinner, it is only an ignorance, or a disease, or a weakness, or a misfortune, and there is no real moral law nor a moral government. And, again, in the salvation of men, something must be done by God, if sin is a bad Will, a depravity of heart, a wreck of character, a lack of good power, a love of evil, or a corruption of spirit life.

This something to be done by God, had to be done after sin was actual. Anything that could have been done in advance by God, to make later doings unnecessary, could only have operated to nullify moral laws, and to make moral government a mere pretense and illusion.

We have said (page 106), "Reason cannot forecast the methods and acts by which The Creator would effect the rescue of men." We, therefore, only survey the doctrine which The New Testament actually presents to us. This doctrine says *Vicarious atonement by Jesus.* that God, not only became, in Jesus, a teacher of men, and a leader towards goodness, but He adopted human life, and put himself into the system of life and relations in which sin existed. He took on that nature which was under moral law, and assumed such human nature that He was vicarious for men before God, and for God before each man.

We have sufficiently surveyed the New Testament's declarations and descriptions of the Deity of Jesus. These might, if taken by themselves, be construed as teaching that He was not a man, but wholly God. The declarations of his complete manhood are, however, equally full and positive. The most of these representations are too familiar and simple to need statement here; we therefore survey only those which present specially important philosophical principles.

Among these representations, are those which declare the blood of Jesus a great element, or factor, in the vicarious atonement.

The blood of Jesus.

We have already noted* that the Hebrews had been taught, by Moses, that "The soul of the flesh is in the blood." This doctrine has its elements of scientific truth, and is now more accepted by scientists than ever before. It has also a popular acceptance, for the word *blood* is generally accepted as the best of all symbols of community of race or family. 'Family blood,' 'Blood relationship,' and 'The blood,' are terms familiar and significant."

The New Testament's doctrine respecting the blood of Jesus first makes note that his blood is the evidence, agency, and symbol of his human being.

Jesus himself is the leader in this, as in other doctrines. In that great discourse in the sixth chapter of St. John's Gospel, in which He declares so many principles of the way of salvation, He asserts himself the Saviour. He speaks of the work and value of The Word and The Spirit, but He proclaims his human personality as indispensable in the salvation of souls.

" Work for the food which abides unto eternal life, which the Son of Man shall give you, * * * Except ye eat the flesh of the Son of Man, and drink his blood, ye have not life in yourselves. * * * My flesh is indeed food, and my blood is indeed drink. He that eats my

*See page 163.

flesh and drinks my blood abides in me, and I abide in him."

In these words, Jesus seems to declare, that in his human nature (joined, of course, with all else that was in Him), there was mediation, and atonement, securing the best spiritual life to souls, that accept it in and from Him.

The doctrine of salvation by the blood of Jesus, is chief among the doctrines of the New Testament. But there is no doctrine that requires more careful study and statement. It is in two parts, and must be so recognized; for each would be without effect apart from the other. These two parts are, blood in the life of Jesus, and death of the blood of Jesus. Each is, in its place and way, a symbol of the complete union of his life with the lives of men. If the union in the living blood had not been complete, vicarious atonement would have been apparently impossible. Without the death, the union would have lacked a finish.

Who shall say which part of the one mediation is chief? Conscience looks on the death, and applauds and trusts, while it trembles. Love looks on the living Son of God and of Man, and worships Him who could for love "Empty himself, and become in the likeness of a man," and could for love assume the life that flows in its channels with blood, and courses on to its death.

The atonement, or mediation, in both its parts, is perhaps most philosophically represented in the *Epistle to the Hebrews*.

"It befitted him on whose account, and through whom, are all things, to make the leader of their salvation complete through sufferings (or experiences). For both the sanctifier and the sanctified are from one. Wherefore, He is not ashamed to call them Brothers. * * * Since then, the children had community of blood and flesh, He also, likewise, shared the same. * * * It was due that He should become like his Brothers, to become a merciful and trusty High Priest in matters relating to God, to conciliate in respect to the people's sins." *Heb. ii.*

"In the days of his flesh * * * though He was a Son, yet He learned obedience from what things He suffered (or experienced). And when complete, He became, to all who obey Him, a cause of eternal salvation." *Heb. v, 7, 9.*

This doctrine, that God became incarnate in Jesus, is not, however, philosophically simple, nor easily accepted, even for persons whose souls may glow with admiration, and even love, for Him who was such an ideal man, such a super-human and love-winning man. We must, therefore, survey further the principles involved in this doctrine.

Vicarious-
ness in
blood.

We have* somewhat discussed the necessity and the nature of vicariousness, or vicarious representation. We have seen, that it is not an idea invented to meet an exigency in theology, but is a principle universal in personal life, having an enormous, a beneficent, and an indispensable, place in the system of moral life.

If we pursue our survey on the same lines, we see that vicarious assumption of the place of men was not, in the judgment of philosophy, possible without a participation in the actual human life that is in the blood of men. Anything else done by The Creator would have been an act of God, a creative act, a masterful act, an act wholly on the divine side of the realm of life. No matter how like men The Creator might have made him-

* Pages 321 to 323.

self, if He did not become of the actual connection of the race, the vitally linked system of personal human life, that flows in the one line of blood, vicariousness would have been impossible. No act of power could, apparently, have created vicariousness, when the fact did not exist.

But the most of human minds, probably, occupy themselves far less with questions of the actualness of the incarnation, than with inquiries as to its necessity and its results.

The necessity of vicarious assumption of men's place by The Creator, by some kind of engagements, before creation, we have already recognized. This is required by philosophy and moral science. It is in the system of Nature, not of physical Nature, but of moral Nature, the system of personal moral relations. This vicariousness-before-creation seems capable of reaching its completion only in some actual taking of the place of mankind in fact.

The results, effects, and values of vicariousness, who can measure? If we see some of them, these are probably but a few, and perhaps not the best, of the results of the incarnation. In studying the incarnation, we are like a porter stationed at his open door, and seeing only the opened wall, and perhaps the form of him who enters. But if he who passes in is The King, the door does not measure his power, works, and gifts. When God comes into human life, only eyes that can measure Heaven can see all the glory and good that are brought into the life of human spirits.

Vicarious atonement is too often surveyed in a narrow and limited scope. It is variously regarded as a traffic, a bargain, a purchase, or else as a persuasion of unwilling

God, or as something else of an intervention, pleasing
to some minds, but causing a revolt of others. In fact,
it is something infinitely broad and comprehensive. All
men somewhat recognize it, so that even in pantheism
and monism it has its subtle influence, among first and
basic principles. Better understood and illuminated, it
enters into the principles of moral law and relations;
better still understood and illuminated, it affects, and is
the glory of, all that life of personal influences, personal
transfers, exchanges, participations, gifts, and finally
grace and love, that gives value to the world of spiritual,
voluntary, inter-connected life of the Children of God.

Probably, to the most of human minds, the vicarious
atonement of Jesus will present itself chiefly as a bearing
of the penalty of the sins of others, a sort of purchase, a
sort of traffic, not altogether free from arithmetical cal-
culations, and puzzles about the possibility and rightful-
ness of substitution. These puzzles we will not attempt
here to solve. They have a base in the conceptions that
honor the infinite holiness and law of God, and they
have also a base in what man learns practically in the life
of society, on this World that God made for man's home.
But vicarious atonement is vastly more than this, more
than even a regenerated and glorified Earth can teach.

Vicarious atonement is that which brings human souls
and The Father together. Somehow, the minds that
cannot philosophize love Jesus. Souls that cannot define
their own thoughts trust Jesus. Hearts to which creeds
are puzzles and vexation rest in Jesus. And Christianity
says to them, Love, and trust, and hope, in Jesus. Christianity values a right creed, because it is a statement of
the right man's intelligent beliefs; but Christianity's creed
is the person and work of the Son of God and of Man.

Vicarious atonement is such that a penitent soul can say, I looked on the infant cradled in a manger; I heard him explain Moses to our teachers; I saw his life of labor, and of all human duties and sympathies; I heard* him say that, as a merchant, and as a field buyer, he gave his all for the World; I saw his feeble steps when he came from forty days of fasting, and of bearing human nature, in the mountains; I stood with the sobbing group when he was silent in cruel Pilate's praetorium; I waited with the heart-crushed women that saw him dying, when† he said, "Father! Forgive them. They do not know what they are doing," and I know that, in Him, God has come to me, and I have come to God.

The place of the death of the blood of Jesus, in the vicarious atonement, is the place of honor, the central and highest place. Like the sin which it remedies, it is clothed in awfulness. Like the misery which it relieves, it draws a veil before the eyes that would see the infinite love in the Father's face. But it is the darkness before the day. It is the red rays in the sky, before a blended glory of sunlight and of whiteness bursts from rent clouds. It is like the sadness when the last hour comes to our dearest friend on Earth, when a soul's life is ripe, and as his spirit vision is opening on immortal splendors, he murmurs,‡ "It is finished."

Of the importance, in the vicarious atonement, of the peculiar features and cruelty of the death of Jesus, we do not, in discussing philosophy, need to say much. They belong to the pathos of life. They are part of the influences that move human hearts to make them better.

*Matt. xiii, 44, 45.
†Luke xxiii, 34.
‡John xix, 30.

Jesus lived the human life to its end; and he dropped
the human frame, not softly, as one lays aside a robe,
but with suffering of those agonies of keen pain, and
those blows of hatred and contempt, which make death
the climax of human woes.

While we may not be able to tell wherein the efficacy
of the death of Jesus most inheres, because we puzzle
over the question, whether his vicariousness
was for death, or the death for the vicariousness, all men can feel that the death was the
finish, and proof, of his complete human personal being.   Without that death the actualness of his physical
life would remain in doubt, and the fact of his human
life would have remained unfinished.   Granting that He
began his human life for vicariousness, humanity would
have stood appalled at the spectacle of the God who
dared not, could not, or would not finish it.

Atonement
in death.

But there was no failure.   If we conceive Jesus, as
Son of God and of Man, returning to the presence of
United Deity, after he has cried, " *Tetélestai*" (It has
been finished), we see Him, not alone followed by the
spirits of the living, but vicar of the greater host of the
dead, even of all the infinite army, that, through life, have
passed, or shall pass, into death, before reaching the
aionios life.

The death of Jesus has that in it which holds the gaze
of the world fixed on it, as the central spectacle of history—a spectacle that has made history—a pivotal spectacle, around which the forces of earthly life revolve.
And the death of Jesus is made by The New Testament
the prominent, central, moral fact of its philosophy of
salvation.

The texts, in which this philosophy is declared, are so

many that we cannot, and need not, take space to quote them at length.

"The bread which I will give is my flesh, for the life of the world." *John vi, 51.*

"Christ Jesus, whom God set forth, to be a propitiation by his blood." *Rom. iii, 25.*

"He was delivered up for our trespasses." *Rom. iv, 25.*

"While we were yet sinners Christ died for us. * * Being now justified by his blood, we shall be saved from wrath through him. For if, while we were enemies, we were reconciled to God through the death of his Son." *Rom. v, 9, 10.*

"Through the obedience of the one shall the many be made righteous." *Rom. v, 19.*

"Our old man was crucified with him." *Rom. vi, 6.*

"To this end Christ died and lived, that he might be Lord of both the dead and the living." *Rom. xiv, 9.*

"Christ died for our sins." *II. Cor. v, 14.*

"I have been crucified with Christ * * * If righteousness is through law, then Christ died needlessly." *Gal. ii, 20, 21.*

"Ye that once were far off are made nigh by the blood of Christ." *Eph. ii, 13.*

"We have redemption through his blood." *Eph. i, 6.*

"Having made peace through the blood of his cross." *Col. i, 20.*

"Obtaining salvation through our Lord Jesus Christ, who died for us." *I. Thess. v, 9.*

"We see Jesus, on account of the suffering of death, crowned with glory and honor, in order that, by God's grace, on behalf of everyone, he may taste death." *Heb. ii, 19.*

"Since the children are sharers in flesh and blood, he also himself, in like manner, partook of the same, in order, through death, to bring to naught him that hath the power of death." *Heb. ii, 14.*

"This he did, once for all, when he offered up himself." *Heb. vii, 28.*

"Through his own blood, he entered in, once for all, into the sanctuary, having found an eternal ransoming." *Heb. ix, 11, 12.*

"Jesus, to sanctify the people through his own blood." * * * *Heb. xiii, 12.*

"Ye were redeemed * * * with precious blood * * * Christ's." *I Pet. i, 16.*

"Who, his own Self, bore our sins in his body on the tree." *I Pet. ii, 24.*

"Unto him that loveth us, and loosed us from our sins by his blood, be glory and dominion forever." *Rev. i, 5, 6.*

"Thou wast slain, and didst purchase unto God, with thy blood, of every tribe, and tongue, and people." *Rev. v, 9.*

In some passages of The New Testament, and especially in The Epistle to the Hebrews, the atonement
is represented as analogous to, and perfect-
Priestly
atonement.
ing, the priestly atonements of The Old Testament.

We have (page 137) surveyed that old priesthood. We saw that its chief feature is the vicariousness of the Priest for the penitent men. We saw it teaching great principles of men's moral relations to God. It showed us that the Priest was a vicar, only in so far as he was a man, and brought the worship of sincere souls, and was accepted by God as a vicar for men.

Such a priesthood is philosophical. It is a crown
and finish of a rational conception of a vicarious atonement. It has no element of a Savage's fear of his fetish.
It has, indeed, sacrifices, but only as an expression of
conscience. The Priest, The Mediator, The Advocate,
The Paraklete, is the chief thing in the priestly ministry, after the suppliant's intent and heart.

We saw that, in the biblical doctrine, and in the
Hebrews' apprehension of it, as expressed by Philo, it
was not the sacrifice, but the attitude and heart of the
worshiper, that constituted the preparation for the
Priest's atonement. In the Epistle to the Hebrews the
same principle is declared. "Gifts and sacrifices, that
cannot, as to the conscience, make the worshiper perfect." *ix, 9.* "It is impossible that the blood of bulls
and goats should take away sins." *x, 2.* In the priestly
atonements, the worshipers accepted the Priest as a
vicarious mediator, but the sacrifices could not be anything more than emblems, because beasts are not in the
line and order of human life, and cannot be vicarious for
men. But, in Christ's mediation, the Priest and the
sacrifices are one person; and the victim is a representative man; and the worshiper accepts both Priest and
sacrifice for representatives of himself.

In this the representation and vicariousness are raised
to the highest grade, and the worshiper declares that
the victim's fate is not only like what he deserves, but is
his very fate, which is, however, overpowered by the
divine mediatorial part of the vicarious efficiency of the
Redeemer.

The New Testament's doctrine of Christ's priesthood
also presents it as, not merely in correspondence with
the Mosaic ritual, but as in principle like the older

patriarchal priesthood, of which Melkizedek* was one representative.   Such Priests represented their own families, and their mediation had many elements of true vicariousness.

In general, we may say, that in the principle of priesthood (so long as it is separate from prophetic, judicial and executive authority) there is something that is true to the best philosophy, and responds to what is best in human nature. So long as it puts a hand under man, and not on him, and so long as it does not veil the face of God, but throws open a door, and says, "Let us go in together," it is a colleague with conscience, before The Father.

And the priesthood of Christ is the ideal perfect priestly office. In the priestly services of the pagans, the Priest stood between the offering from the penitent and his God, and barred the way to the altar with his arrogance and avarice. In Christ's office, the Priest is the sacrifice, and everything concentrates in the vicarious personality of the Mediator. And his gain is the penitent worshiper's gain.

In pagan sacrifices, the priestly office claimed to transfer the victim's death, from the class of slaughters, to the class of holy things; but in Christ's office the sacrifice perfected the Priest. Perhaps we shall always debate the question, whether sacrifice is for vicariousness, or vicariousness is for sacrifice; but, as we gaze on Christ, the vicarious personality becomes more and more glorious, and includes so much, that even the transcendent glory

---

*The peculiar language of *Heb. vii, 3,* is understood to apply to Melkizidek, only as to his priesthood, which was not, like that of Levites, a matter of a special family, and set and limited, time, but continuous (not forever, but *sunekés*).

of the deeds of our Lord does not fill so large and splendid a place as the glory of His Self.

In Him, vicariousness, which human pride and selfhood scorn and hate and mock, comes to the help of human conscience, penitence, and weakness, and becomes the one chief messenger of light and hope to despairing souls. It drops with man to the lowest depth of his extremity, but keeps its place in God, and turns back with the rescued one to the skies.

In a general way we may say that vicarious atonement in Jesus is something so crowning and perfecting the whole moral system, and so interwoven with all personal moral life, that no one act embraces it all, and no one definition can describe it. To select any one feature, and say, " This is the atonement," is to belittle it. On whatever line of philosophy we look towards God, or outward from man, the vistas all cross in this divine and human vicariousness and atonement.

Vicarious atonement not in any single act.

And, in all these views, the element which must never be forgotten, nor disparaged, is that of the personal relations and influence of The Son of God and of Man, with The Triune God. Perhaps, as long as we are human, we shall regard the vicarious atonement as something like a balancing of accounts, and think, " So much for so much." But, in fact, personal dealings refuse to be compassed by arithmetic of numbers or bulk. Who can measure, or weigh, personal relations and influence? Who can measure goodness or badness, which, at the last, are sentiments of the Person who has the right to judge and rule them. Who will say, So much good, for so much bad? Vicarious atonement is defined, in

Element of personal relations and influence.

the judgment of philosophy, more by quality than by quantity.

If we conceive Jesus as suffering "So much for so many," we far more conceive him as pushing to the end, even to the death agonies of a man, in order that the atonement might be perfect in its kind, by the honoring of the law and its Maker, and by bringing into loving relations in Him, through spiritual power, the erring children and the holy Father.

In this vicarious atonement, the redeemed soul makes Jesus its Lord. But there are no jealousies in the Triune God. In the love that clings to its personal Lord, and in which sins of hearts, and crimes of hands, are forgiven, The Father is glorified. That is The Father's Will. "God was in Christ, reconciling the world unto himself." *II Cor. v, 19.* The glorification of The Father is the consummate work of Jesus. He says, indeed, "No man cometh but by me;" but He says, "Cometh to The Father." He promises to acknowledge whosoever shall acknowledge Him; but these are the souls given to Him by The Father. *John xvii, 6, 9.*

Yet one more characteristic must be observed in this vicarious atonement. It is a salvation by the "Grace of God." Our philosophy has said that salvation must begin in God, and that sin is ill-desert, so that by no possibility can salvation come to men except out of God's grace. To this, The New Testament responds with the fullest and sweetest possible representations that, "By grace ye are saved." The vicarious atonement is the perfection of gifts. The giver obtains the power to give by infinite cost to himself; and the gift is ever the boon of transcendent love. And the word *grace* is one of the most frequent words in

Atonement is grace.

The New Testament. It flows from the pens of the writers, in their most precious sentences, like a line of gold and light. It sounds in those sentences as the melody of the perfect tune, and as the voice of The Father in Heaven.

If, in the preceding pages, we have been correct in our philosophy and our biblical interpretation, The Bible's representation of the way of salvation of human souls is perfect. It is concentrated in the person of The Christ. It was conceived before creation, and initiated in the creating act. He who was wronged is the rectifier. He who was great enough to endure rebellion, is good enough to make its rectification possible. The rectification comes to us as advocacy. Expiation is in it, but not expiation to a theory, or to an ideal, or to a law, or to an impersonal holiness; for guilt is a personal relation to the personal Moral Ruler, and He has become "The Advocate," made perfect by experiences, and a vicar and priest by community of life. Reformation is in it, made possible and perfected by spiritual work of The Spirit of God, made just and possible by the advocacy of Christ.

Like Thomas, we look on our smitten Advocate, and cry, "My Lord and my God!" We rest on the promise, "Every one who shall confess me before men, him shall the Son of Man confess before the angels of God." *Luke xii, 8.*

§ 8.   ADOPTION, OR INSTALLATION, OF THE CHILDREN OF GOD.

When the lives of the people of this World, and their history, are surveyed, it is not strange that so many men say, "These are not Children of God." Neither is it strange that, among the great and strong thinkers, and noble men, there should be those who can say that only the pure and good and wise souls are Children of God. Neither is it strange that some Christian men should say that God's fatherhood is not real, and we only become Children of God by a kind of new birth, an adoption.

Nevertheless, either of these theories, when scanned philosophically, and pursued logically to its end, runs into irrational conclusions and inconsistencies. Moral science demands inflexibly that all men shall be recognized as related to their Creator by such likeness of being, and to God's Spirit by such derivation of spiritual being, that the name "Child of God The Father" is a proper and the best name for that relation.

We have now followed the lines of the philosophy and psychology in The Bible, until they have brought us to a position where we see these Children of God corrupted in character, wilful against God, and unwise. We have seen The Father's love, coming from his side of the conflict, making such provisions that the restoration of the Child of God, to a child's place, is proclaimed to be the purpose for which the power and love of God have been manifested and working in all the ages.

Now The Bible, chiefly in The New Testament, comes, showing how the children are restored in the character, and replaced in the position, of Children of God. It calls this a *huiothesia* which has been translated *adoption*, but means Son-placing, which is an adoption, when an alien receives it, but is an installation of a child, when the receiver is a child returning to his native place.

Adoption or install- ation of children.

The philosophy of The New Testament shows everything made ready, on the divine side, for a reinstatement, as soon as the child is ready, in Will and character, to take the position of a Child of God. It sees great psychological and philosophical hindrances in the child. It does not attempt to explain how all of these may be removed, any more than it attempts to explain other mysteries of the life that is below consciousness.

It even emphasizes these hindrances. It represents the change required in souls as being so great that it is like a new birth. It uses baptism to make prominent this conception that the restored New birth. child is like one reborn. We have noted how Christ's words to Nicodemus (*John iii*) show that this doctrine had a great place in his preaching. And although we insist * that the word *ánothen* means *from above*, rather than *again*, it is still true that Christ's teaching affirmed, that, because men were born from above, they could receive a restoration that was like a new birth, and that they must receive this in order to have place in the new " Kingdom of God."

The philosophy of The New Testament meets the necessities of wrecked human nature, in the only way that they can rationally be met, but as no other religious system of the World proposes Agency of God's Spirit. to meet them. It presents that doctrine of God's Spirit which we have already surveyed.† In this it confirms that description of human being which we have detailed‡ in categories. It declares such likeness of spiritual life, in The Father and the children, that holy enlightenment, holy impulses, holy influences, and spiritual help, can come, and do come, into the souls of those who accept the atonement in Jesus, and do install them in the character and positions of Children of God.

*See pages 165, 166, 222, 285.
†See pages 135, 271, 272, 280.
‡See page 72.

Multitudes of men deride this doctrine, and yet have a certain enthusiasm for a degraded and vague form of it. They applaud the theory of Spiritual agency, so long as the spirit is supposed to be impersonal or material. The New Testament, however, with its doctrine that spirit is personal, yet immaterial, offers the only doctrine that is true to psychology, or to philosophy, or to moral science, or that brings cheer and hope to the wandering Children of God.

The New Testament uncovers, before the eyes of God's Children, pictures of glory and of happiness.

Glory and bliss of the children. Heaven presents, in symbols, its places and its ministries, surpassing all earthly facts and conceptions. A new Earth offers them its affluence. Waters of life flow for them. Cities of gems and gold open their gates. The hosts of Heaven assemble to behold, and join, their bliss. They stand before the throne of their Lord, and sing. They wear crowns, and lay them at his feet.

The philosophy of The New Testament demands, also, that this glory shall begin here. It

Holiness here. demands purity of bodily life, rightness towards God, and ministry with justice and love towards men. It proclaims the possibility of all this by personal relations of the spirits of men to the Spirit of The Father.

Is this actualized in Christian experience? Millions innumerable answer that this experience is a fact, and

Christian experience and living. that intelligence of reasonable moral ideas comes through it, as it does from no wordy arguments, and that association with The Holy Spirit is a joy and a strength. Countless hosts will testify that, in them, the new spiritual knowledge of

Jesus has been a revolution of disposition, and a transformation of conceptions and of loves.

Blessed is that spirit in whom dwells love to the Father and to the family of God, whether that love has been like a native character when, "Trailing clouds of glory do we come from God, who is our home," or, perhaps after wildness or crime, or self-loathing or despair, has come in with a flash of truth, like the breaking of a rift in a cloud in a dark and furious storm.

Blessed is he to whom The Father says, "Bring out the best robe, and put it on him; for this, my Son, was dead and is alive. again." Thrice blessed is that spirit in whom there reign at once, a loving trust in The Father, a knowledge that "Grace and truth came by Jesus Christ," and a sense of joy in, and responsiveness to, the presence and ministry of The Spirit of God.

Still more blessed is that soul who comes to the perfection of *obedience* to his Lord; for obedience is installation. When the child of Earth has for his wisdom the thoughts of God, and for his sentiments the loves of God, and for his will the law of God, he has become a Child of Heaven in the home of His Father.

And this child of Heaven prays. All the Bible has proclaimed that, because God is a person, his children may pray, and will be answered. And we have seen that this is philosophical (pages 97, 98). But the re-installed children pray the prayers of communion, praise, and trust. As conquerors in the war of ages, and acknowledged as children and heirs, they sing, as they pray, "Our Father, who art in Heaven! Hallowed be thy name! Thy kingdom come! Thy will be done!

APPENDIX.

COMPARISON OF THE APOCALYPSE AND THE PROPHETS.

Revelation.	Isaiah.	Zechariah.
Spirit, i. 4, 10; ii. 7, 11, 17, 29; iii. 6, 13, 22; iv. 2, 5, 6, 8; v. 14; vi. 1; vii. 1; ix. 15; xxi. 10; xxii. 17; viii. 1.	xi. 2; xxvi. 9; xxxii. 15; xliv. 3; lxi. 1; lix. 21.	iv. 6, 10; vi. 15; vii. 12; xii. 1. Ezek. i. 12, 21; ii. 2; iii. 12, 14; viii. 3; xi. 5, 24.
Name of Lord, ii. 17; iii. 12; xiv. 1; xix. 1.	vii. 14; ix. 6; xxvi. 8; xlii. 7; xliii. 14, 15; xliv. 6; xlv. 6; xlix. 1; li. 15; lii. 6; lvi. 5; liv. 5; lxii. 2; lxv. 16.	xiii. 9; xiv. 9.
Creator, iv. 11; x. 6; ⁓xiv. 7.	xl. 28; xli. 20; xlii. 5; xliii. 15; xliv. 21; xlv. 12, 18; xlviii. 13; li. 9, 13, 16; lxv. 17.	xii. 1.
Jerusalem, iii. 12; ix. 6, 7; xxi.	xxx. 19; lii. 1, 9; lx. 14; lxii. 10; lxv. 18; lxvi. 10, 13, 20.	i. 14, 16, 17; ii. 5, 8, 12; iii. 2; viii. 3, 8; xii. 6, 8; xiv. 8, 11, 17.
Hunger, Feasting, ii. 7; iii. 20; vii. 16; xix. 17.	v. 17; xxv. 6; xxx. 29; xlix. 9, 10; lxii. 9; lxv. 13.	xi. 9, 16.
Temple, iii. 12; vii. 15; xi. 1, 19.	xliv. 28; lxii. 9; lxvi. 6.	vi. 12, 13, 15.
Fire, xiv. 10; xx. 10, 14.	lxvi. 16, 24.	ii. 5; ix. 14; xii. 6; xiii. 9.
Water, vii. 17; xxi. 6.	xxxv. 6, 7; xli. 18; xliii. 20; xliv. 3; xlix. 10; lv. 1; lvi. 10; lviii. 11.	xiii. 1, 8; xiv. 8.

Revelation.	Isaiah.	Zechariah.
Priests of the Lord, i. 6; v. 10; xx. 6.	liv. 5; lxi. 6; lxvi. 21.	vi. 13.
Presence of the Lord, vii. 17; xiv. 1; xix. 11; xx. 4; xxi. 3, 22.	xlix. 10; lviii. 9; lxiii. 9; lxiv. 1.	ii. 5, 10, 11.
Root, rod, branch, v. 5; xxii. 16.	xi. 1, 10; liii. 2.	iii. 8; vi. 12.
Calling, coming, i. 7; ii. 5; iii. 11, 20; vi. 17; xvi. 15; xxii. 7, 12; xxii. 17.	xliii. 22; lv. 6; lviii. 8, 9; lxv. 24.	xiii. 9.
Holy city, xi. 2; xxii. 19.	i. 26; xlviii. 2; lii. 1; lx. 14; lxii. 12.	viii. 3.
Babylon, xiv. 8; xvi. 19; xvii.; xviii.	xiii.; xiv.; xlviii. 14.	ii. 7; vi. 10.
Light, xviii. 23; xxi. 24; xxii. 5.	ix. 2; xlii. 6; xlv. 7; xlix. 6; li. 4; viii. 8, 10; lx. 1, 3, 19, 20.	xiv. 7.
"First and last," i. 8, 17; iii. 14; iv. 11; xxi. 6; xxii. 13.	xli. 4; xliv. 6; xlviii. 12.	
Sword (of mouth), i. 16; ii. 13, 16; xix. 15, 16.	xi. 4; xlix. 2.	
Keys, i. 18; iii. 7.	xxii. 22.	
Apocalypse (Revelation), i. 1.	xlii. 6. (See Luke ii. 32.)	
Immortality, xiv. 10, 13; xix. 20; xx.; xxi. 8.	xxv. 8, 19; xxvi. 19, 21.	
New creation, xxi. 1, 5.	xlii. 9; xliii. 7; xlvi. 9; lxv. 17; lxvi. 22.	
Fear of the Lord, vi. 15, 17.	lix. 17, 19.	
Convulsions of Nature, vi. 12, 14; viii. 5 to 12; xi. 13; xvi. 20, 21.	xiii. 10; xxix. 6; xxx. 26, 30; xxxiv. 4.	
Singing, v. 9; xiv. 3; xv. 3.	xxvi. 1; xxx. 29; xxxv. 6, 10; xlii. 10; xliv. 23; lii. 9; lxv. 14.	
Bridegroom and bride, xix. 7; xxi. 9.	xlix. 18; liv. 5; lxi. 10; lxii. 5.	
Book, v. 1, 2, 3, 4; x. 2, 8, 10; xiii. 8.	xxix. 11, 18; xxxiv. 16.	Ezek. ii. 10; iii. 1, 2, 3.
Trodden wine-press, xiv. 19, 20.	lxiii. 1 to 6.	
The Shepherd, vii. 17.	xlix. 9, 10.	

Revelation.	Isaiah.	Zechariah.
Lamb, v. 8, 12, 13; vi. 1; vii. 14; xii. 11.	xi. 6; liii. 5, 6, 7; lxv. 25.	
Heavens removed, vi. 6, 12, 14.	xxxiv. 4; li. 6.	
Eyes, iii. 18.	xxix, 18; xxxv. 5; xlii. 16, 18, 19; xliii. 8.	
Tears, vi. 15; xiv. 7.	xxv. 8; xxx. 19; lxv. 19.	
Past, Present and Future, i. 19; xxii. 6.	xlvi. 10.	
Assembling of God's People, v. 11; vii. 1 to 15.	xi. 12; xliii. 6; lx. 3, 14; lxv. 9; lxvi. 20, 23.	
Dragon, Serpent, Devil, xii. 3, 4, 7, 9, 13, 16, 17; xiii. 2; xvi. 13; xx. 2.	xxvii. 1; li. 9.	
Judgment, Justice, iii. 10; xiv.; xx.	iii. 14; xxvi. 21; xxviii. 6; xxx. 33.	
Brimstone, xiv. 10; xix. 20; xx.; xxi. 8.	xxx. 33; xxxiv. 9.	
Blood, v. 9; vii. 14; xii. 11.		ix. 11.
Stone and Name, ii. 17; iii. 12.		iii. 9.
Kingship and throne, iii. 21; iv. 2, 5, 9, 10; vii. 15; xx. 11.		vi. 13; ix. 9; xiv. 9.
Two olive trees and candlesticks, xi. 4.		iv. 3, 11, 12, 14.
Hill and valley of Megiddon, xvi. 16.		xii. 11.
They that pierced shall see Him, i. 7.		xii. 10.
Candlesticks, i. 12, 13, 20; ii. 1, 5; iv. 5; xi. 4.		iv. 2, 11, 14.

If, as we suppose, each of the seven sections of *The Apocalypse* is the same as the others in respect to its chief subject-matter and its outline, and they differ only as to their emphasis of special features, and each is a reiteration or explanation of *Daniel vii*, we may expect to find, in each of the seven sections, something analogous to Daniel's vision of animals.

Daniel saw (*vii, 4, 5, 6*) four beasts come out of the sea. One was a lion with an eagle's wings and a man's feet and heart. The second was a bear. The third was a leopard, with wings and four heads. Then there came (*vii, 8, 11, 20*) a fourth beast, terrible and powerful, having iron teeth and ten horns, actual or incipient. He devoured and trod down. Three horns were plucked out, but another sprang up having a man's eyes and a mouth speaking great things against the Most High. It pretended to do the works and exercise the prerogatives of God. It was allowed to rage for three and a half periods (*vii, 25*), but was finally slain and burned; but the first three beasts still lived, although restricted, for a season and a time, after which came the kingdom of The Son of Man and the saints (*vii, 9, 10, 13, 14, 22*).

The four beasts are explained (*vii, 17*) as kings, but later it is said that the fourth beast is a kingdom, and each of its horns is a king (*vii, 23*). Evidently these names, King and Kingdom, are symbolical of forces and of character, or of numbers of persons, rather than of individual rulers.

Now, there is, in each of the seven sections of *The Apocalypse*, more or less of the following scheme of representation, viz.: *First*, Satan, the primal wickedness, as some beast or beasts; *second*, violent human wickedness, as some form of beast; *third*, human seductive false theology and philosophy, which leads to vice, as some form of beast; *fourth*, the ever-present Messiah, especially present in the middle point of moral history; *fifth*, the conflict of God with sin; *sixth*, human immortality, with blessedness of the saints in heaven; *seventh*, a judgment of spirits; *eighth*, the triumph of the Lord, and the overthrow of the beasts of sin.

In the first section of *The Apocalypse* (*chapters vi, vii*) the symbols of wickedness are horses and riders. The fourth horse is peculiar and murderous. He is named Death, and is followed by Hades.

In the second section (*viii to xi*) Satan is a falling star. He is also called "King of the abyss" and Abaddon (a Hebrew word meaning *destruction*, and *abyss*, as in *Job xxvi, 6; xxviii, 22*). His disposition and forces are figured as locusts, like war-horses, with human faces, lions' teeth, scorpions' tails, and iron breastplates. These are followed by a second army of horses, with lions' heads, breathing fire and sulphur, and having tails that are like scorpions, and have heads. Their power is in their mouths and their tails. In *xi, 7* one of these swarms of beasts is called, in one word, "The Beast," and he overcomes God's witnesses for three and a half days.

In the third section (*xii, xiii, xiv*) there is the Adversary, as a great red dragon, having seven heads and ten horns, and a tail that destroys men. He prevails for twelve hundred and sixty days, or three and a half periods. Then a beast comes out of the sea. It resembles the dragon in having seven heads and ten horns, and resembles Daniel's vision in being like a leopard, a lion, and a bear. It serves the dragon, and has authority for forty-two months. The number of the letters of its name is 666, which is Cain's number. Soon after its appearance it receives a mortal stroke, which, however, is healed, and this suggests *Genesis iv, 15*. In connection with this beast it is said (*xiii, 10*), without apparent reason, "If any man shall kill with the sword, with the sword must he be killed," and this reminds us of *Genesis iv, 14*.

The first beast is followed by a second (*xiii, 11*). This one speaks like a dragon, pretends to exercise divine powers, and deludes men into worshiping the first beast and receiving his mark.

In the fourth section (*xv, 5 to xix, 16*) there is a scarlet beast, covered with names of blasphemy, and having seven heads and ten horns. It is said of this beast that it had lived, was not then living, but would arise from the abyss and go into perdition (*xvii, 8*), and yet, with apparent inconsistency, it was said of its heads (*xvii, 9, 10*), that they are mountains and kings, of which five had fallen, one then existed, and one was to come for a brief period. And it is incomprehensibly said of this beast that it is of the seven kings, and yet it is an eighth (*xvii, 11*). And its ten horns are ten kings, of one mind, not then in authority, but favoring the beast (*xvii, 12, 13*). This language is, in itself, unintelligible, but in comparison with the language of the descriptions in other sections, and with *Daniel vii*, *8, 11, 20*, it explains itself as a description of a dragon and two beasts, as seen at the middle point of their history.

In the fifth section (*xix, 17 to end*), which is a consummation tableau, the beast and the false prophet are cast into a volcano.

In the sixth section (*xx, xxi*) there is a binding of the dragon in the abyss for a thousand years, after which it is loosed until the judgment is complete, when, with the beast and false prophet, it is shut up.

In the seventh section (*xxii*) it is said, "Without are the dogs, etc., and every one that loveth and maketh a lie."

SAINT PAUL'S APOCALYPSE.

The language of Saint Paul in the epistles to the Thessalonians, written about twenty years earlier than Saint John's *Apocalypse*, seems, when compared with Christ's words in *Matthew xiii, xxiv, xxv*, to indicate that the general ideas of *The Apocalypse* were taught to the disciples by Jesus.

The First Epistle to the Thessalonians (*iv, 13 to v, 11*) has the same essential ideas as in *Daniel*, viz., the life and blessedness of the deceased saints with Christ, the future special presence of Christ, the judgment of all souls, the present life a conflict, and the future bliss of saved souls perpetual.

In the Second Epistle Saint Paul returns to the subject of "The Day of The Lord" and his presence (*parousia*) (*ii, 1 to 13*), when there will be a "Gathering of the saints to him." He says, "God chose you *from the beginning* unto salvation" (*ii, 13*), and exhorts them to "Hold the traditions which ye were taught" (*ii, 15*). He foretells that many will willingly believe lies, and that the day of The Lord will not come until false religion, which was then active (*ii, 7*), has made a strong fight. He says that there will be an *apocalypse* of the "Man of lawlessness," "The Son of destruction (in the Syriac version *abaddon*), who opposeth and exalteth himself against all that is called God, or that is worshiped, so that he sitteth in the temple of God, setting himself forth as God."

Saint Paul adds that he had before told these things, and that this *lawlessness* is a *mystery*, and that finally the Lawless One will be uncovered (*apocalypsed*), "Whom The Lord Jesus shall slay with the breath of his mouth, and do away by the display of his own presence."

THE APOCALYPSE OF JOHN THE BAPTIST

Any attempt, in the chapter on John The Baptist, to indicate the systematization and fullness of his words, as a philosophy, would have been premature, would have required a wearying discussion, and probably would have seemed forced and fantastic. Now, however, after analyzing the book of The Revelation, and words of Christ, we can say that John The Baptist's words are wonderfully parallel to those of *The Apocalypse*, and that the two Johns explain each other, as declarers of a complete system of truth.

There is, in both, the same philosophy, founded on the same recognition of The Creator, the personal God, the Trinity, the completeness of the end in the beginning, the nature and causes of sin, the presence of The

Saviour, the conflict of sin and righteousness, the immortality of souls, the general judgment, and the bliss in Heaven.

If our understanding of baptism is correct, its symbolism may be expressed in words, by saying that it means the same as, The end is in the beginning, or Alpha and Omega are joined, or The last is the first; for it says that The Creator and Father saves souls for an endless spiritual and blessed life. Now this is the system of truth that is drawn out, in graphic detail and emblems, in *The Apocalypse;* for that book is a delineation of the fact that, The Lord is "The Beginning and The End," and that creation and heavenly bliss are one system.

A careful reader of both John and The Apocalypse will further note, that in the record of John's words, which we are told are only a small part of what he said, there is not only a general resemblance to *The Apocalypse,* but also a close likeness in phrases, details and symbols. We find this oldest part of The New Testament, which is authenticated by all four of the Evangelists, exhibiting the same outline of features which the last book exhibits for the ripest product of the teachings of Christ and The Spirit. We have in this the evidence that both John's words and *The Apocalypse* are, in substance, Christ's own words; and we have another, and not the least remarkable, instance of the unity of the sacred Scriptures, another case in which the beginning and the end are joined, in God's wonderful word.

In our preceding pages (225 to 260 and the *Appendices*) we show that the prophecy of *Daniel,* the words of Jesus in *Matt. xiii., xxiv., xxv.,* and the book of The Revelation, explain each other, and all present one and the same array of principles, prophecy and facts. Referring to those pages for details, we give here a parallel comparison of the outlines of chief features:

The Apocalypse and Daniel.

1. A provision, before creation, for the salvation of sinners; and this represented in symbols significant of the creative days (or lights), and The Lord as a lamb slain before creation.

2. God's adversary symbolized as a beast.

3. Human wickedness, as beasts.

4. The Redeemer present at the middle point of moral history, as Son of Man, Son of God, King, Lamb of God, etc.

The beginning of "The kingdom of the God of Heaven."
God's Spirit, symbolized as lamps, stars and eyes, very active.

6. The conflict of sin with God.

7. Promises from God to many out of the twelve tribes, and to hosts of others.

8. A judgment. Punishment of the impenitent.

9. Immortality of all souls. Blessedness of saints. Christ a bridegroom.

The Baptist.

1. Baptism an emblem of God's Creatorship and Fatherhood, and of men's first birth and a renewal, and of beginning and end.

2. A parent viper.

3. Offspring of vipers.

4. "There cometh One," etc.
"Behold the Lamb of God."
"This is my beloved Son."
"The kingdom of Heaven is at hand."
God's Spirit as a dove.
Baptism with Holy Spirit

6. "Repent!"
"The axe is laid at the root of the trees," etc.

7. Remission of sins. Children of Abraham from stones.

8. "Fan is in his hand."
"Will burn the chaff."
"Wrath to come."

9. Will gather wheat into his granary. Christ a bridegroom. "He that believes The Son has everlasting life."

That John's proclamation was, in fact, Christ's own message, is plainly indicated in *John iii. 27 to 36*, where, among other things, The Baptist says, "The friend of the bridegroom rejoices greatly because of the bridegroom's voice. This my joy is therefore complete." ... "He that comes from heaven testifies what he has seen and heard, and his testimony nobody is receiving. He that has received his testimony has borne witness, as under a seal, that God is true. He whom God has sent speaks God's words . . . and The Father has given all things into his hand."

In our analysis of *The Apocalypse*, and in Appendix II, we have shown how large, and important, a place certain living creatures have in the symbols used by Daniel and Saint John.

In *Rev. xiii. 18*, it is said that the name of the beast (or rather the living creature, to *zōŏn*) is spelt with letters which, in the Greek way of writing numbers, have the total numerical value 666, and that a certain man's name has the same numerical value. Here arises the question, with an important bearing on biblical interpretation, Is the correspondence of the symbolical language of the two Johns so complete, that the number 666 should be in the name *viper?* In fact, *viper* is, in common Greek, ἔχιδνα, and the value of these letters is 5, 600, 10, 4, 50, 1, making 670. But, in Asiatic Greek ε (ĕ) is often changed to *a*; and in the Syriac version of The Baptist's words in *Matt. iii. 7*, and *Luke iii. 7*, the Greek name for *viper* is used, and is spelled with an initial a. With this change ἄχιδνα is 666. We have shown that the man's name in *Rev. iii. 18*, is probably Χάïεν (Cain) having the letters of ἔχιδνα except δ.

The mention of a name by its number has **not**, in

Greek, any characteristic of frivolity; but is often quite a plain way of telling a name which, for some reason, it is undesirable to mention. In Hebrew, and in Greek, all numbers were written in letters of the respective alphabets; and, to a Greek, the numerical value of a letter was as familiar as its sound. Every short word instantly suggested a number. The mention of a number of the name of the living creature, in *Rev. xiii. 18*, is, therefore, so significant, that it seems designed to indicate that, from the days of John The Baptist, there had been a recognition that the "Generation of Vipers," mentioned by him, signified the same as "The Beast" of Daniel, as does also "The Living Creature" in *Rev. xiii. 18*. The likeness of letters in ἔχιδνα and χάϊεν is very suggestive of reasons for speaking of them as Saint John does.

Some of our readers may think the number of words, which may make the number 666, is large, and that the really indicated words must remain wholly conjectural. Having, however, reached by exegetical methods, the conclusion that the indicated words are χάϊεν and ἔχιδνα, we make another study and perceive the following facts.

The mathematical and shortest way of writing 666 in Greek, is with the letters χξς. This combination contains no vowel, and cannot be a word. To obtain a vowel, one of the three numbers, 600 or 60 or 6 must be divided into two numbers represented by two other letters. But no division making a combination of four letters, makes any actual word. If, proceeding further, we divide two numbers into their highest and lowest elements, making a combination of five letters, we immediately have χαιεν, as the first and shortest word that makes the number 666. The number of other possible combinations of five letters, making this number, is less than twenty, and none of them makes a known name. If, however, taking χαιεν as a strating base we proceed to divide 5, the last obtained number, into two elements, 1 and 4, we immediately have ἄχιδνα, as the first word of six letters that makes the number 666.

It is certain that 666 is not the number of the name of any other animal creature that is mentioned, or suggested, in the Bible: and the conditions of the use of letters as numbers are such, and so simple, that it is certain that very few actual short Greek words numbering 666 exist, and the probability that the name of any other animal creature makes exactly that very peculiar number is infinitely small.

INDEX OF TOPICS.

Abba, The Father, 310.
Above (from above), see *anothen*.
Abraham's offering, 182.
Abstraction, 73.
Activities of beings, 21, 29, 38, 39, 73, 145, 170, 305.
Activities of God, 121, 149, 150, 211, 265.
Adaptations to experience, 71, 72.
to relations, 71, 72.
Adonai (Lord), 114.
Adoption of God's children, 339.
Advents of Messiah, 214, 225, 227, 228, 233, 241, 256, 259, 262.
Advocate (Paraklete), 174, 175, 189, 278, 279, 280.
Agnosticism, 85, 86.
Aïdios, 90.
Aŏni, 90.
Aiōnes, 193.
Alphabetical numerals, 186.
Alternative law, 102.
Altruism, 73.
Amr (Word and Lamb), 183.
Ancient of days 202, 225, 226, 235, 241, 242.
Angels, 155, 156, 245, 259.
Anointed (*Messiah Christ*), 228, 248.
Anothen, 160, 165, 166, 201, 222, 286, 287, 341.
Anthropomorphism, 86.
Apocalypse, 237 to 259.
A priori ideas, 28, 35, 44, 45.
Arbitrator, 174.
Assistance, 73.

Association of ideas, 42, 43, 73.
Atoms, 78.
Atonement, 132, 141, 199, 318 to 339.
Attention, 42, 73.
Authority, 209.
Axioms of intuition, 72, 73.

Babylon, a symbol of sin, 255.
Balaam, Balaamites, 251, 258.
Baptism, 196, 275, 296, 341.
of Jesus, 198.
of spirit, 275.
for dead, 296.
Baptist, John, 195.
Basis of moral science, 56.
Beasts in Apocalypse, 246, 250.
(number 666) 252.
Being, 22, 25, 37, 38, 39, 47, 64, 72, 88, 291, 292, 293.
Birth from water, 163, 283, 287.
from spirit, 198, 275, 283, 285.
from above, 285, 287, 341.
new, 341.
Blaspheming the spirit, 277.
Bliss, 141, 257, 342.
Blood, 163, 164, 283, 284, 285, 326.
its voice, 121, 236.
of Jesus, 236, 326, 328, 331.
Body, 282, 308–311.
Book of life, 236, 242, 243, 256.
Breastplate of judgment, 133, 134, 175, 176, 280.
Breath of God, 138, 159, 165, 284.
Brothers, 328.

Cain, 121, 251, 252.
(his number 666) 252.

Categories of knowledge, 32.
  Kant's, 33.
  of man, 69 to 73.
  Philo's, 170.
Cause, the First, 75, 76, 92, 115, 145 to 152, 181, 213.
Causal relation, 92.
Causation, 49, 91, 145, 146, 172, 292, 299, 305, 322.
  in moral science, 54 to 61, 74, 145, 299.
Chaos (apocalyptic), 243.
Character, 100, 125, 136.
Cherubs, 120, 131, 249.
Children of God, 59, 67, 162, 294 to 298, 339.
Christ, 217, 228, 233.
Church, 187.
Coherence, 72.
Combination, 73, 76.
Common sense, 17.
Community, 68, 270.
Conceptions, 37.
Conscience, consciousness, 15, 18, 39, 41, 47 to 52, 57 to 64, 67, 70, 93, 105, 116, 118, 171, 172, 173, 174, 176, 181, 182, 204, 207, 269, 305.
Conscientiousness, 62.
Continuity, 24, 72.
Conviction, 173, 174, 176, 206.
Correlation, 73, 76.
Creation, 108, 109, 110, 145, 146, 214.
  of atoms, 78, 83, 109.
Creator, 49 to 52, 56, 58, 59 to 63, 74, 77, 78, 90, 95, 109, 126, 149, 213 to 216.
Crime, the first, 121.
Crisis of world, 182.

Daimones, 156.
Daniel's prophecies, 225, 229, 231, 233, 234, 242, 246, 250, 253.
Days, 243.
Death, 117, 119, 196.
  the second, 256, 258.
  of Jesus, 331 to 334.

Decrees of God, 135, 189.
Defense, self, 22.
Deity of Jesus, 220.
Design, 51, 75.
Desolation, 254.
Devil, 249, 251.
Dianoia, 30, 149, 158, 167, 313.
Dimension, 44.
Divine Word, 153.
  Person, 74, 109 to 122, 211, 213.
  Spirit, 135, 160, 269 to 295, 341.
Division, idea of, 44.
  by word (logos), 207, 216, 217.
Doings of person, 21, 30, 38 to 46, 49, 62, 72, 78.
Dove, 199.
Dragon (Devil), 251.
Duty, 56, 57, 59, 99, 102, 321.

Eden reversed, 255.
Education, Mosaic, 124.
  of conscience, 63, 116, 118.
  of Jews, 283.
Ekklesia, 187.
El, Eloh, Elohim, 110, 114, 115.
Elders (24), 242.
Elements of matter, 78, 160.
Emotions, 22, 63.
Empirical thought, 71, 73.
Endor, Witch of, 140.
Ends of life, 55, 58, 76.
Equation, the personal, 40, 72.
Essence, 26, 33, 291, 295.
Essenes, 134, 188.
Eve's sin, 118.
Evolution, 80.
Experience, 72, 342.
Expiation, 339.

Faculties of persons, 24 to 52.
  of God, 149.
Faith of Abraham, 123, 182.
Fall of man, 118, 119.
False prophet (Balaam), 251, 258.

Fatherhood, God's, 59, 60, 67, 68, 93, 96, 107, 115, 137, 146, 149, 166, 195, 230, 288, 293, 343.
Father of spirits, 288, 293.
Fifteenth century B.C., 124.
First Cause, 55, 75, 92, 115, 145 to 152, 181, 213.
First born son, 158, 229.
Force, 78, 291.
Freedom, 306, 312.
Freewill, 23, 54, 72, 99, 130, 170, 300, 315.
Fulfill, 198.

Genesis, book of, 108.
Ghost, see Spirit.
Ghostism, 139, 282.
Gift of Holy Spirit, 276.
Gnostics, 193, 251.
God, 83, 91, 94, 110, 114, 115, 119, 149.
  Philo's second, 151.
Goodness, the Platonic, 150.
Grace, 141, 338.
Groaning of spirit, 286.

Habit in morality, 125.
Hades, 139, 254.
Half-seven, 227, 247.
Heart, 290.
Hebrew philosophy, 142.
Heirs of God, 294.
Help from God, 106, 135, 141, 314.
Hhoshen mishpat, 133, 175, 189, 280.
Holy spirit, 273, 274, 275, 276, 280.
Hope, 122, 199.
Human person, 20, 281.
Humanity of Jesus, 284, 285, 326.
Huiothesia, 340.

Iakach, 174.
Ideal humanity, 307 to 315.
Idealism, 84.
Image of God, 68, 111, 152, 178.

Immortality, 68, 137, 138, 158, 167, 188, 253, 256, 295 to 299.
Incarnation of God, 231, 329.
Indignations of God, 102, 179.
Ineffable God, 116.
Infinity, 87, 89.
Influence of spirit, 274, 337, 341.
  personal, in salvation, 200, 319, 337.
Insanity, 51.
Inspiration, 212.
Installation of moral relations, 115.
  of God's Sons, 339.
Instruction about God, 124, 129, 283.
Intellect, 24 to 52, 158, 167.
Intelligence, 29.
Involution, 81.

Jah, 114, 115.
Jahoh, 114, 121.
Jehovah, 114, 116, 121, 126, 127, 136, 223.
Jesus, 217 to 228, 314 to 337.
Jezebel, 257.
John, The Baptist, 195.
Judgment, 226, 248, 252.
Justice, 61, 129.

Kant, 27, 28, 29, 33, 34, 35, 75, 77, 93.
Kingdom of God, 225, 226, 232, 252, 253, 254.
Knowledge is of activities, 38.
  of concretes, 37.
  relation, 40, 41.
Kosmos noetos, 158.
Kurios, 114, 149, 223, 224.

Lamb of God, 142, 182, 200, 202, 223, 234, 236, 242, 244, 257.
Law (from logos), 113, 135, 158.
  moral, 57, 113, 118.
  is God's will, 39, 101, 113, 126, 299, 301, 304, 308.

Lawdeified, 79.
  punitive, 102.
  alternative, 102.
Lego, 31.
Lex, 135.
Life, an enigma, 13.
  the future. See Immortality.
Light, 182, 221, 222, 257.
Logos, 31, 151 to 158, 168, 169, 207, 214, 216, 236.
Logeton, 134, 135, 158, 175, 176, 189, 280.
Logic, 15, 31.
Logismos, 149, 167.
Lord, 114, 122, 149, 223.
Love, 179, 313.
Loves of God, 101, 102, 313.

Man, 20, 69, 72, 162, 281.
Manchild, 249.
Mar, 114, 223.
Materialism, 79, 190, 283, 290, 291.
Matter, 78, 83, 110.
Mediation, 280, 318 to 337.
Mediator, 142, 174, 319, 337.
Memory, 42.
Messiah, 191, 228, 233, 247.
Metaphysics of Bible, 203, 210.
Mind, 64, 149, 166.
Millennium, 256, 259, 260.
Miracles of Jesus, 263.
Modality, 34, 70 to 73.
Monism, 88.
Moral nature, 55, 61, 72, 116.
  science, 52, 57, 117, 141.
  character, 73, 100.
  law, 5ⁿ, 101, 118, 129, 299.
  relations, 54, 58, 68, 77, 91, 99, 116, 150.
  sentiment, 55, 63, 101, 125, 343.
Mosaic education, 124 to 128.
Mutuality in relations, 68, 77.

Names of Christ, 223, 258.
Nature, 157, 158, 269, 320, 329.
Necromancy, 139.

Neo Platonism, 193.
Nikolaos is Balaam, 251.
Nikolaitans, 251, 258.
Nobility, 59, 72, 306.
Numerals are Syriac letters, 186.

Obedience, 52, 125, 300, 328, 343.
Obligation, 57.
Ownership, 54.

Pantheism, 82, 290.
Paraklete, 174 to 181, 278, 279.
Pardon, 105.
Parousia, 259, 262.
Passion of self-defense, 22.
Past life permanent, 104.
Patriarchal theology, 123.
Perception, 36, 41.
Person, 20, 25, 64, 200, 281, 299, 306.
  the divine, 74, 125, 129, 148, 200, 213.
Personal God, 92, 125, 150, 152, 201.
  equation, 40, 72.
  influence, 200, 319, 337.
Persistent relation, 98, 104.
Pharisees, 189.
Philo, 143 to 183.
Philosophy, 13, 203, 208, 281.
  the basis of theology, 108, 203, 281.
  the supernatural, 209.
Physical man, 282, 289, 308 to 311.
Plato, 25, 173.
Pleasure, 22.
Plero, 198.
Plural consciousness, 47, 52.
  God, 94, 111, 149.
Powers of God, 149.
Prayer, 98, 343.
Presence of Christ, 259.
Priest, High, 166, 182, 206.
Priesthood, 131, 135, 166, 334.
Proof, 15.

Prophecy, 224.
  of Daniel, 225, 231, 238.
Prophet, the false, 207, 215.
Pros, 251, 256.
Providence, 98.
Psuché, 65, 164.
Psychical man, 72, 289.
Punitive law, 102, 129.
Purification, 131.
Purity, 59, 131.
Purpose, 51, 75, 220.
Principles of pure understanding, 71.

Quality, 44, 72.
Quantity, 44, 72.

Reason, 16, 30, 32, 157, 167, 171, 173.
Reciprocity in relations, 68, 77, 270.
Reconciliation with God, 104, 132, 141, 318.
Reformation, 104, 180, 339.
Relations of persons, 91, 97, 150.
Relativity, 70, 77, 270.
Remedy of sin, 104. See atonement and salvation.
Repentence, 180, 339.
Resurrection, 226, 248, 252, 296, 297.
Revelation of God, 106, 211.
  Apocalypse, 237 to 258.
Right, 56, 129, 298 to 315.
Right reason, 31, 145, 168 to 172.
Rights, 60, 125.
Ruler, God, 114, 141.

Sabbath, 127, 187, 190.
Sacrifices, 131, 142.
Sadducees, 190.
Saints, 240.
Salvation, 104, 132, 140, 178, 187, 315 to 339.
Sanctification, 277.
Sanctuary in Eden, 120.
Satan, 251, 256, 258.

Science, 50, 108, 264.
Science, moral, 52.
Second death, 258.
Sects of Jews, 188.
Self, 20.
Self-knowledge, 18, 173.
Sensation, 37.
Sense, common, 51.
  perception, 36, 41.
  of value, 57.
Sentiments, 22, 62, 73, 269.
Serpent, 247, 251.
Sheol, 139.
Silence, 183.
Sin, 117, 129, 135, 308, 316.
  is death, 196.
Skepticism, 85.
Skill, 51.
Society, 60, 121, 314.
Son of God, 152, 158, 176, 215, 228.
  of Man, 230, 231, 249.
Song of Moses, 254.
Soul, 65, 163, 283.
Space, 44.
Speech, 168, 181.
Spirit, 66, 94, 111, 160, 269, 282, 288, 293, 306, 312.
  of truth, 278.
  of God, 135, 159, 160, 199, 250, 269, 280, 293, 312.
  as a dove, 199.
  is aether (Philo), 160, 165.
  is created (Philo), 160, 165.
Spiritual agency, 107, 135, 141, 212.
  life, 288, 306, 341.
Spiritualism (Ghostism), 139.
Star (morning), 257.
Substance, 33, 88, 89, 291, 295.
Suneidesis and *suneidos*, 91, 172, 173, 176, 205.
Suntéleia toû aiônos, 226, 234.
Supernature, 98, 209.
Sword (the word), 154, 207, 216, 241, 257.
Symbolization, 44.
Symbols in the Apocalypse, 238.

Synagog, 187, 190.
Syria, 124, 184.
System of Nature, 55, 80.
　of God, 90, 300, 304.
　of infinity, 89.

Tabernacle and temple, 131.
Taste, 23.
Teleology, 55, 93.
Theodicy, 101, 103.
Theology precedes philoso-
　phy, 90.
　of patriarchs, 122.
Therapeutae, 190.
Thummim, 133.　See *Hhoshen*.
Times and a half, 227, 247.
Trees, the two, 117, 119.
Trial.　See Judgment.
Trinity, 260, 320, 324.
Triumph of Christ and his
　people, 255.
Truth, 15, 37.
Types, 130.

Unit, 39.
Unity, 69, 89, 94, 160.
Unitism (monism), 88.
Unknowable God, 116, 147,
　194.
Urim, 133.　See *Hhoshen*.

Values of life, 58.
Vicariousness, 321 to 324, 328
　to 337.
Virtue, 71.　See Right.

Water, 162, 196.
　and spirit, 163, 285.
　in baptism, 196, 282.
　of life, 289.
Will, 23, 72, 170, 265, 315.
Will of God is law, 59, 100,
　118, 126, 128, 150, 301 to
　308.
　of God is the cause, 92, 150,
　299.
Wisdom, 51.
Witch of Endor, 140.
Word of God, 112, 151, 154,
　201, 207, 214 to 217, 241,
　255.　See Logos.
　of God is law, 112, 158.
　(Jesus), 214, 255.
Wrath of God, 102, 225 to 228,
　254.

Zero (cypher) is Syriac letter
　I, 186.
Zodiac, 185.

Laurel-Crowned Letters.

Lightning Source UK Ltd.
Milton Keynes UK
UKHW012306300119
336486UK00010B/1026/P